INSURGENT IMAGINATIONS

This book argues that contemporary world literature is defined by peripheral internationalism. Over the twentieth and twenty-first centuries, a range of aesthetic forms beyond the metropolitan West – fiction, memoir, cinema, theater – came to resist cultural nationalism and promote the struggles of subaltern groups. Peripheral internationalism pitted intellectuals and writers not only against the ex-imperial West but also against their burgeoning national elites. In a sense, these writers marginalized the West and placed the non-Western peripheries in a new center. Through a grounded yet sweeping survey of Bengali, English, and other texts, the book connects India to the Soviet Union, China, Vietnam, Latin America, and the United States. Chapters focus on Rabindranath Tagore, M.N. Roy, Mrinal Sen, Mahasweta Devi, Arundhati Roy, and Aravind Adiga. Unlike the Anglo-American emphasis on a post-national globalization, *Insurgent Imaginations* argues for humanism and revolutionary internationalism as the determinate bases of world literature.

AURITRO MAJUMDER is Assistant Professor of English at the University of Houston. He writes extensively on world literature, critical theory, and intellectual history. He is on the editorial board of *Mediations* journal and an executive member of the Modern Language Association's South Asia forum.

INSURGENT IMAGINATIONS

World Literature and the Periphery

AURITRO MAJUMDER

University of Houston

Shaftesbury Road, Cambridge CB2 8EA, United Kingdom

One Liberty Plaza, 20th Floor, New York, NY 10006, USA

477 Williamstown Road, Port Melbourne, VIC 3207, Australia

314–321, 3rd Floor, Plot 3, Splendor Forum, Jasola District Centre, New Delhi – 110025, India

103 Penang Road, #05-06/07, Visioncrest Commercial, Singapore 238467

Cambridge University Press is part of Cambridge University Press & Assessment, a department of the University of Cambridge.

We share the University's mission to contribute to society through the pursuit of education, learning and research at the highest international levels of excellence.

www.cambridge.org
Information on this title: www.cambridge.org/9781108725743

DOI: 10.1017/9781108763899

© AuritroMajumder 2021

This publication is in copyright. Subject to statutory exception and to the provisions of relevant collective licensing agreements, no reproduction of any part may take place without the written permission of Cambridge University Press & Assessment.

First published 2021
First paperback edition 2025

A catalogue record for this publication is available from the British Library

ISBN 978-1-108-47757-4 Hardback
ISBN 978-1-108-72574-3 Paperback

Cambridge University Press & Assessment has no responsibility for the persistence or accuracy of URLs for external or third-party internet websites referred to in this publication and does not guarantee that any content on such websites is, or will remain, accurate or appropriate.

For my mother, Jayanti Majumder

What was interesting was that the details of the [Nairobi literature] debate were the same: all sides were agreed on the need to include African, European, and other literatures. But what would be the center? And what would be the periphery, so to speak? How would the center relate to the periphery? Thus the question of the base of the take-off, the whole question of perspective and relevance, altered the weight and relationship of the various parts and details to each other.

Ngũgĩ wa Thiong'o, "The Quest for Relevance,"
Decolonizing the Mind

Contents

Preface	*page* ix
Acknowledgments	xiii
1 Peripheral Internationalisms	1
2 The Memoir and Anticolonial Internationalism in M.N. Roy	47
3 The Lumpen Aesthetics of Mrinal Sen: *Cinema Novo* Meets Urban Fiction	83
4 Black Blood: Fictions of the Tribal in Mahasweta Devi and Arundhati Roy	118
5 The Disappearing Rural in New India: Aravind Adiga and the Indian Anglophone Novel	164
6 Conclusion	197
Works Cited	201
Index	221

Preface

Insurgent Imaginations: World Literature and the Periphery contends that peripheral internationalism provides a radical new perspective on world literature. A non-Western humanist and internationalist imagination vigorously negotiated the struggles of subaltern groups in the periphery. A wide range of aesthetic forms came to resist cultural nationalism: I trace the notion of peripheral internationalism across a range of cultural forms – fiction, cinema, theater, memoir, and essay – through a situated study of Anglophone and Bengali texts. The book's chapters focus on well-known and relatively marginal figures such as Rabindranath Tagore, Manabendra Nath (M.N.) Roy, Mrinal Sen, Mahasweta Devi, Arundhati Roy, and Aravind Adiga.

Insurgent Imaginations connects India to 1920s and 1930s Mexico and the Soviet Union; 1960s and 1970s Vietnam, Cuba, and the Congo; and present-day China and the United States. I discuss how literary texts came to highlight marginalized groups across national boundaries, provincialize dominant histories, and articulate the distinctive yet interconnected problematic of peripheral literature. These interactions shaped – and transformed – indigenous aesthetic traditions: this meant in turn that not only individual authors but also cultural forms such as vernacular and Anglophone fiction, film, and drama evolved globally in dialogue with one another. What is significant here is that an understudied constellation of writers outside the "West" was drawing more on one another than on the imperial center when it came to their aesthetic sensibilities. This is vital for correcting the assumption that the colonized were always responding, or writing back, to their former masters. In a sense, these writers were marginalizing the center and placing the periphery in a new center.

Peripheral internationalism is also very different from what is now called "world literature." Unlike the latter's emphasis on a "post-national" globalization, the former insists on national sovereignty and self-determination. Internationalism pitted intellectuals and writers not only against the ex-imperial center but also against their own national elites. In our own moment, such an imperative assumes enormous ethical and creative urgency. The categories of modernism and realism, too, were far from being matters of individual artistic choice, taste, or fashion. Rather, these notions were intimately tied to powerful ideological currents and major social conflicts, locally as well as globally. Their negotiation of a vernacular internationalism, I reckon, problematizes Anglophone understandings of the global and the cosmopolitan. Indeed, by highlighting culture as a site of emancipatory struggle in the periphery, one returns to a central debate in the theoretical humanities today – what it means to be human. Mediating against critical theory's valorization of the post- and the non-human, artistic and political movements in the majority world continue to push the boundaries of humanist emancipation. The "insurgent imagination," while not beholden to the liberal-Enlightenment notion of a coherent self, testifies to the possibility of progressive social change. This pushes back against pessimistic ideas of a posthuman present where there is no scope for human agency.

In addition, the book brings attention to peripheral modernism and realism in an indigenous source language, Bengali (the second language after Hindi in South Asia and the seventh globally in terms of numbers of native speakers) as well as its complicated influence on Anglophone production. Bengali occupies an anomalous position in Anglo-American cultural studies that my book seeks to address: on the one hand, leading postcolonial scholars such as Ranajit Guha, Gayatri Spivak, Partha Chatterjee, and others draw on nineteenth-century Bengal to make their case for colonial discourse; on the other hand, the rich history of twentieth-century Bengali internationalism and the diverse influence of Russian, Chinese, and "third-world" anticolonial currents, manifested most prominently in literature, are almost entirely unknown to Anglo-American readers. By focusing on internationalist literature (Mahasweta Devi, Samaresh Basu, Manik Bandopadhyay, and many others) and its relationship to theater and cinema (Bijan Bhattacharya, Utpal Dutt, and Mrinal Sen et al.), I illuminate important conjunctures of aesthetic development in South Asia that resonated with parallel currents in Asia, Latin America, Africa, and elsewhere in the peripheral world.

Chapter 1 advances a redefinition of world literature with specific focus on the periphery. Annotating a politically charged terrain of intellectual history, I maintain first that the humanist imagination emerged as a key topic of debates since the early twentieth century and, second, that anti-imperial currents emphasized the role of the imagination in envisioning an alternative conception of the world. As part of this internationalist constellation, the chapter discusses the intertwining histories of Rabindranath Tagore's pioneering lecture on "World Literature" (1907) and Mao Zedong's Yenan lectures on art and literature (1942). Such a constellation sheds new light on Fredric Jameson's much-debated notion of "third world literature as national allegory" (1986), going beyond extant critiques. It further complicates, I argue, the conventional separation between twentieth-century anticolonial, postcolonial, and contemporary globalization-era literatures.

Chapter 2 highlights the understudied literary genre of the memoir. I focus on the writings of the peripatetic activist-intellectual Manabendra Nath (M. N.) Roy. Exploring his diverse engagements with early twentieth-century Black radicalism in the United States and anticolonialism in Mexico, the Soviet Union, China, and Germany, my reading of *Memoirs* (1964) illuminates how literary form negotiates the politics of anticolonial internationalism. Roy contributed to the debates of the Communist International, famously differing with Vladimir Lenin on the "National and Colonial Questions." Roy also posited the imbrication of race and caste through his critique of cultural nationalism in India. An icon of the interwar era, Roy presented formulations in *India in Transition* (1922) that complicate both Euro-American universalism and the influential paradigm of decoloniality that favors postcolonial nationalism in terms of its cultural difference from the West.

Chapter 3 explores non-Bollywood, regional Indian cinema. I take up the depiction of urban struggles in Mrinal Sen's *Calcutta 71* (1972). Sen's "city films," as these are called, are trailblazing experiments in stylistic form and anticolonial theory. They explicitly draw from Latin American *Cinema Novo*, particularly "Imperfect Cinema" and "Third Cinema" popularized by the Cuban Julio Garcia Espinosa and the Argentinians Fernando Solanas and Octavio Getino, respectively. On the other hand, Sen is equally indebted to Bengali literature on the city, which includes the work of the poet Jibanananda Das and the prose writers Manik Bandopadhyay and Samaresh Basu among others. Sen's cinema sets in motion a conceptually daring relationship between film, literature, and politics. He authors what I call a "lumpen-aesthetics," which turns a pejorative term for the dissident poor (the lumpen) into an objective assessment of peripheral society. It is a cinema that is adequate to the task of representing the city and articulating its peculiarly peripheral fractures.

Chapter 4 examines representations of tribal or *adivasi* movements by two of India's best-known writers, Mahasweta Devi and Arundhati Roy.

Roy's creative nonfiction essay "Walking with the Comrades" (2011) created a stir in India for its sympathetic portrayal of rebellious tribal activists. I maintain that Roy's key inspiration is the earlier short story by Mahasweta Devi, "Draupadi" (1978). Describing a tribal woman leader Dopdi Mejhen, Devi's story, translated into English by Gayatri Chakravorty Spivak, is a widely anthologized text in postcolonial literature. However, the text's global career fails to capture its complex history: this includes the Cold War and the contest between the Soviet- and American-led blocs for regional hegemony in South Asia; the impact of antiwar people's theater of the 1960s, including plays on Vietnam and the Black Panthers; and the tradition of progressive Bengali women's fiction within which Devi is properly located. The chapter surveys the relationship between Devi's Bengali-language story and Roy's English-language essay through a host of little-known (to the Anglophone world) intermediaries. In doing so, it demonstrates how various grassroots movements for the rights of *adivasi* and ethnic minorities continue to inflect creative nonfiction in the contemporary era.

Chapter 5 discovers an unlikely source of caste and class politics in Aravind Adiga's Anglophone novel of individual ambition *The White Tiger* (2008). I propose that the novel recodes, through a series of parodies and formal allusions, rural lower-caste militants, who regularly appear at the margins of the plot and whose contrapuntal significance the majority of commentators have overlooked. The chapter re-illuminates the complex maze of subterranean flows that undercuts the novel's surface narrative of a new India. I hold that traditions of the protest novel, epistolary narrative, and modernist and indigenous satirical genres are at work in the novel: these gesture to suppressed narratives of peripheral internationalism. My reading of the novel elaborates the evolving significance of internationalism in twenty-first century India, where the rural and the subaltern have been all but banished from cultural discourse.

Chapter 6, a concluding section, annotates the contributions of this book to contemporary scholarship on non-Western world literature and intellectual history. It provides a critical assessment of humanism and literary form and makes suggestions for realignment and expansion. I locate twentieth-century modernity as an interlinked and asymmetrical relationship between the metropolitan core and the global periphery. This is a relation that continues to structure the twenty-first century world and the struggle for liberation in interesting and unforeseen ways.

Acknowledgments

I am grateful to Crystal Bartolovich, Keya Ganguly, Timothy Brennan, and Subho Basu, who sustained the project at crucial junctures. Thanks for their indulgence are due to (alphabetically) Susan Andrade, Deepika Bahri, Amit R. Baishya, Sandeep Banerjee, Pradip Basu, Craig Brandist, Marshall Brown, Nicholas Brown, the late Dipankar Chakraborty, Mrinalini Chakravorty, Supriya Chaudhuri, Serajul Islam Choudhury, Amlan Das Gupta, Sharae Deckard, Manan Desai, Gerard H. Gaskin, Ahsan Habib, Daniel Hartley, Nalini Iyer, Pranav Jani, Philip Kaisary, Suvir Kaul, Salimullah Khan, Ania Loomba, Don Mitchell, Don Morton, Zobaida Nasreen, Monica Popescu, Nimanthi Rajasingham, Henry Schwarz, Amritjit Singh, Gayatri Chakravorty Spivak, and Rashmi Varma. My colleagues at Houston provided generous support: Hosam Aboul-Ela, Margot Backus, Jason Berger, Paul Butler, Ann Christensen, Chitra Banerjee Divakaruni, Chatwara Duran, Sarah Ehlers, Karen Fang, James Kastely, Sebastian Lecourt, Keith McNeal, Alex Parsons, Kavita Singh, Roberto Tejada, Cedric Tolliver, Lynn Voskuil, Lois Zamora, and Lauren Zentz. Finally, I am indebted to my partner, Sreya Chatterjee: this is her book as much as mine. The great Walter Rodney once remarked that to claim – in a book's preface – all mistakes and shortcomings as solely one's own is "sheer bourgeois subjectivism": that is quite unavoidable in the present case.

Archival research was made possible by the English Department and the College of Liberal Arts and Sciences at the University of Houston. Thanks to the staff at P.C. Joshi Archives on Contemporary History, New Delhi, as well as the National Library, and the Little Magazine Library and Research Center, Kolkata. I am grateful to Ray Ryan, commissioning editor, and the anonymous referees at Cambridge University Press. Portions from Chapter 1 appeared earlier as "World Literature, the *Geist* and the East, 1907–1942," in *History, Imperialism,*

Critique: New Essays in World Literature, ed. Asher Ghaffar (New York: Routledge, 2018): 13–28, and "The Case for Peripheral Aesthetics: Fredric Jameson, the World-System and Cultures of Emancipation," *Interventions* 19.6 (2017): 781–796. These have been revised for the book.

CHAPTER I

Peripheral Internationalisms

The *Geist* and the East

While the idea of a world republic of letters has a long history in Europe, expressed by Dante in the fourteenth; Erasmus and More in the sixteenth; and Goethe, Marx, and Engels in the nineteenth centuries, it is only in the twentieth century that its promise is realized and displaced on a world scale. The latter includes, arguably, such events as the establishment of the World Literature Publishing House in the Soviet Union in 1918, the All-India Progressive Writers Association in India in 1936, and the Afro-Asian Writers Association founded in Sri Lanka in 1958 and finalized in Egypt in 1962. These institutions and the ideas they traced, albeit little recognized today, constitute a vast corpus of anticolonial theory and literature. Disparate manifestos present aspects of this demotic humanist vision, such as the Indian Rabindranath Tagore's lecture on *visva-sahitya* (world literature) in 1907; the Hungarian Georg Lukács's "Narrate or Describe" in 1936; the Chinese Mao Zedong's Yenan Forum talks on literature in 1942; the German Erich Auerbach's "Philology and Weltliteratur" in 1952; and, lastly, the Ngũgĩ wa Thiong'o–led Kenyan group's (with Taban Lo Liyong and Henry Owuor-Anyumba) "On the Abolition of the English Department" in 1972. I mention nationalities of these writers, who represent widely divergent positions, for no other reason than to illustrate the wide reach of their arguments. Here, broadly speaking, one finds an emphasis on the coevality of imperial and colonized cultures; a focus on the oral, the vernacular, and the folk; unity of thought and action; and last but not the least, the centrality of creative, purposive human agency in the task of social transformation.

In his book *Borrowed Light: Vico, Hegel, and the Colonies*, Timothy Brennan (2014) advances that the eighteenth-century Italian thinker Giambattista Vico prefigures and in many ways nuances Hegel's concept of the *Geist* or Spirit as the self-realization of human freedom. It is Vico who avers that the earliest human knowledge is expressed through oral myth and poetry (literature), and that it is the human imagination, at work, that grounds social and political change, rather than positivistic science or instrumental rationality. What I take to be a key methodological point in Brennan is the account of philosophical modernity as centered on the concept of *agon* or processive struggle.[1] Immanent in various philosophers' ways of viewing the world, and something of which they themselves were often acutely aware, is a methodological "war of positions": not a priori assumptions imposed from without, but a logical working out of inherent tensions and contradictions, and a processive evaluation of intellectual legacies and disavowals. As a reading practice, this is the core of Hegel's famed truth procedure, a challenge to read negatively without presuppositions. Equally, if the Vichian-Hegelian lineage of the Enlightenment challenged Cartesian rationality and Nietzschean ontology – three distinct trajectories, very far from our settled opinions of a monolithic Enlightenment – it did so through the category of *labor*. This is labor understood, expansively, in the Hegelian sense of the term, as intentional, purposive human activity.

Such conceptions were by no means limited to eighteenth-century Europe; rather, they impinged on, and were reworked by, a wide range of intellectuals in the nineteenth and twentieth centuries.[2] Focusing through a Vichian-Hegelian lens, this chapter explores the conceptual overlaps between Western Marxist thought, with humanism and the collective oral imagination as its twin leitmotifs, and anticolonial intellectuals and their equally Vichian critique of class and foreign domination. Human thought-activity provides a figuration of political and aesthetic resistance, what I call the "insurgent imagination." The rational thought characteristic of the *Geist* is neither in counterpoint to the imagination nor is it reducible to the economic sphere in the figure of homo economicus.

This chapter places Rabindranath Tagore's lecture on world literature (1907), possibly the first of its kind in the non-Western world, in conversation with Mao Zedong's Yenan Forum talks on art and literature (1942). Tagore's lecture traces the beginning of a continent-wide upsurge that peaks with Mao's talks. Tagore – the first non-European to win the Nobel Prize for literature – registers a historical juncture that is especially significant in terms of anticolonial sentiment in Asia. Around this time, Japan's victory over Russia, a major European power, in 1904 marked the beginning of Japanese ascendancy in the Far East, providing the first trigger in a chain of European upsets at the hands of Asian nations. In the aftermath of the Russian defeat, the two revolutions of 1905 and the Bolshevik

Revolution of 1917 successfully dismantled the three-hundred-year-old Tsarist Empire. The fledgling Soviet Union, with its policy of supporting – some would say hegemonizing – nationalist movements in the East, exercised enormous influence over Asian anticolonialism including in China, India, and Turkey. After the partition of Bengal in 1905, likewise, the rise of the *swadeshi* (national self-sufficiency) movement in British India resonated with parallel developments elsewhere, especially with Japanese, Korean, as well as Chinese nationalisms. In China, following the revolution of 1911 and the May Fourth cultural movement of 1919, debates around Westernization and indigeneity closely paralleled the Indian discourse of *swadeshi*. The May Fourth movement and the Red Army campaign in the 1930s, preceding the Chinese Revolution of 1949, form the twin backdrops to Mao's controversial Yenan talks on the role of literature and the popular arts in national liberation.

It would be an understatement to say that Tagore's pioneering articulation of world literature has received scant attention in Anglo-American scholarship. More generally, the worldly underpinning of his thought, either in philosophical or intellectual history terms, has been lost in translation.[3] On the other hand, Tagore's receptions in Latin America, Central-Eastern Europe, or – as we see later – the Soviet Union and China – offer a very different understanding of his politics-poetics.[4] The comparison between Tagore and Mao, unfathomable, perhaps, to *our* contemporary Anglophone conceptions, grounds a little regarded phase of cross-cultural exchange. If Tagore locates literature's worldliness, that is, literature's relation to the world, Mao in turn articulates the linkage between local form and foreign influence. These lectures foreground a historically distinctive relationship between writers, texts, and readers: between them, Tagore and Mao (and their mutual interlocutors) theorize an Asian and global trajectory, a *situated conception* of literature that emphasizes the counter-hegemonic role of intellectuals, the processive forging of popular sovereignty, and anti-imperialism. Between Tagore and Mao, to put it modestly, we witness the consolidation of an Asian notion of the "East," with a remarkable emphasis on the idea of culture as a site of emancipatory practice. These texts forge the foundations, arguably, for a tradition of world literature that provincializes the "West." Simultaneously, the Hegelian-Marxist categories of dialectical philosophy, previously restricted to elegant explanations of bourgeois Europe, encounter and have to grapple with a new, foreign, and properly world-historical object of study. The intimate connection between speculative thought and social being, and between concept and actualization, poses a properly universal, that is ex-European, problematic only in the twentieth century, explored alike by socialist thinkers within Europe and anticolonial intellectuals in Asia and elsewhere.[5]

February 9, 1907, is a significant date in literary history. In Calcutta, Tagore spoke to the National Council of Education, a fledgling body set up a year earlier to develop university education independently of colonial control. *Visva-sahitya* – in Bengali – or world literature was Tagore's term for "comparative literature." Given that the lecture has very little to say about specific literary texts, per se, its title is somewhat misleading. Rather, Tagore theorizes how literature mediates the individual's perception of and relation to the world. In *visva-sahitya*, he freely articulates a parallel vision to that of Vico, Hegel, and Marx in Europe – namely, an idea of "socialist universalism." The first term of this pairing is often obscured, and even ignored, in focusing on the second. But clearly, Tagore, in speculating on the scope of individual freedom, locates that freedom in the development of humanity-in-common: to "seek," in the individual, "a union of its particular humanness with all humanity" (*samasta manusher maddhe sampurnarupey apnar manushatter milan*) (141).[6]

In Tagore's expansive view of interrelations, what is posited is a double connotation of the "world." On the one hand, the world is the concrete manifestation of intention and action; on the other hand, the truth about the objects of this world can be perceived, only progressively and intangibly, through subjective understanding and experience. Here it is noteworthy that Tagore does not devalue subjective understanding. If subjective, immediate understanding is "incomplete," which it is – when it is "by itself," Tagore adds – that is simply because the self (*atman*) is in the process of discovering and actualizing "truth," which is a matter of diachronic development. Tagore notes, "One can apprehend one's innermost spirit (*antaratman*) in the outside world most readily and comprehensively in other human beings ... [t]he more I apprehend that unity, the greater my good and my joy" (139, 141). The thrust of his argument, which rejects the a priori notion of Being and instead connects the individual to collective becoming and dialogue, once again deserves underscoring.

Tagore's notion of the world, as well as the truth of the world, points to historical knowledge, which is "fashioned by many people through many years" (142). Of course, he goes several steps further. Included in this epistemology is sensory perception, such as "sight, hearing, and thought," "the play of the imagination," and "the attachment of the heart" (139), that contributes to the knowledge of the world as it is perceived, felt, and ultimately known. It is in relation to sensory perception that literature finally emerges in Tagore's discussion. Dividing the realm of human activity into work and literature, *karma* and *sahitya*, it is to the latter that Tagore assigns the crucial task of forming "affective bonds with truth," one that goes beyond self-centeredness in seeking a universal realm of humanity.

At this point, the difficulty that arises in locating Tagore's essay within not only a dialectical but also materialist – in other words, Hegelian-Marxist – tradition is the seeming devaluation of labor or work (*karma*). Tagore appears to suggest, first, that work is driven by instrumental, self-serving reason. Second, it also bears noting that Tagore speaks of work as an "offshoot" (142) of human expression, almost a mark of humanity's fallen state rather than its true purpose. Finally, he seems to view literary expression more positively as "the prodigal wing of human nature," as that which repeatedly thwarts the designs of "reason, the parsimonious steward" (143). Yet, it would be quite superficial to interpret these remarks as pitting literary endeavor against laborious work, or favoring sensuous imagination over cognitive reason. Such a reading is untenable when one considers the text as a whole. Far from bracketing the social conflicts that literature mediates, Tagore emphasizes, in Vichian terms, the active role of the imagination in shaping the material world. Tagore's method, in other words, finds supplementary relationalities rather than dualist antitheses between imagination and labor.

Tagore's most astute insight is the suggestion that literature is at once the most intensely personal exploration of the world around us, driven by the self's urge to express itself, while literary work seeks to overcome the "obstacles" created by the "self-interest" (146) of socialized, alienated labor. Literature and work, *sahitya* and *karma*, rather than being antithetical, are "parallel" to and "complement each other" (142) in the desire for freedom. What literature embodies is a *special* kind of work. If the self is at its most free when it is able to express itself fully, such as in literary expression, this "total autonomy" also leads to "isolation," and to a state of – Tagore uses a strong word here – "uncivilized" existence. Equally, the growing freedoms of modernity result not only in a loss of human authenticity and essence, but also even the civilization fostered by such reified freedom is but the negation of the actual concept. Meanwhile, it is in literature that the self, in articulating, simultaneously fulfills and abolishes itself, thereby approaching totality and a higher realization of the self (*atman*). Tagore's conceptual framework is that of *samsara* (the sum of the whole), for processive totality that is not simply the sum of parts but their dynamic and transforming interrelation.

This is the kernel of Tagore's argument: while literature comes to serve as the expression of the universal spirit, what he terms "concrete form in the world" from "inchoate ... abstract ideas," it does so through self-consciousness revealing "itself to itself" (142). Rather than rejecting the individual in the face of the general or the universal, literature as imagination testifies to the importance of individual self-consciousness in any manifestation of the universal spirit. As he says, "Incomplete in itself, it [individual consciousness] is relieved if it can somehow turn its inner truth into the truth of the world" (143). At the opposite end of the spectrum, the other possibility, as it were, is the greater alienation and stunting of the self (*oudasinya*), a resigned withdrawal from the world that Tagore compares to death (*mrityu*).

A few additional comments are in order about the other salient points in his argument, which are not about literature but point toward social issues. As a matter of fact, the essay has very little to say about the conventional pleasures of literature, as previously noted, and instead links creative expression to the irreconcilable points of social antagonism. In *visva-sahitya*, Tagore defends the right to property, and more controversially the passing of property from father to son. But it is necessary to point out that he does so on the basis of socialized property rights and insists rather radically that this applies to everyone rather than only to the elite. Still, he is troublingly silent on the patrilineal aspect of inheritance.

Similar too is Tagore's defense of war in *visva-sahitya*. Tagore sees modern warfare as the positive expression of the collective spirit of nations! Yet he is equally quick to point out that such intentions have been subverted by "Western" nation-states that instrumentalize war through mechanical means (weapons), and wage war for the accumulation of resources and profit. In other words, to paraphrase his contemporaries Vladimir Lenin and W.E.B. Du Bois but almost a decade before them, Tagore here is making a distinction between oppressor nationalisms and those of the oppressed (colonized nations) and emphasizing the right of the latter to self-determination by all means, including war.[7] But Tagore remains firmly opposed to exclusionary conceptions of nationalism. Finally, and I extrapolate here, by positing history as entirely human-made, he advances a view of secular (non-ideological and non-identitarian) modernity that is based on progress, denying an unreflexive admiration for the achievements of the past. While *visva-sahitya* points to the growing stratification and alienation that is a direct result of capitalist modernity and its instrumental use of reason (which, it is needless to say, would hardly appear otherwise to a colonial intellectual), Tagore insists on affirming the historical development of human reason (*buddhi*) and its complementary relation to affect and emotion (*hriday*).

By linking the development of human consciousness to an analysis of societal formations, Tagore offers a nuanced view of the role of literature in the context of modernity. He is a philosopher of the modern, someone who insists on the need to engage with the world as it exists and as it *could* exist, without withdrawing from it in despair or taking recourse to nostalgia for the past. Tagore is no garden-variety admirer of the modern either; in fact, it is his critical unpacking of the pitfalls of modernity that most resonates with our own contemporary consciousness (Bannerji, "Beyond the Binaries," and *Always Towards*).[8] He did not live to see the outcome of the twentieth century, but already by the time of his death (in 1941), Tagore described a globalized world marked by endless war, poisoned nationalisms, environmental destruction, vast immiserated populations, uprooted communities, and the isolation of the precariously free individual. As a special kind of laboring work, it is literature (*sahitya*) that offered him a way of narrating – as determinate and imaginative negation – the "not-yet" of this world (*visva*). Such an articulation of the contradictory unity of the material world and the former's registration in human thought-activity, therefore, places Tagore in contradistinction to current versions of theoretical *posthumanism*. In the conceptual schema that Tagore put forward in *visva-sahitya*, modernity, rationality, and universality are processive notions to be achieved through human – sensuous, cognitive, and intentional – effort. It is closer in the philosophical sense to Marxian humanism (Amiya Bagchi, "Rabindranath Tagore"), albeit with notable non-Western inflections from the *Advaita* philosophers to the Sufi *fakir* oral traditions.[9]

In terms of creative labor, of course, Marx and Tagore were addressing distinct notions of the proletariat, as befitting their different historical locations and preoccupations. Both, however, would have commonly understood the term to be referring to those who, by virtue of their self-activity, were singularly responsible for the reproduction and perpetuation of the material world without, necessarily, having attained the full consciousness of doing so in language (Marx and Engels, *The German Ideology*).[10] In the Asian context, our second text under discussion, Mao Zedong's Yenan Forum talks, further clarifies the relation between labor, consciousness, and the creative imagination posed by Tagore, Marx, and Hegel, but before them, Vico.

In *The New Science*, Giambattista Vico observes in his well-known passage on "Method" that to trace the development of human thinking:

> With the philosophers we must fetch it from the frogs of Epicurus, from the cicadas of Hobbes, from the simpletons of Grotius; from the men cast into this world without care or aid of God .... Our treatment of it must start from the time these creatures began to think humanly ... we ha[ve] to descend from these human and refined natures of ours to those quite wild and savage natures. (100, par. 338)

Mediating between the "refined" and the "savage," Vico indicates the highly uneven aspect of popular consciousness. This was an awareness sustained by the Neapolitan philosopher's understanding of eighteenth-century Italian city-states and their competing claims to sovereignty. The problematic of uneven consciousness – what Hegel terms the "national" component of the *Geist* or Spirit – is taken up, nearly a century later, by Hegel in his *Lectures on the Philosophy of World History*. In the twentieth century, alongside Tagore, we see this in Vico's compatriot, the Marxist intellectual Antonio Gramsci. Vichian thought offers a unique perspective on cultural materialism, not simply as an analytical framework but also as a form of resistance politics. Vico sees language and literature as informed by processes of global class struggle; similarly, his insistent return to the subjects of popular myth and orality and critique of class and foreign domination offers templates for peripheral and semi-peripheral intellectuals. The Vichian influence clearly emerges in the interwar era: as much within Europe in Italy, Russia, and Ireland, as without in India, Peru, or China.[11]

In the Yenan lectures of 1942, the key methodological point that Mao makes about intellectual work directly parallels Vico's advice to the philosopher. Namely, one makes sense of the creative imagination – Tagore's *sahitya* – but only in relation to the material conditions under which people operate. This is what Vico terms "divinity": to divine, in secular "gentile" fashion, is to imagine. Mao Zedong, who takes up a similar thematic in his Yenan talks, is responding as much to his contemporaries in the May Fourth movement, to the debate between the various stripes of Westernizers and neo-traditionalists, as to the Chinese readers of Vico.[12]

Mao takes two seemingly antithetical positions at once. It is not sufficient, Mao holds, for intellectuals to look at the culture of the past and to deduce from it the character of the people; such an approach mistakes forms, which are but ideal projections, and substitutes them for social relationships. Intellectuals have to critically engage, he says, with "the hangover of petty-bourgeois ideology among many proletarians and backward ideas" (4). On the other hand, he asserts that many intellectuals "were acquainted neither with their subjects nor with their public" (6). The former suggests a vanguardist notion of consciousness raising from above; at the same time, much of what Mao says about the intellectuals' lack of familiarity undercuts and, in many ways, fundamentally alters the previous position to propose a different vision of literature and art. Just as Vico had, quixotically, proposed moving from Epicurus, Hobbes, and Grotius to undertake a study of the "frogs," the "cicadas," the "stones," and "rocks" to illuminate the "savage natures" of the early humans and emphasized the role of the "philologians" in the undertaking, so too does Mao. Impatient with "abstract ideas," Mao claims: "In the life of the people there lies a mine of raw material for art and literature" (21). A fairly commonplace suggestion: what is distinctive is Mao's twofold insistence that the "life of the people" be understood first and foremost through things traditionally considered by intellectuals to be "dirty" (7) and "crude" (21), that is, belonging to lower, marginalized, and supposedly backward strata; a second aspect, following from this previous one, is a call for a historical-materialist philological enquiry, that "language" (6–7) itself be investigated afresh.

Mao places language – and philological enquiry – at the very heart of the objective study of human society (10). He emphasizes that language is key both to the development of inner psychic life and to cultural expression; the latter includes oral and plastic art (e.g., handicrafts), in addition to written texts of literature. Language not only registers but also determines proletarian existence, including "their [people's] emotions, their manners ... [as well as] wall newspapers, murals, folk songs and folk tales" (16). Changing patterns of human interaction with the material world, as well as the historical evolution of modes of living, are traced in the field of language. Language, then, is a dynamic index of human experience.

Nonetheless, the Yenan lectures propagated a "party line" view of cultural production, for which they have been justly criticized. Such assessments are important. The published text of the lectures underwent several rounds of revisions in the post-revolutionary period, as Liu Kang contends, each reflecting a greater dogmatism about the "correct" kind of socialist-realist art.[13] For his part, Mao refutes the conflation between politics and art and, in fact, devotes the last two sections of the lectures to making the point that political and aesthetic criteria are differently based, not the same thing, and should not be substituted for each other. In short, artists and intellectuals enjoy a degree of autonomy separate from political activism; their concerns are also somewhat distinct from the prevailing milieu. A significant number of statements and passages, even from the authorized text version of the lectures, could be cited to support this view. Equally significant is his view of past traditions and national cultural forms. In the face of the traditionalist, neo-Confucian insistence that ancient culture contains the necessary wisdom for China's future growth, the Yenan lectures posit the past as "foreign," something that is to be neither accepted nor rejected wholesale but to be refashioned.

If Vico, in *The New Science*, had presented the past as something that is truly comprehensible only to those who lived it and therefore foreign to the present, Mao takes the Vichian position further. Echoing Vico, Mao holds that national character is historically uneven at any given time, including the present moment. Depending on levels of human self-actualization, different historical epochs coexist within the same nation (45). Such unevenness further implies that cultural forms belonging, strictly speaking, to different historical eras are found coexisting with one another at any given conjuncture. Mao proposes a form of creative adaptation – to "use ... the artistic and literary forms of the past," while "reshap[ing] them and filling them with new content" (14). He reasons that the socialist cannot be blind to the past like the modernizers, or to the outside world like the nativists. The correct approach is immanent and relational, "not reject[ing] the legacy of the ancients and the foreigners, even though it is feudal or bourgeois," but combing these with "our own creative work" (22). Arguably, this is similar to theories of world literature where the past and the transnational, as foreign forms, intersect with the form and content of the local and immediate present (see, e.g., Moretti, "Conjectures"). For Mao, however, this entails a practice of constellation, activating these diverse elements under new conditions so as to articulate previously unavailable truth.

In Mao's text, there emerges a new awareness of the relation between speculation (concepts) and totality (history). Rooted in the specifics of 1930s China, it is nevertheless generalizable to anticolonial culture at large. This is to say that Mao's original contribution does not rest solely on de-emphasizing the classical Marxian proletariat to incorporate the categories of the people and the peasantry. The Yenan talks formulate a continual dialectic of human self-consciousness actualizing itself in the realm of *popular language*, and within *reconfigured* cultural forms of the oral and plastic (and not only the textual). Such theorization resists the positivist reduction of culture to successive and linear modes of economic production, just as it denies any retrograde longing for the past. Rather, to use Rebecca Karl's evocative phrase, it is the "economic as lived experience" that comes to articulate the "semi-colony" in the fold of history.[14] I will return to this issue in the next section.

Likewise, my reading of the Yenan talks seeks to reclaim the humanist elements, and insights, against the grain of their dogmatic institutionalization in post-revolutionary China. The critic Raymond Williams, no supporter of repressive Communist regimes, perceptively noted that the aspect that was "theoretically most interesting in Mao's argument [in the Yenan lectures]" was "the emphasis on the transformation of social relations between writers and the people" (*Marxism and Literature* 203). The lectures conceptualize, Williams writes, "not only the integration of writers into popular life, but a move beyond the idea of specialist writer to new kinds of popular, including, collaborative, writing. The complexities of practice are again severe, but at least theoretically this is the germ of a radical restatement" (203).[15] As Williams correctly points out, such an emphasis renews the material, *practical* link between artistic expression and sociopolitical contestation. At the level of theory, the Yenan talks established the ground for influential counter-hegemonic conversations that were – and still are – not reducible to statist Communism.

If Tagore and Mao represented two ends of an "impossible" dialogue during the interwar era, the tensions resulting from this pairing were addressed extensively in localized debates – for example, in the pages of literary magazines and in intellectual circles in India, China, and elsewhere. These involved some of the most significant if unremembered voices of the era; comparing and contrasting the two, Tagore and Mao, many critics, artists, and writers collectively put together a framework connecting literature to the imperatives of decolonization. The dialogue was free-spirited and accretive, marked by visceral feuds, sparkling polemics, and high-minded convictions alike, just as much it was worldly in scope and form. As Arif Dirlik avers in a different context: "If Mao did not explicitly address questions of modernism and anti-modernism, the problems presented by modernity were integral to his historical context – not just the context of Chinese society but the global context" ("Modernism and Antimodernism" 59). On the other hand, Tagore was the preeminent literary figure for many Indian intellectuals, and his corpus received widely varied receptions. In addition, the near congruence of the two epochal events of Indian independence in 1947 and the Chinese Revolution of 1949, albeit with distinct trajectories, provided the context in which the potential of Tagorean and Maoist aesthetic-political ideals were debated and elaborated by various stripes of writers and critics.

Such cross-cultural interactions formed part of a broader network too vast to summarize here. Recent scholarship has uncovered other comparable and similarly fraught exchanges: to take just two examples, the influence of the Yenan lectures on postcolonial African writers, the Nigerian Omafume Onoge or the Kenyan Ngũgĩ wa Thiong'o or the reciprocal relation between African American authors and activists, such as W.E.B. Du Bois and Robert F. Williams, and Maoist internationalism during the height of the Cold War.[16] The translation and dissemination of the Yenan talks in post-partition India occasioned a similar discussion that effortlessly traversed territorial boundaries.

Much earlier, Tagore had visited China between April and May 1924. He delivered lectures, later published as *Talks in China*, to the Beijing Lecture Association as well as in Nanjing and Shanghai. Prior to his visit, Tagore was already a well-known figure in China. Chen Duxiu, co-founder of the Chinese Communist Party (later expelled by Mao for the former's Trotskyism) translated portions from Tagore's book of songs, *Gitanjali*, from English to Chinese in 1915. Another translator was the novelist Mao Dun, later minister of culture in the People's Republic. Notable others such as Liang Shuming, Liang Qichao, Qu Quibai, and Hu Shi engaged with Tagore's work, sometimes admiringly and sometimes with frank criticism. While his poetry, patriotism, and sense of pan-Asian solidarity were widely appreciated among Chinese intellectuals, Tagore's spiritual approach was often identified with obscurantist Confucianism and mysticism.[17]

A similar situation obtained during Tagore's visit to the Soviet Union, one that both endeared him to, and attracted criticism from, the Left. The poet traveled for a two-week trip in 1930. His observations, published as *Letters from Russia*, evince an admiration of the new system common to many anticolonial intellectuals of the era. Tagore presciently noted the restrictions on dissent, however, and worried what that might portend for the future development of Soviet society. At the same time, Tagore praised the massive strides made in Soviet primary education, an initiative he saw as paralleling his own efforts in Santiniketan. As well, Tagore saw the Soviet attempt to accommodate hitherto marginalized nationalities within the socialist state as a possible model for decolonization in British India. Later, in 1937, his sharp criticism of dogmatic "socialist realism" and its influence among sections of Indian writers annoyed pro-Soviet intellectuals. On the other hand, eminent Soviet intellectuals and artists, such as Nikolai Roerich, Konstantin Stanislavsky, Fyodor Shcherbatskoii, and Mikhail Tubianskii, with some reading him in the Bengali original, took and continued to take an intense interest in Tagore before, during, and after the revolutionary period.[18]

In sum, the Soviet sojourn marked a turning point in Tagore's humanist philosophy: a "fundamental shift" that is best described by the prominent scholar of Indic philosophy Debiprasad Chattopadhyaya: "From 1930, when he [Tagore] visited the Soviet Union, to 1941, the year he died, it remained as some kind of unshakeable conviction for the poet that the humanism he always dreamed of could be scientifically implemented by following the path of the Russian revolution" (Chattopadhyaya, "Tagore" 230). This development was intimately and not only incidentally related to Tagore's increasingly stringent critique of colonialism and exclusionary nationalism. Yet, what I previously termed Tagore's "socialist universalism" – with balanced emphasis on both terms – is elided in seeing him as an incipient "postcolonial" critic of anticolonial nationalism; such are the vicissitudes of intellectual history. Meanwhile, key elements of his mature conception that resonated with the revolutionary upsurge in Russia and beyond (such as the emphasis on humanism, the generalized critique of reified being, or most strikingly of all the affirmation and simultaneous interrogation of the "national spirit") are discernable much before 1930, at least as early as the 1907 *visva-sahitya* lecture. In general, however, things get especially complicated after 1930.

Both liberal anti-Communist as well as Marxist intellectuals laid claim on Tagore's legacy; if anything, the case was more bitterly contested in the sundry Marxist camps. (An interesting aside, the poet's grandnephew Saumendranath Tagore was one of the leading anti-Stalinist Marxists of the interwar period.) In his natal land, many recognized that Tagore's greatest accomplishment had been the democratization of modern Bengali literature, not only in terms of theme (content) but also style (form). Perhaps more than any previous modern writer, Tagore brought Bengali literary language closest to expressing the life of the people, while imbuing both subject and object with the philosophical gravitas of a deep humanism. This was much more the case in Tagore's poetry, songs, dance-dramas, and short stories, perhaps, than novelistic prose.[19] The nuanced recognition was already an advance over his reception in the West as an Oriental "sage" (separated from the "savage" by a solitary syllable) after the Nobel Prize.

But even sympathetic intellectuals remained divided over Tagore. To some of his more strident critics on the Left, Tagore appeared a sentimental figure at best, his humanism outdated, and his "feudal" critique of bourgeois society not very attuned to the demands of progressive literature (*pragati sahitya*) in the interwar period. Perhaps the Hungarian literary critic and philosopher Georg Lukács's characterization of Tagore – on reading the latter's novel *The Home and the World* – as a "metaphysical" and "reactionary" thinker is the best-known example of this trend. Yet Lukács's caustic review "Tagore's Gandhi Novel," published in the German magazine *Die Rote Fahne* in 1922, was not the isolated judgment of a European, and Eurocentric, critic as it might initially appear.[20] Similar charges had been leveled against Tagore in China in 1924. In Bengal, a succession of modernist and Communist intellectuals, including such leading figures as Buddhadev Bose, Saroj Dutta, Chinmohan Sehanobish, Pradyot Guha, and Bhabani Sen, made visceral criticisms throughout the 1930s and 1940s, in the pages of such influential periodicals as *Kallol*, *Agroni*, and *Marxbadi*. Equally, on the other hand, several other writers and intellectuals recognized significant overlaps between Tagorean humanism and the future goals of socialist humanism. Arguably, one of the most spectacular rereadings of "humanism and critical practice" (to borrow from Said, *Humanism and Democratic Criticism* 2) was underway.

For this latter group, interestingly, Mao's texts such as "Analysis of the Classes in Chinese Society" (1926), "On New Democracy" (1940), and the Yenan Forum talks (1942) were particularly influential in the appraisal of Tagorean humanism. The *Parichay* magazine played a key role in bringing together Tagore and Mao: in its spring issue of 1948, coedited by Gopal Haldar and Niren Roy, *Parichay* published the first Bengali version of the Yenan lectures, translated by Jagannath Chakrabarty, and another translation of Mao Zedong's poem "Snow." In addition, various poems addressed to Mao and China, written by the likes of the stalwart poet Subhas Mukhopadhyay, as well as Bimal Ghosh, Anil Kanjilal, Nirmalya Bose, and others were published in adjacent issues of the periodical. The next year, Dhananjoy Das and Mihir Sen coedited the first Bengali poetry anthology, titled *Mahachin* (Great China), memorializing the 1949 Chinese Revolution. Alongside the poets, Hiren Mukherjee, eminent public figure and future member of Parliament, published an essay in *Parichay* that underscored the significance of the Chinese triumph for national liberation movements all over Asia (Dhananjoy Das, *Marxbadi Sahitya Bitarka* 152–154). These sentiments of Indo-Chinese solidarity were widely shared (an illustrative case in point is the Kotnis-led Indian medical mission to Yenan in 1938–1939, arranged by leading Congress socialists such as Jawaharlal Nehru and Subhas Chandra Bose). Mao's reception in India, and specifically post-partition West Bengal, emerges in this context.

Around the same time between 1949 and 1950, *Parichay*, mainly, but also a number of other periodicals such as *Daak* and *Notun Sahitya* published a number of important revaluations of Tagore. These included essays by Sanat Basu, Nirendranath Roy, Amar Home, Amarendra Mitra, Satindranath Chakrabarty, and the historian Sushobhan Sarkar.[21] Drawing on the Yenan Forum's distinction between contradictory and uneven elements of the national past, as well as other Mao texts on aspects of bourgeois and feudal culture in China, these critics averred that Tagore's championing of collective liberation (*mukti*), if not Marxist, far exceeded the limits of his contemporaries. Similarly, Tagore, a committed anti-fascist through his later years, challenged the irrational and reactionary strands of Indian (read Hindu Brahminical) nationalism. If Tagore the writer sometimes posited idealistic (according to contemporary standards) solutions to social ills, he was not averse to exposing the exploitation of labor, the oppression of women, and the depredations of imperialism and fascism. In these ways, members of the group argued, Tagorean humanism represented an achievement of past culture that was worthy of retrieval and reconfiguration.

More importantly, they emphasized that the "truth" of Tagore could not be decided through critics' judgments alone, howsoever nuanced or sophisticated these may be, but rather by transforming the context of his reception, what Raymond Williams terms in relation to Mao, the "integration of writers into popular life." The humanist, rationalist, and universal aspects of Tagore could only be strengthened, nay actualized, by forging greater and deeper connections between his corpus and the marginalized culture of the non-elite classes, *loksongoskriti* in short. In practice, such a task would be complex and severe (to paraphrase Williams, again). Conversely, this critical view militated against the glib "tendency to make him [Tagore] pass as a modern revolutionary or materialist" (Chattopadhyaya, "Philosophy" 115). By emphasizing the tentative nature of ideas as unrealized activity, and simultaneously resisting their appropriation by hegemonic elite groups, as reified "icons," such pronouncements once again underscored the *materiality* of thought – as decentered, mutable, and ultimately subject to contestation.

Something else is worth mentioning here. Simply put, in reading Tagore in conjunction with Mao (and many others), these critics were answering Lukács's criticism of Tagore in Lukácsian terms. For Tagore's critical defenders, Mao's Vichian emphasis on collective practice as the final arbiter of truths proved more helpful than Lukács's seeming reliance on the individual critic's judgment of cultural classics. While these Bengali commentators display little knowledge of Lukács or his writings as far as one can tell, the critical *mode* in which they seek to recuperate Tagore corresponds almost exactly with Lukács's defense of bourgeois realism.[22] Lukács's collaborator, the noted literary critic Mikhail Lifshitz, finds mention too, though without referencing the latter's affinity with Giambattista Vico.[23] The discussions situate Tagore and Bengali literature both in relation and in distinction to the development of modern literatures of Europe, Russia, and China. Just as Lukács, in essays such as "Narrate or Describe" (1936) and individual case studies such as those anthologized in *Studies in European Realism* (1950), had distinguished between "objective illumination" and "bourgeois apologetics" in the nineteenth-century realist novel, so too did a section of Marxists rescue Tagore's corpus from crude class reductionism. This meant a practice of reading – without presuppositions or assumptions – the diverse local-indigenous and foreign traditions represented by Tagore and excavating the contradictions and contestations of colonial culture immanent therein. In this manner, Mao's writings on peripheral culture provided a significant if overlooked model for evaluating the many legacies of Tagore. This pioneering work was generative, too – knowingly and otherwise – for the development of Bengali literary criticism and aesthetics-politics. One thinks here of figures such as Munier Chowdhury, Ranesh Das Gupta, Ahmed Sofa, Serajul Islam Choudhury in Bangladesh, and Gopal Haldar, Samar Sen, Kshetra Gupta, Ramkrishna Bhattacharya in West Bengal, to name only a few.[24]

The Panchsheel Treaty of 1954 formed the high point of an "official" Indo-Chinese alliance in postwar Asia, preceding the better-known institutional moments of Bandung and the Non-Alignment Movement. The state relations between India and China steadily deteriorated thereafter, following episodes of the Indo-China border conflict (1962), the Indo-Pakistan conflict (1965), and the Bangladesh liberation struggle (1971), for reasons too varied to summarize here. But cultural solidarities went much further. By the late 1960s and 1970s, during and after the Cultural Revolution, Mao Zedong's influence reached its contradictory apotheosis in eastern South Asia. The contemporary cult of Mao is aptly captured by the pithy Bengali slogan, *chiner chairman amader chairman* (China's Chairman Is Our Chairman). This was especially true for two Communist-led movements, the Naxalites in West Bengal and the Sarbohara Party in Bangladesh. Led by Charu Mazumdar and Siraj Sikder, respectively, both parties declared their full-throated allegiance to "Mao Zedong thought." Complicating matters further was the case of theologian and politician Maulana Bhashani, whose combination of Maoism and Islamic socialism was influential before, during, and after the Liberation War in Bangladesh. The Cultural Revolution discourse about destroying the "Four Olds" – old customs, culture, habits, and ideas – proved particularly potent in the two regions. In a stunning reprisal of the 1940s, Leftist militants in West Bengal once again raised questions about the past, about the legacy of the nineteenth-century "Bengal Renaissance" and "bourgeois icons" such as Rammohan Roy, Tagore, and Ishwar Chandra Bidyasagar. In Bangladesh, by contrast, Tagore was claimed as the representative figure of Bengali nationalism against West Pakistan's colonial-military rule, and his 1906 song, *amar sonar bangla*, adopted as the national anthem in 1972, with its own set of attendant contradictions (see Saha, *An Empire of Touch* 86–87).

Still, "Maoist" and especially the ideas of the Cultural Revolution were not always blindly emulated in South Asia, as has been sometimes implied.[25] Even sympathetic fellow travelers raised oblique-to-direct critical questions about Communist China's trajectory, while remaining equally if not more critical of their own dominant nationalisms. If an earlier generation, in the 1940s, sough to conjoin the appraisal of Tagore's ideas to the demands of mass politics, many in the 1970s subjected Maoism, and the growing personality cult of Mao himself, to a similar litmus test. Once again, we see the ideas of Tagore and Mao juxtaposed and measured in relation to social formations and contests.

When Hemango Biswas, one of the leading figures of the Indian People's Theater Association (IPTA), visited China in 1957, Tagore was foremost on his mind. On the occasion of Tagore's birthday, May 8, 1959, Biswas published an article on "Rabindranath and China" in the editorial pages of *Renmin Ribao* (People's Daily), the official organ of the Communist Party of China. Biswas clearly reprised a Marxist take on his compatriot, noting that while Tagore always sang of generalized freedom (*chhuti*), he specifically desired liberation (*mukti*) from the bonds of labor in capitalist society (*dhonotantrik samajer sromer bondhon*). According to Biswas, after witnessing the physical labors of the Chinese workers of Hong Kong, Tagore had formulated a possible future of a China where labor was not measured by the value it produced, but by the communist principle of each according to her need (*Abar Chin Dekhe Elam*, 5–7).[26]

When Biswas went back a second time, in 1974, he was much more critical of the Communist regime supposedly carrying out Tagore's vision of non-alienated communist freedom. Biswas admits to his Bengali readers that the principles laid down by Mao in the Yenan Forum lectures, which were a "lodestar" to leftist artists and writers worldwide in 1958 (during Biswas's previous visit), had been thwarted by the development of bureaucratic and anti-democratic tendencies in China. He recounts that in 1931, the Gorky School, so named after the iconic Russian writer Maxim Gorky, was set up in Ruijin, Jiangxi province, to train Red Army soldiers in not only warfare but also theater and songs. These institutions sought to embed an internationalist ethos in the daily lives of ordinary people – millions of peasants, soldiers, and workers – that had been neglected by the urban-based efflorescence of the May Fourth intellectuals. Biswas lamented the bureaucratic managerial classes that had, to some extent at least, reversed the processes of democratization and revolution from below (*Abar Chin* 284–286).

If Biswas glossed over the contradictions of post-revolutionary China somewhat, another Bengali Indian colleague was more perceptive to, and frankly critical of, the Cultural Revolution's violent suppression of artists. This is the case of Utpal Dutt, noted Brechtian dramaturge, stage and screen actor, and cultural critic. Like Biswas, Dutt visited China in the 1970s and published a largely positive account, *China Jatri* (1979); additionally, at the height of the Naxalite movement, he performed a series of plays in West Bengal that were modeled on the Peking Opera, including plays on Vietnam, Cuba, and Mao Zedong (more on that in Chapter 4). But Dutt pointedly criticized the "lumpen 'revolutionaries'" of the Cultural Revolution who beat up veteran Peking Opera players under the banner of *Kulturkampf* (cultural struggle). He drew explicit parallels to India, noting that the same tendency of mob violence appeared in 1948 under the "left deviation," and in the late 1960s and early 1970s during the height of Naxalism (*Revolutionary Theatre* 37). In these remarks, unfavorably comparing the Cultural Revolution to Nazi Germany, Dutt pinpoints the destructive impact of Communist dogma on culture. While committed to the principles of socialism, Dutt decries the latter's violent appropriation of collective identity, in China as much as in India.

Similarly, commenting on the Naxalite controversy around Tagore, Dutt unequivocally opposed the "petit-bourgeois" intellectual vogue for censoring classics as per the latest fashion whether that is "the Swastika or the Red flag." The emancipation of the working classes, he correctly reasons, cannot be imposed from above. Rather, Dutt argued, "It is the worker who must read the classics and then it is he [sic] alone who will judge what he needs and what he does not. No other class has the right to sift the classics and hand the worker a censored selection" (*Revolutionary Theatre* 105).[27] Dutt's statements revisit, albeit in slightly modified form, the problem of intersecting classics with *loksongoskriti* as discussed earlier. At the same time, they reveal a greater and ultimately unresolvable tension between upholding the artist's or intellectual's freedom to explore *while* denying her the right to adjudicate over culture. Either as an instrument of the state or swayed by the latest market trend – where "boredom becomes his source of politics" (105) – the artist-intellectual impedes rather than enables the creative processes of culture. By contrast, Dutt locates two vectors of solidarity at the heart of cultural work: internationalist solidarity, to be constantly renewed rather than passively advocated, and counter-hegemonic solidarity with oppressed social groups. His stance is illustrated by a telling anecdote. Asked, in a 1971 interview, to explain his notion of revolutionary theater, Dutt replied simply: "Our 'program' is to bring the stories of the gallant revolutionary struggles of another people to our own people so that they too will be inspired to fight" ("Theater as a Weapon" 225). This was in reference to Dutt's group staging a play, in West Bengal in 1966, on the contemporary Vietnamese struggle against US occupation.

The repeated constellation of the foreign and the worldly, as well as Tagore and Mao, in the work of these intellectuals signals a broader practice of solidarity. Such solidarities radiated outward and downward – in theory, embracing ever broader regions of the world, while capaciously incorporating the resistance of those below. The extent to which such ideals were realized or miscarried in practice, articulated in different forms and in multiple directions, forms the focus of the present book. Taken as a whole, my account traverses vital if unequally illuminated conjunctures of the long twentieth century: interwar notions of the anticolonial East, the contradictory legacies of Communism and national liberation, and the advent and crisis of neoliberal globalization.

In the next chapter, complementing – and completing – the Asian *Geist* of the interwar era, I trace an overshadowed history of solidarity coursing through India and the Soviet Union by way of the United States, Mexico, and Germany. Though not a literary figure in the traditional sense, M.N. Roy, whose narrative *Memoirs* I discuss, is a cultural worker in the broadest sense. Compared to his better-known compatriot Tagore, Roy's advocacy of internationalism, signaling a heterodox trajectory of activist and intellectual history, is largely forgotten today. Similar but not identical strands of heterodox internationalism are elaborated in subsequent chapters of the book that delineate interactions between India and Latin America, Vietnam, Black America, and China across a range of cultural forms – cinema, fiction, drama, and nonfiction. The Naxalite movement in India, so named after the 1967 Naxalbari uprising in West Bengal and confined to central and southern Indian provinces today, forms a running thread in these chapters, further illuminating Mao's reception and mobilization in postcolonial India.

Between Chapters 3 and 5, I move from Bengali literary and cultural depictions of the movement's earlier phase of the 1960s and 1970s to Anglophone representations of the post-2000s era. Respectively, I discuss the work of Mrinal Sen and Mahasweta Devi, and Arundhati Roy and Aravind Adiga, from the earlier and later periods, as well as explore many lesser known others. The political ideology of the Naxalite groups and other significant Left constellations such as the parliamentary Communists (who were elected to power for a record thirty-four years, 1977–2011, in West Bengal) are outside the scope of the present study.[28] Rather, the ebbs and flows of Naxalism register, as I show, historically determinate notions of solidarity and critique linking the intellectual to the struggles of the urban underclass or "lumpen proletariat" and the rural landless indigenous or *adivasi* peasantry. Each of the artists and writers adopts as well as adapts – at times with contradictory impulses – foreign and indigenous ideas, forms, and genres. They juxtapose, for example, experimental film with short stories, feminist fiction and Brechtian theater, and reportage and the novel. To be sure, each of these figures is quite distinct in matters of style, temperament, and even political sensibility. Nonetheless, I suggest, the content as well as the techniques and strategies of their creative works are shaped by something more than artistic preference. By putting dissimilar forms in conversation with each other, these texts not only rework extant literary-aesthetic traditions but also locate global literary forms in conjunction with persistent social contestations. Localized and peripheral struggles – connecting not only those in Asia, Latin America, and Africa but also within Europe and North America – come to take center stage, eclipsing and thoroughly reconfiguring the metropolitan and Anglo-centric conception of the world.

What emerges from these diverse encounters, I argue, is a profile of peripheral internationalism as a series of *insurgent imaginations*. The idea of humanism is at the heart of the matter. It is humanism that informs its principle of solidarity, animates each of its texts, and undergirds the constellation as a whole. In the words of Tagore's *visva-sahitya*, peripheral internationalism embraces the "union of its particular humanness with all humanity." This includes not only neglected or unrealized dialogues among the geo-historical regions of the peripheral world, as activists, writers, and other militants engage with one another across cultural and national boundaries. But also, such engagements and interactions, constellations and groupings, activate an alternative conception of world literature. Peripheral internationalism articulates a decolonizing vision challenging the unidirectional traffic of ideas from the metropolitan core to the peripheries, and highlighting the narrowness of Anglo-centered ideologies of cosmopolitanism and transnationalism.

I locate peripheral internationalism as not simply a formation in time and space, composed of a number of texts, figures, and connections. Such an account, properly speaking, is the task of the empirical historian. Rather, I read into the specific conjunctures of the world as they are articulated in the text: namely, how people felt, perceived, and ultimately imagined their connections to others. As much as anything else, this constitutes a *reading method*. In the remaining pages of this chapter, I flesh out my methodology and its implications for a peripheral world literature through the concept of the "national allegory." Reading within and against the grain of empirical and imperial reality, such a method focalizes human thought as a material presence. Furthermore, mediating between the particular and the universal, my reading explicitly illuminates the connections between artistic and socialized labor.

The National Allegory

To locate conceptual, imaginative *thought* as negation of the past and present, foregrounding the not-yet of the future, recall Adorno's observation in the brief essay "Resignation": "Whatever was once thought ... can be suppressed; it can be forgotten and can even vanish. But it cannot be denied that something of it survives" ("Resignation" 168). To reduce thought to an objective, that is, positive teleology, is to resign one's critical faculty. Adorno contends that the intellectual's role is not to submit her critical autonomy to the current fashion, no matter how convincing or appealing it may be (his own reference is to the events of May 1968 and his nonparticipation therein). While it is not necessary to commend Adorno's skeptical attitude toward activism, the importance of his remarks lies in another direction. Adorno reminds us that thinking – thought-as-activity – is at its most potent when it continues to resist the historical defeat of its actualization. Resistance – in and through thought – lies in the negation of failed utopias as well as victorious reactions. Rather than accepting the demise of emancipatory horizons, the task of critique is to remain true to its negative charge (see also Adorno, *Hegel: Three Studies*).

Influential books and essays, such as Pascale Casanova's *The World Republic of Letters* and Franco Moretti's "Conjectures on World

Literature," have injected fresh vitality into the concept of *weltliteratur*.[29] What is common to critics such as Casanova and Moretti is an interest in delineating a "literary world-system," tracing the production, circulation, and reception of ideas, forms, and genres. One of the notable gains from the world literature conversations of the past two decades, it seems, is the renewed awareness of what Edward Said, in the 1980s, had termed the "worlding" of texts (*The World, The Text* 31–53). Complicating the then-dominant view of language and literature as wholly autonomous entities, Said's remarks on the text's relation to the world proved remarkably prescient.[30] Thus, Franco Moretti, borrowing from Immanuel Wallerstein et al., speaks of "one world literary system . . . [that is] profoundly unequal" ("Conjectures" 56). Pascale Casanova, influenced by Pierre Bourdieu, similarly describes the "field" of literature as mediated by the cultural circuits of the French metropole and its capital city, Paris (*The World Republic* 23–34). Whatever their sins of omission, the work of literary critics such as Moretti and Casanova deserves commendation for its incorporation of economic history and sociology into the study of literary texts.

The resurgence of world-systemic analysis is not a new contribution per se, but a belated, and partial, correction of earlier errors. A framework deemed obsolete two decades ago, namely materialism/Marxism, is being reanimated by cultural scholars, critics, and students to make sense of the contemporary world, albeit often without the goals of struggle, democratization, and emancipation that marked materialist critique. On the one hand, it has become unexceptional to suggest that the economic does play a role vis-à-vis the cultural; on the other hand, the role of either in a politics of emancipation is seldom probed. What has returned in recent decades, unanticipated, is cultural materialism. This is also to say that such returns have been partially obscured and misrepresented.

Today, one locates not only a vigorous and welcome interest in non-metropolitan literary traditions but also, more crucially, the recognition that texts operate in and are mediated by hierarchical structures of accumulation and differentiation between the core, semi-periphery, and periphery: a capitalist world-system in short. Certainly this has not been the only or even the principal line of enquiry; nevertheless, it has been a significant one. Drawing on theorists such as Immanuel Wallerstein and Neil Smith on scale and, even earlier, Leon Trotsky on combined and uneven development, world-system thinking resituates the comparative study of minor aesthetic modalities, the parallels between regional

The National Allegory

modernisms, and the translational and transnational circulation of literary and cultural texts.[31]

In recent times, there is arguably greater acknowledgment of the mimetic function of literature, as well as the latter's registration of what Raymond Williams termed "the experienced tensions, shifts and uncertainties, the intricate forms of unevenness and confusion" that mark "lived [social] experience" (*Marxism and Literature* 129–131). To the extent that such discussions are rooted in a materialist understanding of literature and are not simply reiterations of a traditional model, describing the diffusion of stylistic influence from the European metropole to the peripheries and semi-peripheries, they represent a genuine advance. Materialist world literature moves beyond, on the one hand, the poststructuralist insistence on seeing literature as a randomly assembled order of signs, signifiers without signifieds, as well as the postcolonial criticism, on the other hand, that claimed that Western conceptual tools were simply inadequate for deciphering the non-Western world, and as such any unitary, materialist-humanist model of interpretation à la Williams perforce needs discarding.[32]

A counterpart to Raymond Williams's account of the countryside and the city in British literature, the Brazilian critic Roberto Schwarz traces the relation between novelistic form and the social form of the periphery in *Misplaced Ideas: Essays on Brazilian Culture* (English translation 1992). Yet Schwarz, one of the key theorists of Brazilian literature, finds no mention in Pascale Casanova's discussion of peripherality in the Latin American novel, or in her much-quoted notion of the "Greenwich meridian of literary taste" (92–101, 232–234). In turn, Moretti, discussing the export of metropolitan literary forms of the novel and their interaction with diverse local contexts in the colonial and non-colonial peripheries, has this to say about Schwarz: "Now, that the same configuration [of export of ideas] should occur in such different cultures as India and Japan – this was curious; and it became even more curious when I realized that Roberto Schwarz had independently discovered very much the same pattern in Brazil" ("Conjectures" 58). Schwarz's originality is neither "independent," as Moretti wants us to believe, nor can Schwarz be adduced so easily to Moretti's supposedly "un-American," "distant reading" (57–58). Schwarz – and his theory of objective form – belongs to a tradition of criticism that includes his teacher at the University of São Paulo, Antonio Candido, as much as the key figures of interwar Marxism, Georg Lukács and Theodor Adorno.[33] While Moretti sees Schwarz's negative method as the precursor to his own positive model of distant reading, I believe – and genuinely wish to emphasize – that they are quite separate.

Contemporary critics such as Casanova and Moretti accept the structuring role of imperial and capitalist unevenness as determinate conditions for literary production. Yet in the last instance, these critics' aim becomes descriptive – that is, an attempt to classify the social form of capitalist modernity in quasi-scientific and even pragmatic terms of *models*. This already represents a retreat from earlier, and robustly anti-positivist, traditions of materialism per se. A second tendency, best exemplified by Susan Stanford Friedman's magisterial study *Planetary Modernisms*, is even more ambitiously revisionist: it discards any notion of modernity as the historically specific and concrete social form of capital emerging on a world scale in the sixteenth century. Friedman, following Fernand Braudel's notion of *longue durée* and Bruno Latour's network theory, sees modernity and modernism everywhere and at every time, thus – in effect – nowhere.[34] In such accounts, the constitutive role of capital as limit, especially the mediation of colonial-capitalism, is relegated to a second order of explanation if not discarded wholesale.

What is left out, arguably, is a conception of substantive rather than nominal democracy. By sharp contrast, it is precisely such a concern that animates the revolutionary humanism of world literature's European founders – Goethe, Marx, and Engels. It is not incidental that the "German Enlightenment," represented by these three figures (and Hegel), was first forged in the peripheral milieu of a backward Germany, trailing behind England and France (here I paraphrase the argument put forward by the Brazilian theorist Paulo Arantes and his notion of *ressentimento*; an earlier formulation is found in Lukács, *Goethe and His Age*). Similarly, freedom or *mukti* is a defining aspect of Tagore's *visva-sahitya*. Marking the early stirrings of Indian or more properly Asian anticolonialism, Tagore's *visva-sahitya* militated against utilitarian or nominal freedom while retaining an emphasis on universal humanism. This is of course a nonrepresentative list of thinkers (along gender lines, for example). But over the past two centuries, there emerged a definitive linkage between emancipation, progress and the keenly felt awareness of peripheral status. To recount these interventions is to yoke world literature anew to the desire for emancipation.

Roberto Schwarz's discussion is noteworthy on this count. In the central essay of *Misplaced Ideas*, "Brazilian Culture: Nationalism by Elimination" (1986), commenting on the cultural imbalance between Brazil and metropolitan nations such as England or France, Schwarz observes that "the painfulness of an imitative civilization is produced not by imitation – which is present at any event – but by the social structure of the country" (15). Rather than seeing the intrusion of core-metropolitan ideas in the structurally dependent periphery (Brazil, in his case) as an ontological lack, a "copy" of a European "original," Schwarz sees Brazilian literature as articulating a social structure of unevenness or mixed norms. Significantly, Raymond Williams, writing slightly before this time, had theorized a similar "structure of feeling" in describing the changing literary representations of the countryside in Britain. In Schwarz's study, a tiny Europeanized intellectual class imbued with "imported" ideas of liberty and progress struggled to express the social reality of a country undergirded by slave labor and an export-oriented plantation economy. The distinctive form of social classes in Brazil was tripartite: a liberal elite, an intermediate group of *agregados* or free men and women, and the directly enslaved. "Backwardness" and "national dependency" in such a context, to be sure, are coeval: belonging to "the same order of things as the progress of the advanced countries" in the metropolitan core (14). "Our 'backwardness,'" Schwarz claims, is "part of the contemporary history of capital and *its advances*" (16, original emphasis). Drawing, above all, from Adorno, Schwarz contends that it is literary form that best captures the contradictions of social form in the periphery, more than thematic content.[35]

The resulting differential calibration of realist and modernist form in non-metropolitan literatures will be familiar to most scholars of world literature.[36] Such differentials need not be restricted to Brazil but extend to other peripheral literatures. What is less familiar, I want to point out, is Schwarz's *partisan* approach in the old political sense of the term. For Schwarz suggests, rather emphatically, that the crisis of aesthetic autonomy in the periphery can be resolved only through greater popular access to culture, and not by rejecting metropolitan/foreign ideas in favor of autochthonous ones. The peculiar contradiction of peripheral representation rests "on the exclusion of the poor from the universe of contemporary culture" (16). This is of course a general point about capitalist culture tout court. Schwarz argues for more than economic justice for the poor. He suggests that culture itself is impoverished by being restricted to the "elite" and the "dominant class," necessarily locked into a condition of dependence on the metropolis, since these are "the beneficiaries of ... [the] given situation" (15).

By focusing on the exclusion of the poor from the universe of culture, what Schwarz testifies to is the partisan nature of cultural activity. His work gives concrete theoretical shape to that which is immanent within a given cultural formation, but which is activated only by purposive labor of the collective. Or to put it differently, the negation of the present order rests with the "workers gaining access" to their conditions of existence, and "redefin[ing] them through their own initiative" (16). Situated squarely within the realm of creative human practice, the outcome of such processes is unpredictable, "either promis[ing] ... or catastrophic." The form of Schwarz's dialectical argument is negative: successively engaging nativist, postmodernist, and ontological reading practices, only to reveal the inadequacy of each. If dialectical criticism is posited as a contrarian method in Adorno, it emerges, in Schwarz, only in opposition to prior available options and with an emphasis on demotic practice. Critique folds within itself the present order of things, transforming identity into non-identity and back again – what Hegel describes in the *Phenomenology* as the schema of negation, fulfillment, and sublation.

Schwarz's approach constitutes the conceptual ground for reading what I contend is a peripheral aesthetics, attentive to the particular histories of societies and the literatures these engender. Rather than venerating a small canon of postcolonial texts, all more or less divorced from context, this entails a rigorously historicized examination of diverse national literary traditions, their mediated autonomies, and their interconnectedness. Furthermore, instead of viewing these texts and contexts as unique or culturally irreducible, these are properly seen as interlinked instantiations of a literary world-system shaped by "capital and its advances," and articulating the specific limit-conditions for the abolition of the latter.

To concretely ground the notion of the periphery, I draw on the world-system theorist Andre Gunder Frank's remarkable formulation, the "development of underdevelopment," which is in turn derived from the mid-twentieth-century work of Latin American *dependista* economists such as Raúl Prebisch, Theotonio Dos Santos, Fernando Henrique Cardoso, and others (see Cardoso, "Consumption"). The methodology that Gunder Frank put forward in the collection *Dynamics of Global Crisis* (1982) might just as well be used to describe the literary world-system of cores and peripheries. Frank asserts that crisis

> should perhaps be interpreted not simply as spreading outward from the Western center, but rather as developing out of the imbalances in changing productive capacities, supply and demand, and international trade flows [of the world-system] .... With adequate historical and futuristic scope, such analysis would facilitate appreciation of the changing roles of the world's productive, trading, and consuming units of the West, South, and East in the capitalist international division of labor. (112)

It should be noted that in the last phase of his career, particularly *ReORIENT* (1998), Frank departed from dependency theory. Sweepingly, and with some justification perhaps, *ReORIENT* points to the Eurocentrism of key materialist thinkers from Marx to Wallerstein and notes, again correctly, that "Asia and not Europe held center stage for most of early modern history" (xv).[37] In thinking of literature, the focus on the relations of production, exchange, and consumption does not imply reducing representation to economics but rather on the dialectic that binds the two. Frank gestures in the cited passage to a second related point: like Schwarz, he suggests that the question of ideational dominance of the metropolitan cores over the semi-peripheries and peripheries should be approached in the context of structural imbalances and capacities, supply and demand of the international division of labor. The periphery is a relational entity based, in the final instance, on appropriated labor.

Already in the early 1980s, Frank helps to rethink the literary-cultural relation of domination between the advanced metropole and the backward periphery. Frank suggests, correctly, that there can be no account of Eurocentrism in the periphery that operates exclusively at the level of discourse.[38] Nor can one speak of associated notions such as epistemic imperialism, teleological progress, and colonial rationality only on the plane of linguistic ideas. Instead, as another scholar notes, taking stock of contending materialities, one needs to "emphasize the importance of examining all parts of the world in irreducible, mutually implicating relation to each other ... [and] understanding *capitalism* (not "Eurocentrism" or "cultural imperialism") as underwriting those relations in their historically specific form of 'combined and uneven development'" (Bartolovich 10, original emphasis).

Peripheral aesthetics arises out of – and responds to – the mutually implicated yet uneven world created by socialized capital. To postulate our hypothesis: the condition of possibility of peripheral aesthetics is combined and uneven development. This is the juxtaposition of capitalist and non-capitalist modes of production and their determinate social relations in a given order, with the former – the capitalist mode – dominating (Trotsky, *History*). Such pairings generate a series of contradictions marking social life. This engenders a modernism as a set of representational strategies and concerns, which corresponds to the disjunctive and discontinuous experience of modernity. Peripheral aesthetics not only arises out of unevenness but also, as a resisting impulse, seeks to abolish its conditions of emergence.

Such a delineation of peripheral aesthetics recalls that proposed by Fredric Jameson in his much-debated essay "Third-World Literature in the Age of Multinational Capitalism" (hereafter, "Third-World Literature"). I turn to this essay because its argument about "national allegory" and "third-world aesthetic" holds maybe even more relevance today than when it was first published. In the Anglo-American context, it remains the pioneering attempt at a systematic delineation of the relation between the world-system and peripheral literary cultures. Jameson not only establishes a materialist perspective on world literature; he also anticipates many of the strands of the current debate.[39] His richly sophisticated account of modernisms and modernities in the third world and their development vis-à-vis the West concretely situates the determinate relation between artistic representation and historical circumstance – that is, the objective form of the national allegory.

My aim here is limited to illustrating a particular aspect of Jameson's argument. Like Schwarz's account of nineteenth-century Brazil, Jameson's reading of late twentieth-century third-world literature contains the crucial and much overlooked suggestion that culture is, in fact, a site of *emancipatory contestation*. The notion of third-world aesthetic rests on an oppositional critique whose conceptual basis bears retrieval. Moreover, the persistent significance of Jameson's theorization rests on a paradox: it is relevant despite the disappearance of the third world as a geopolitical entity, as well as the disintegration of socialism not only in the erstwhile second world but also in the present-day "socialist" countries such as China, Vietnam, North Korea, and Cuba. In other words, a fresh evaluation of "Third-World Literature" emphasizes the fact that the processes of peripheralization are *not* exclusive to the third world. Furthermore, I wish to stress that the terms "first," "second," and "third world" do not simply name geographical or temporal but conceptual entities. These terms indicate an evolving trajectory – between the 1950s and 1980s – of capital and its uneven expansion. If the era of global or multinational capital (the latter signified in the title of Jameson's essay) has offered one lasting lesson, it is confirmation of the fact that peripheralization and the attendant issues of uneven development do not wither away but continue to determine the imperialized world. Since the 1990s, these are realigned within newer parameters of metropolitan centers and semi- and full peripheries.[40]

Jameson proposes "a literary and cultural comparativism of a new type," deriving "a more typological analysis of the various socio-economic situations from which they [literary texts] spring and to which they constitute a direct response" ("Third World Literature" 86–87). More controversially, he holds that such a study should proceed from a premise that is distinct from the modern "West." Jameson claims the following, "by way of a sweeping hypothesis":

> All third-world texts are necessarily, I want to argue, allegorical, and in a very specific way: they are to be read as what I will call *national allegories*, even when, or perhaps I should say particularly when their forms develop out of predominantly Western machineries of representation, such as the novel. (69, original emphasis)

One of the key criticisms voiced against Jameson's method, to frame it in the words of its chief opponent, Aijaz Ahmad, is that "there is no such thing as a 'third-world literature,' which can be constructed as an internally coherent object of theoretical knowledge" ("Jameson's Rhetoric" 4). Ahmad pinpoints some of Jameson's missteps and oversights. There is sound logic to his counterposition (which I address in the final chapter of the book). But Ahmad, quite mistakenly, faults Jameson for not saying what the latter actually does say: namely, that the third world is an internally coherent concept, an abstraction, but only in relation to *capital*. In fact, Jameson is keenly aware of this determination when he speaks of third-world cultures as "locked in a life and death struggle with first-world cultural imperialism – a cultural struggle that is itself a reflection of the economic situation in such areas of their penetration by various stages of capital" (68). Despite sharing typological similarities, literary texts from the third world are different from one another as well as from those of the West. From his title onward ("Jameson's Rhetoric of Otherness"), Ahmad imputes to Jameson a notion of essentialized, civilizational divides between the West and the third world; in doing so, Ahmad highlights – and underrates, in Jameson – the uneven globalizing and universalizing tendencies that locate the peripheries in comparable yet distinct relationships of dependency and penetration with respect to metropolitan capitalism.

Rather than a supposedly Eurocentric essentialism, I want to contend, it is the awareness of combined unevenness that marks Jameson's use of the terms "third world," "nation," and crucially "allegory." The third world, encompassing the regions formerly dominated by colonial capitalism, marks a distinctive type of cultural experience, notes Jameson, because it is witness to the uprooting, displacement, and annihilation of pre-colonial ways of life, and the top-down replacement of older, precapitalist modes of production with capitalist wage-labor, monetization, and commodity forms of production (68). As the constitutive space of European (and

North American) colonization and combined and uneven modes of production, the third world, symptomatically as it were, foregrounds the fact that culture is imposed (everywhere), as Benita Parry terms it, by "violent imperialism":

> The peripheries and semi-peripheries of core capitalism extended and still extend to a larger geo-political expanse than the colonized regions ... [but] the extent and degree of the coercions visited on those [colonial] societies ... register a consciousness of a violent imperialism that we will not expect to find in Eastern Europe or Portugal [i.e. non-colonized peripheries]. (Parry, "Aspects" 28–29)

It is important to emphasize two related points here. First, the uprooting, displacement, and annihilation of older social formations – while characteristic of capitalist penetration everywhere per se – are still particular, and dependent on local factors. The degree of this transformation varies from region to region but also between semi-peripheral and peripheral nations, and between ex-colonies and those peripheries with no colonial history. These are not identical in nature and scope. Second, and therefore, these differences symptomatically gesture *toward* a worldwide system that is constituted in and through these particularities. In Jameson, it is in this specific vein that national allegory serves as an interpretive method for the diverse sets of representations that arise from the third world.

Neither the national nor the allegorical moreover is limited to the third world. The term "national allegory" first appears in Jameson, in a 1979 text that is prior to, and in some senses anticipating the arguments of, the "Third-World Literature" essay. This is in Jameson's discussion of the English author Wyndham Lewis in *Fables of Aggression*. Imre Szeman has drawn our attention to this. Jameson claims that Lewis's novel *Tarr* (1918) sets up a "dialectically new and more complicated allegorical system ... [T]he national allegory in general, and *Tarr* in particular, presuppose ... the objective existence of a system of nation-states" (Jameson *Fables* 90–91, 94 qtd. in Szeman 57–58). In *Fables* as well as in the "Third-World Literature" essay, Jameson asserts a single and theoretically consistent point: the nation-state, as an inherited historical form, is born out of capital's continuous rearrangement of the territorial markers of the world-system. The modern nation-state constitutes not only a fundamental unit of political and literary analysis but also implies coevalness of the West and the third world. While emancipatory politics need not be restricted to the nation-state, it is also true that this particular form, and the attendant popular struggle over discrete nationalisms, cannot be simply wished away. To do so is to deny the overdetermined and hierarchical condition of empire in which diverse nation-states and nationalisms coexist and interact.

The imperative to read third-world literature as national allegory does not impose an a priori reduction of the "other" as a belated image of the "Western self." Rather, this imperative is properly born out of the recognition of a "structural tendency in the narrative forms" of the periphery. As Neil Larsen notes in his commentary on the Jameson-Ahmad debate:

> If... the third world nation exists, on one plane at least, only as an abstract possibility – as a volatile and unstable form of social identity resting on the already volatile and unstable "Bandung" alliance of third world capital and labor – then it follows that attempts to represent this nation ... will reflect this abstraction within the formal elements of the medium itself. (*Determinations* 19)

In other words, even if each and every literary text from the third world does not project the allegorical narrative of the nation, it is within the condition of possibility that it does so.

Likewise, third-world national allegory is not some ascription of ritualistic correspondence between reality and representation. Nor does it imply that the cultures in question lack any distinction between the private and public, or between individual and collective history. Far from it: as Jameson defines it, "the allegorical spirit is profoundly discontinuous, a matter of breaks and heterogeneities" ("Third-World Literature" 73). Jameson's understanding of allegory is a consistent one, something that, once again, his critics appear to misrecognize. In *Marxism and Form* (1972), Jameson reads Walter Benjamin and especially Benjamin's *The Origin of German Tragic Drama* as a "theorist of allegory"; he follows Benjamin in noting that "both – the Baroque and the modern – [are] in their very essence allegorical" (60).

This earlier essay goes on to offer a detailed and, it has to be said, richly nuanced discussion of the trajectory of allegorical representation in the West, encompassing Dante, the Baroque era, Baudelaire, Proust, and T.S. Eliot.[41] To provide a specific example of the relevance of allegory for the discontinuous cultural experience of the periphery, recall the literary and visual investment in the transculturated New World Baroque among twentieth-century Latin American intellectuals, such as José Lezama Lima, Frida Kahlo, Alejo Carpentier, and Gabriel García Márquez (Zamora, *The Inordinate Eye*; Kaup, *Neobaroque*). Jameson's reflection on Benjamin's Baroque is equally applicable in the Latin American context, both predating the third world. As in feudal Europe's transition to early mercantile capitalism, in a like manner one can speak of the periphery's incorporation under imperialism: "allegory is precisely the dominant mode of expression of a world in which things have been for whatever reason utterly sundered from meanings, from spirit, from genuine human existence" (*Marxism and Form* 72). In this light, Ahmad's criticism that Jameson uses national allegory to separate the third world from the West, as "metatext as well as the mark of its constitution and difference" ("Jameson's Rhetoric" 11), seems quite off the mark. Interestingly, Ahmad cites *Marxism and Form* in his discussion; however, he reads it to the opposite purpose, not in terms of the continuity between allegorical representation in early modern Europe and the imperialized periphery of the early twentieth century, but something that reconfirms Jameson's Eurocentrism (13–14).

Allegorical representation is intimately tied to modernism, which as Jameson argues, is "seen as uniquely corresponding to an uneven moment of social development ... the coexistence of realities from radically different moments of history" (Jameson, *Postmodernism* 307). Modernism, in this register, is tied closely to the cognitive experience of what Ernst Bloch called the "simultaneity of the non-simultaneous" [*die Gleichzeitigkeit des Ungleichzeitigen*]. It articulates the contradictory mediations that mark lived experience, between feeling and articulation, more acutely manifested if anywhere in the peripheries than in the metropoles. As Jameson remarks elsewhere, this is "a formal mode ... [that presupposes] a type of historical raw material in which disjunction is structurally present ... [and which] articulate[s] [the] superposition of whole layers of the past within the present" ("On Magical Realism" 311). It is this structural condition of unevenness that gives peripheral modernism its peculiar, and arguably distinctive, charge.

Neil Lazarus has observed that the reception of national allegory "mutate[d] from [Ahmad's] Marxist critique of 'Third-Worldism' into a 'Third-Worldist' critique of Marxism" (*The Postcolonial Unconscious* 99). This change had a lot to do with the general theoretical sentiments of the 1980s and 1990s, as Lazarus suggests, which might seem less important today. What I think is the most underutilized aspect of Jameson's thesis is his claim about the political function of the third-world intellectual, and that of culture as a site of humanist emancipatory struggle: "In the third-world situation the intellectual is always in one way or another a political intellectual. No third-world lesson is more timely or more urgent *for us* today, among whom the very term 'intellectual' has withered away, as though it were the name for an extinct species" (74, emphasis added). Not only he does go beyond the liberal-cosmopolitan politics of representation (to let the subaltern speak, so to say, the very opposite of Spivak's thesis), Jameson links the role of the intellectual to the very different terrain of socialist politics.

It is a sentiment that one may well heed. Surely, in "withering away," the intellectual has simply been re-enmeshed into the bourgeois public sphere. To paraphrase Gramsci, it appears as if "independent intellectuals," keenly cultivating their individuality, paradoxically end up reiterating the ruling class view that change – in the sense of transformative emancipation – is impossible. Intellectuals have lost their oppositional role, or put in other words, the very term "opposition" has been evacuated of historical meaning.[42] These are the very terms of the withering away of the intellectual, indexing "our imprisonment in the present of postmodernism" ("Third-World Literature" 66). Jameson's anecdotal counterexample, about attending a discussion on the role of intellectuals in a college-preparatory school in Cuba, a third-world and socialist country, seems to suggest that this is not the case everywhere (75). Surprisingly, few discussions of Jameson's essay seem to take notice of his trenchant critique of intellectual pessimism and retreat.

What the essay implies by the intellectual's renewed participation in "cultural revolution" is the "old mystery, the unity of theory and practice" (76). Jameson invokes Mao Zedong in this context, though without referencing the multiple genealogies flowing from Mao both within and outside China. In that sense, Jameson obscures the scope of his own argument – just as he fails to sufficiently dwell on the fact that Lu Xun's "A Madman's Diary" (1918) that he analyzes is not, actually, a third-world text, strictly speaking, but from an earlier period. Similarly, Maoism, despite its somewhat attenuated presence in radical theory today, such as in the philosophical work of Alain Badiou and Slavoj Žižek, does not enjoy the status that it did once. Unlike the instances of a domesticated Gramsci or a Fanon, it is perhaps because contemporary cultural theory has been unable or unwilling to appropriate Mao.[43] Maoism – and the Cultural Revolution in particular – are invoked more often than not to delegitimize any "nostalgic" association between organized politics and the political role of art. The example of Maoism unfailingly reminds us of the pitfalls of instrumentalization, of reducing art to politics. However, such accounts fail to grasp the contradictory legacies of the Chinese revolution, mediated through prerevolutionary writers such as Lu Xun and, especially, the figure of Mao himself. To clarify, this is not to say that the authoritarian violence of the Mao era (1949–1976) or afterward should not be unequivocally condemned.[44]

The "political intellectual" (Jameson's phrase) is intimately linked to the notion of creative activity as a "struggle" or *agon*. In the Yenan Forum lectures from a much earlier moment, Mao delineates such a view:

> What we demand is the unity of politics and art ... [The] works of art, which lack artistic quality, have no force, however progressive they are politically. Therefore, we oppose both works of art with a wrong political viewpoint and the tendency towards the "poster and slogan style" which is correct in political viewpoint but lacking in artistic power. On questions of literature and art we must carry on a struggle on two fronts. (36)

To be sure, aesthetic and political work are two different things, and one cannot stand in for the other. They are not entirely separate either, but rather exist in complementary relation to each other. This is the connection between aesthetics and politics, or as Mao puts it – in the heat of a military campaign – between "pen-front" and "gun-front." Such is also the "lesson" that Jameson, somewhat haphazardly, without fully tracing the contours of his argument as it were, adduces from the political intellectual of the third world.

Finally, Jameson makes an important point about artistic autonomy and its relation to socialized identity:

> In the west, conventionally, political commitment is recontained and psychologized or subjectivized by way of the public/private split ... [whereas] in third-world texts ... the relationship between the libidinal and the political components of individual and social experience is radically different from what obtains in the west. ("Third-World Literature" 71)

This is not a claim about essentialized cultural differences. Rather, to repeat, the West and the third world – as much as the second world of officially existing socialism – instantiate a particular conjuncture of the capitalist world-system. The distance between fully and incompletely – read unevenly – reified capital determines the differential calibration of the "public" and "private" in the core and in the periphery.

It is the fully realized reification of capital, as Lukács pointed out much earlier in *History and Class Consciousness*, that enables the turn to a purely private subjecthood and the peculiar autonomy of the work of art. Jameson similarly traces, along two axes, the constitutive relation between modalities of representation and the psychologizing of social being: on the one hand, the "decline" of "allegorical representation," and on the other hand, the emergence, since "the Romantic revolution of Wordsworth and

Coleridge ... [of] the massive and monumental unifications of ... modernist symbolism or even realism itself [,] ... the homogenous representation of the symbol" ("Third-World Literature" 73). The symbol is the direct opposite of the allegory and substitutes the latter. Structurally, this same process takes a different form in the periphery, where the retreat into the purely personal is held at bay. The allegorical, signaling discontinuity and heterogeneity, keeps resurfacing and interrupting the homogeneity of the symbol. I will offer a few concrete examples by way of grasping this conceptual distinction.

Toward a Peripheral Aesthetics

When William Wordsworth postulated the Romantic aim in his 1800 manifesto, the "Preface" to the *Lyrical Ballads*, it was "the fitting to metrical arrangement [of] a selection of the real language of men in a state of vivid sensation" (5). More than a hundred and twenty years later, in 1921, in an equally famous manifesto for "Modern Fiction," Virginia Woolf would exhort "young writers" (not *all* of them – as she would note contemptuously, only those who "were a free man and not a *slave*, if he could write *what he chose*") to "examine ... an ordinary mind on an ordinary day ... to record the atoms as they fall upon the mind ... upon the consciousness" (740–742, emphases added).

Common to Wordsworth and Woolf, despite the differences of genre (poetry versus prose), period (Romanticism versus Modernism), and gender, is an emphasis on the subjective domain as the only proper object of art. Their respective manifestos register the growing desire to articulate the private and the sensuous as distinctly separate from the social and the political. In biographical terms, the "Preface" marks Wordsworth's rejection of his once-cherished ideals of the French Revolution, just as "Modern Fiction" carves out, once again in the name of aesthetic innovation, the aloofness of Woolf from the epoch-making events of the time, the Russian Revolution of 1917 among others.[45] In both these manifestos, one gets the sense – diffuse yet explicit – of a breaking away from the past, a heralding of a newfound subjectivity with novel philosophies and aesthetic strategies. What is expressed is a potent cultural myth. Rather than the unity of thought and practice, here we have the philosophical counter tradition to Vico, Hegel, and Marx in Europe – that of de Sade, Nietzsche, and Bataille. At play is a Nietzschean bohemianism, which says that practice, now understood as sensuous and corporeal, is only possible by delinking itself from historical thought.

To be clear, this is not to say that such figures sum up the entirety of Western literary and philosophical movement from Romanticism to Modernism. Far from it: rather, these manifestos register certain *tendencies*, especially influential in England, that were passionately contested from a variety of other perspectives. Likewise, as the inheritor of these tendencies, American postmodern culture, as Jameson says, internalized the confident valorization of aesthetic separateness, the primacy of libidinal desire, and the rejection of historicity and social conflict – articulating the mental universe of Nike's famous late 1980s campaign, "Just Do It," so to speak. In literature as in culture in general, to be able to freely choose one's object of enquiry is the result of (metropolitan and racialized) *liberal* privilege.[46] That, as Woolf does not fail to remind us, is unavailable to the slave.

To quickly touch on the contrast, I turn to another iconic manifesto, but this time from the so-called third world, Glauber Rocha's "The Aesthetics of Hunger," the ur-text of Brazilian and Latin American *cinema novo*. I focus on this specific example, again, because it embodies particular contrarian tendencies emerging from the periphery. Unlike the older instances of poetry or prose, cinema is the most "modern" of representational media; yet, and especially in the peripheries where its foreignness is most keenly felt, modernist cinematic representation is circumscribed not by the individual rejection of history but precisely its opposite. Simply put, Rocha's manifesto is characterized by a haunting of the collective past bearing down on the present. Again, this is not limited to the third world alone. Not only the Third Cinema of Rocha, Solanas et al., one also thinks here of the early Soviet pioneers – Eisenstein, Vertov, Dovzhenko, Pudovkin, visual thinkers positioned in the eastern peripheries of imperial Europe, or the postwar European example of Italian cinema, De Sica, Pasolini, and others.

In "The Aesthetics of Hunger" (1965), Rocha captures "the tragic originality of Cinema Novo in relation to world cinema" thus:

> Our originality is our hunger and our greatest misery is that this hunger is felt but not intellectually understood. We understand the hunger that Europeans and the majority of Brazilians have failed to understand. For the European, it is a strange tropical surrealism. For the Brazilian, it is a national shame. He does not eat, but is ashamed to say so . . . only a culture of hunger can qualitatively surpass its own structures by undermining and destroying them. (94–95)

In this manifesto, unlike those of Wordsworth and Woolf, the aesthetic is inseparable from the interplay of nature and history. What is most corporeal, "hunger," is at same time the most historical. In the quoted passage, we do not glimpse any notion of autonomous *being*, but instead an affirmation of identity in relation to natural history, a process of *becoming*. The object of the individual consciousness is conceivable only allegorically, as "a national shame" in the collective psyche. Rocha contends that it is the very nature of Brazilian society and the constitutive condition of its existence.

Here as elsewhere, the linkage between the historical past and the contemporary present perhaps constitutes a distinctive aspect of Brazilian *cinema novo*, one that contrasts sharply with the disavowal of history that we see in the earlier manifestos of English Romanticism and Modernism. To take a few other examples: the same tendency is illustrated in the Ukrainian Alexander Dovzhenko's epic depiction of land collectivization, *Earth* (1930), as it is in the Indian filmmaker Mrinal Sen's *Calcutta 71* (1972). In the latter film, the narrator-protagonist claims, fantastically, that, "I have walked for a thousand years." The significance of deep time, suggested by the title of the film itself, is also evident in the Ethiopian Haile Gerima's mythic portrayal of peasant uprising, *Harvest 3000 Years* (1976). Epic, fantasy, and myth, all are focalized through the lenses of these filmmakers as they articulate collective struggles; in their texts, these come to share the same representational space as the narration of present-day events (I discuss this in detail in Chapter 3).

Contrary to notions of the exotic other, such an aesthetic also rejects celebrating the irrational. If the mythic, the epic, and the fantastic are summoned in the service of a native culture, the goal is not to construct discursive alternatives to Western modernity, but a revolutionary negation of modernity itself. Rocha, for example, speaks for a long line of Latin American intellectuals when he trenchantly dismisses the appropriative tendencies of a "European ... tropical surrealism" with its stylized passion for the primitive. His remarks parallel similar critiques made earlier by both Alejo Carpentier and Aimé Césaire of Nietzsche-inspired surrealism and its thoroughly reactionary, defeatist character in the context of 1930s and 1940s Latin America.[47] Even as peripheral intellectuals and artists acknowledge the determinate presence of the irrational in the social reality they seek to represent, the aim is to probe into the very source of the irrational – imperialism. By probing and seeking the source of conflict, the work of art comes to articulate an explicitly political endeavor, an overcoming of the irrational through the very process of mimesis as *re*-presentation.

These Latin American examples gesture toward a distinctive peripheral aesthetics of *modernismo*. Here, as Neil Larsen has insisted, "representation does not 'break down' in the wake of 'inhuman' abstraction ... [and instead] become[s] distended over the ruptural divide between capital as *ratio* and the flagrant 'irrationalities' that it erects along its path." *Modernismo* is not only driven by the crisis of representation and the crisis of historical agency characteristic of so-called European high modernism but also by "the more urgent project of producing the terrain of synthesis per se":

> The agency of the [modernist art] "work" as a negative closure become[s] suspended by the more pressing drive to *mediate* the split dividing both historical subject and historical object .... The work of art actively transforms and regrounds the modernism of the metropolis by promoting a synthesis of the metropolis ... [with] rural peasant and indigenous tribal cultures. (*Modernism and Hegemony* xxxv–vi, original emphasis)

Foregrounding the interventionist function of art, Larsen reworks Adorno's notion of modernist art's autonomy. Unlike its European high modernist counterpart, Latin American *modernismo* not only negates but also synthesizes "ruptural divide(s)" through the radical incorporation of marginal social groups.

In the opening discussions of Indian, Russian, and Chinese modernisms, we witnessed a similar – but not identical – braiding of art's individual articulations to the broader culture of the dominated classes. Going beyond historical or regional periodizing, such impulses can be traced across modern, postcolonial, and contemporary literary cultures. It might be possible, therefore, to make a few tentative *generalizations* at this stage about the aesthetics-politics of peripheral internationalism. On the one hand, the work of art, through discontinuous and disjunctive modes of allegorization – the juxtaposition of foreign and local aesthetic forms, the retrieval and reconfiguration of older cultural forms, the deliberate insertion of the collective oral and popular elements and so on – formally (objectively) illuminates the social relations pertaining to the periphery. Subjectively, on the other hand, foregrounding the dynamic contradictions between individuals and groups, art – and the individual artist – potentially reclaims the function of social critique. While differently detailed everywhere, the structure of peripheral societies, where imported metropolitan culture invariably coexists with and reconfigures rural peasant and indigenous cultures, provides just the common "national" terrain for such recuperations.

Equally, we are better positioned to define peripheral internationalism as a reading method now than previously. This is to say, such a method recuperates, reconstellates, and recognizes previously unknown relations between disparate objects. These linkages may not be actualized or (non-) exist as absence or negative possibility but are activated through intimate engagement between the reading subject and the represented object as well as their mutual interrelations. In other words, such a dialectical method operates through various levels of close reading, as I discuss in the subsequent chapters.

In the next chapter, I explore the intersection of aesthetic and political forms through the concrete example of the memoir. M.N. Roy attests to Tagore's contention in *visva-sahitya* that individual freedom is realized in unison with universal humanity. Both these thinkers share a common conception of the human and the universal, with more similarities than differences. However, Roy grapples with a distinct postwar phase of the humanist imagination: one that is qualitatively different, and in retreat.

Notes

1. Brennan's *Borrowed Light* posits Giambattista Vico as the largely unacknowledged master of interwar Western Marxism. Drawing attention to a less-discussed aspect of Edward Said, namely the latter's affinity to Vico, Brennan resituates one of Said's singular interventions: the role of language and literature in shaping and not simply reflecting imperial domination and resistance. Brennan's field-defining study, in my view, remaps the connections and departures between humanist Marxist and postcolonial theory.
2. Siraj Ahmed's study *Archaeology of Babel* identifies the emergence of "a new philology" in the eighteenth century as transforming previous understandings of world history and comparative literature. The key figure in this account is the philologist and polyglot scholar William Jones (1748–1794), proponent of the idea of Indo-European languages and founder of the Asiatic Society of Bengal. The British Orientalists shaped in no small measure the so-called Bengal Renaissance of the nineteenth century, with Tagore as its most illustrious legatee.
3. In an important if unremarked intervention, Supriya Chaudhuri's "Singular Universals" outlines the interlocking Germanic and Indic aesthetic-philosophical lineages – especially the *Upanishads* – that Tagore draws on in *visva-sahitya*. Chaudhuri suggests that the term *visva-sahitya* might be rendered more accurately as "universal friendship," and that English translations such as self for *atman* and world for *visva* inadequately convey Tagore's idea of universal humanity. Amit Chaudhuri, *On Tagore*, provides an account of the problems of translation: namely, that the initial orientalizing translations of Tagore into English not excluding his self-translations were the cause of both his fame and subsequent neglect. For an alternative view that emphasizes Tagore's canny bilingualism, see Vadde, *Chimeras of Form*, chap. 1.

4. The Spanish couple, the Nobel Laureate Juan Ramón Jiménez and the poet Zenobia Camprubí, translated Tagore's *Gitanjali* from English to Spanish. In Latin America, Tagore's interlocutors included significant figures such as Victoria Ocampo in Argentina, Gabriela Mistral and Pablo Neruda in Chile, and Octavio Paz in Mexico, among others. See Shyama Prasad Ganguly, *The Kindred Voice*. Ana Jelnikar, *Universal Hopes*, offers a comparison between Tagore and the leading Slovenian poet Srecko Kosovel that interrogates postcolonial studies' neglect of peripheral European literature.
5. Hegel is a subject of renewed interest in Anglophone critical theory only in recent decades. To mention some prominent efforts: the English translation of Losurdo, *Hegel*; Buck-Morss, *Hegel and Haiti*; Žižek, *Less Than Nothing*; Jameson, *Valences of the Dialectic*; Marasco, *The Highway of Despair;* and Cole, *The Birth of Theory*. Compare this to the critical engagement, say, in Latin America, where intellectuals otherwise as varied as José Aricó in Argentina, Paulo Arantes in Brazil, Leopoldo Zea Aguilar in Mexico, and Augusto Salazar Bondy in Peru, among others, produced substantial explorations of Hegelianism.
6. All quotations in English are from Swapan Chakravorty's translation of Tagore's text (Tagore, "World Literature"). Where relevant, I have consulted the Bengali original (Tagore, "Visva-Sahitya").
7. See Du Bois's essay on "The African Roots of War," published, less than a decade after Tagore's *visva-sahitya*, in 1915 in the *Atlantic Monthly*. For Lenin, especially his theory of imperialism and its relation to Indian anticolonialism, see Chapter 2 of this book. In a fascinating recent study, *India, Empire, and First World War Culture*, chap. 10, Santanu Das compares and contrasts Tagore's response to war to not only Lenin but also two influential Indian thinkers, Aurobindo Ghose and Muhammad Iqbal, as "part of an international conversation" (397) on decolonization. Das highlights the multiple and often fraught intersections between ideas of pan-Asianism, universalism, and spiritual religiosity (Hinduism, Islam), none of which was nationalist in any straightforward sense.
8. In these two essays, Himani Bannerji contends that Tagore is critical of notions of development and progress but does not reject them wholesale. Instead, his outlook as per Bannerji is marked by an emphasis on decolonization, where development is measured by the degree of social transformation, and the progressive cultivation of self and its positive relation to others.
9. In locating Tagore within a diverse materialist tradition, scholars such as Himani Bannerji and Amiya Bagchi argue for retrieving the humanist Marx. See also Bagchi and Chatterjee eds., *Marxism: With and Beyond Marx*. Another useful linkage of Tagore, that I can only indicate in passing, would be with the indigenous materialism of Fakir Lalon Shah (d. 1890), who combined Islamicate, Vaishnavite, and Buddhist philosophical lineages in nineteenth-century Bengal.
10. The humanist (and so-called early) Marx has been the subject of intense theoretical debates in twentieth-century Western Marxism. Broadly speaking,

the tradition of Left-Hegelianism and thinkers such as Lukács, Adorno, Bloch, and Marcuse uphold the humanist Marx. The anti-Hegelian Marx has been emphasized in postwar structuralist and poststructuralist theory, especially since Althusser.

11. It is admittedly difficult to illustrate such transnational lineages in compressed form. These require fuller consideration of intellectual histories, such as the one undertaken by Craig Brandist, *The Dimensions of Hegemony*. Nonetheless, the Vichian figures I have in mind would include Antonio Gramsci, Mikhail Bakhtin, James Joyce, Kazi Nazrul Islam, José Carlos Mariátegui, and Lu Xun, among others.

12. Particularly interesting is the case of the literary theorist Zhu Guangqian (1897-1986). Zhu was instrumental in introducing Western aesthetic theory in 1930s Chinese circles, particularly the work of Immanuel Kant and Benedetto Croce. In the 1950s, he moved closer to Marxist humanism and advocated a distinctive view of aesthetics that often clashed with official socialist realism. A keen translator for much of his life, Zhu translated Vico's *The New Science* in the 1980s and also published several influential essays on him.

13. I am following the textual history of the Yenan talks provided by Liu Kang (*Aesthetics and Marxism* 86–93). Kang notes, "Previous 'forms of art' were substituted with 'life' itself, which works of art must reflect faithfully; and the ideological and political mission of artwork was clearly spelled out: to 'propel history forward.' A theorization of the formal and semiotic complexities of aesthetic representation was then rendered into a neoclassicist, pro-Soviet 'socialist realist' dogma" (92). These were post-1949 developments and paralleled the institutionalization of the Chinese revolution. See also Kang's essay, "The Legacy of Mao and Althusser," for the critique of ideology developed in postwar French thought.

14. For a discussion of "semi-colonialism," its multiple uses, and the "economic as lived experience" see Rebecca Karl, *The Magic of Concepts*, chap. 5. Karl recounts the heterodox and ultimately unsuccessful Chinese Marxists' attempts of the 1930s, such as that of the economist Wang Yanan, to develop new interpretations of the economic from Marx's "Asian mode of production." Such analyses often departed from the linear view of historical development advocated by the Comintern and instead emphasized the cyclical nature of history. On Mao's oscillations between orthodox Stalinist and heterodox Marxist positions during the period between 1937 and 1945, see Nick Knight, *Rethinking Mao*, chap. 5.

15. In his commentary on the Yenan lectures, Williams insists that the individual artist's "commitment" is not a matter of preference or choice, but rather predicated on the "writer's real social relations" and "the 'style' or 'forms' or 'content' of his [sic] work" (*Marxism and Literature* 203–4). The issue of commitment in real terms, of course, was more often than not measured by the individual writer's fidelity to the Communist Party's directives, something that not only Williams but also Dorothy Thompson, E.P. Thompson,

Dona Torr, Christopher Hill, and others in the Communist Party of Great Britain's Marxist Historians Group roundly criticized.
16. Among various examples, Omafume F. Onoge's foundational essays, clearly influenced by and citing the Yenan talks, such as "The Crisis of Consciousness in Modern African Literature" and "Towards a Marxist Sociology of African Literature," laid the groundwork for a materialist understanding of African literature (reprinted in Gugelberger ed., *Marxism and African Literature*). The African American civil rights icon Robert F. Williams spoke in Beijing on the twenty-fifth anniversary of the Yenan Forum in 1967 (Bill Mullen, "By the Book"). Between W.E.B. and Shirley Du Bois, Mabel and Robert Williams, several generations of African American radicals came to associate their activism with Maoist China, as Robeson Taj Frazier discusses in *The East Is Black*. On the reception of Soviet and Chinese socialist culture in the non-Communist third world, see Vijay Prashad, *The East Was Read*.
17. Tagore's literary works were disseminated and widely read in China, in English and in translation. This included well-known short stories such as "Chhuti" and "Kabuliwala," novels such as *Ghare Baire*, essays, and plays. Tagore's mixed reception in China had as much to do with the writer himself as with the ideological divisions among contemporary Chinese intellectuals. See the essays in Tan Chung, Amiya Dev et al. eds., *Tagore and China*, and also Sisir Kumar Das, "The Controversial Guest," and Subho Basu, "Framing China." I am grateful to Subho Basu for pointing me to these discussions.
18. The Indologist Mikhail Tubianskii (1893–1943) was the foremost Russian scholar and translator of Tagore and also established the study of Bengali in the USSR (see Brandist, "The Eastern Side of the Circle"). Tagore's positive relation to the Soviet Union is the subject of many books. The interested reader might consult two noteworthy accounts – one translated from Russian to English and another in Bengali: A.P. Gnatyuk-Danil'chuk, *Tagore, India, and the Soviet Union*, and Chinmohan Sehanobish, *Rabindranather Antorjatik Chinta*.
19. By the 1920s and 1930s, aided by philological breakthroughs, a widely focalized topic especially in various counter-hegemonic intellectual circles was how "modern" Bengali elevated urban elite, Hindu Brahminical language over the syncretic forms of the Muslim, tribal, and lower-caste peasantry especially in rural northern and eastern Bengal. On Tagore's contribution to the democratization of the Bengali language, I am paraphrasing the arguments made by noted Bangladeshi intellectuals: Serajul Islam Choudhury, "Unish Shotoker Bangla Godyer Byakaron" and "Ekaki Kintu Shokoler," and earlier by Ahmed Sofa, "Banglar Sahityadorsho" and "Rabindranath" etc.
20. See Kalyan Chatterjee, "Lukács on Tagore," and Köves and Mazumdar eds., *Contributions on Lukács*, especially Sisir Kumar Das's essay "The Wrath of Lukács." Among recent scholars, Ulka Anjaria provides a nuanced assessment of *Ghare Baire* highlighting both the relevance of Lukács's critique and Tagore's formal innovation in the novel that defies easy categorization (*Realism*, esp. 18–24). Benjamin Baer, *Indigenous Vanguards*, chap. 5, further

elucidates Lukács's position in relation to Gandhian nationalism in India as well as Tagore's vexed reception in Germany.
21. These essays are reprinted in Dhananjoy Das, *Marxbadi Sahitya Bitarka*, 232–313. Their immediate purpose was refuting Bhabani Sen's damning criticism of Tagore in 1949 in *Marxbadi*, the theoretical journal of the Communist Party of India. Sen published under the pseudonym Rabindra Gupta, since the party had been banned and members were underground. Sen's essay, whose views he later modified, is reproduced in the same volume (Das, *Marxbadi Sahitya Bitarka*, 98–122).
22. Only the essay by critic Sanat Basu briefly cites Lukács and the latter's discussion of realism in Balzac, Flaubert, Zola, and Tolstoy (*Marxbadi Sahitya* 288). Basu appears to be referring to Lukács's essay, "Ideas and Form in Literature," published in the December 1949 issue of *Masses and the Mainstream*. Lukács is by and large absent in the Bengali discussions of 1949–1950.
23. The critic Nirendranath Roy discusses Lifshitz at some length, particularly the latter's nuanced assessment of Tolstoy (*Marxbadi Sahitya* 237–240). The Russian literary critic Mikhail Lifshitz (1905–1983) was a key figure in the journal *Literaturnyi Kritik* in the 1930s. His best-known work *The Philosophy of Art of Karl Marx*, first appearing in English translation in 1938, pioneered a Hegelian-Marxist theory of aesthetics. Lifshitz was also the leading Soviet authority on Vico's historical theory of knowledge, writing the introduction to the Russian translation of *The New Science* published in 1940.
24. These critics and their interventions are seldom mentioned in Anglophone scholarship. Nonetheless, they represent a strand of vernacular literary and cultural criticism that is no less aware of global currents.
25. See for example Dipesh Chakrabarty's "From Civilization to Globalization." The historian summarizes the contemporary milieu by anecdotally recounting his participation in Maoist activism, almost as a comedy of errors, in West Bengal during the early 1970s.
26. Hemango Biswas (1912–1987) was the foremost exponent and scholar of popular and folk music in eastern India – pre-partition Assam and Bengal. Active since the early 1940s, he played a crucial role in Assamese folk music and activism during the 1950s and 1960s. The example of Biswas, like so many of the other figures I discuss later, attests to the clear continuities between the cultural landscape of the 1940s and the 1970s.
27. Like Biswas's adaptation of folk music, Utpal Dutt (1929–1993) incorporated vernacular forms such as *jatra* in his dramaturgy. The innovation of these artist-intellectuals needs to be underlined, because they consistently redefined and reconfigured the scope of literature. If the literary classics were to reach the marginalized social classes, beyond the professional middle class, then the notion of a "classic" itself would have to assimilate nonliterary ideas of canonicity and value. As we see in later chapters, new relationships between music, theater, cinema, and literary writing emerge over this period.

28. Shah and Jain, "Naxalbari," provide a comprehensive annotated bibliography on the recent phase of Naxalism; other relevant texts and scholarship are cited in later chapters. Elsewhere, I have written on the parliamentary Communists in West Bengal (Basu and Majumder, "Dilemmas of Parliamentary Communism").
29. Nearly two decades later, the field of world literature has generated voluminous scholarship. Of the numerous directions and approaches, a noncomprehensive list might include Emily Apter, *Against World Literature*; Pheng Cheah, *What Is a World?*; David Damrosch, *What Is World Literature*; Wai Chee Dimock, *Through Other Continents;* Jason Frydman, *African American and Caribbean Routes of World Literature*; Thérèse Migraine-George, *Sounding the Break: From Francophonie to World Literature in French*; Aamir Mufti, *Forget English!: Orientalisms and World Literatures*; Joel Nickels, *World Literature and the Geographies of Resistance*; John Pizer, *The Idea of World Literature*; Christopher Prendergast, *Debating World Literature*; Mariano Siskind, *Cosmopolitan Desires*; and Longxi Zhang, *From Comparison to World Literature*.
30. It is noteworthy that Said had already, in *The World, The Text, and the Critic*, taken a position against the notions of indeterminacy and anti-historicism. One recalls his principled disagreement, in the context of discussing the Spanish-Muslim scholar Ibn Hazm (994–1064), with the Foucauldian position that all reading is misreading. Instead, Said emphasizes the locating of "the text's worldliness, circumstantiality, the text's status as an event having sensuous particularity as well as historical contingency, [which] are considered as being incorporated in the text" (39). A fuller lineage of Arab and North African historicism would include such varied figures as Sadiq Jalal al-Azm, Abdallah Laroui, and Mahdi Amel, among others. As a recent study points out, these names and their intellectual positions come up rarely if at all in Anglo-American critical theory (see Aboul-Ela, *Domestications*).
31. For combined and uneven development and the question of scale, see Smith, *Uneven Development*. For discussions of Wallerstein and Trotsky in the context of world literature, see respectively, Palumbo-Liu et al., *Immanuel Wallerstein and the Problem of the World* and Warwick Research Collective, *Combined and Uneven Development*.
32. For an excellent assessment of Williams's significance, see Daniel Hartley, *The Politics of Style*, chap. 5. Recently, Sandeep Banerjee, *Space, Utopia and Indian Decolonization*, demonstrates the utility of Williamsian cultural materialism for exploring anticolonial and spatial utopias in the Indian subcontinent.
33. For fuller accounts of Schwarz and his Brazilian context, see Silvia López, "Dialectical Criticism in the Provinces" and Maria Elisa Cevasco, "The São Paulo Fraction." Nicholas Brown, "Roberto Schwarz: Mimesis Beyond Realism," summarizes Schwarz's key departures from the Frankfurt School.
34. Friedman's book continues the conversation on planetarity and world literature by taking as its point of departure Gayatri Chakravorty Spivak's

formulations in *Death of a Discipline*. An older formulation not to be confused with this new turn is Martin Heidegger's *planetarische* (*Introduction to Metaphysics*). Elsewhere, I discuss Spivak's Marxist theory of the imagination and planetarity at greater length (Majumder, "Gayatri Spivak, Planetarity, and the Labor of Imagining Internationalism").

35. Schwarz shows in his study of Machado de Assis, the preeminent nineteenth-century Brazilian novelist, that the narrative structures of Machado's novels formally articulate the peculiar forms of Brazilian modernity. Narrativizing a society different from, but also tied (beholden) to contemporary France or England in key aspects, Machado departs from the nineteenth-century conventions of European naturalism. His work combines and takes on a dual character of modernist experiment with narrative form and realist critique of the bourgeois order (see Schwarz, *A Master on the Periphery of Capitalism*).

36. In Anglophone scholarship, the early interlocutors of Roberto Schwarz are Neil Larsen, Silvia López, Keya Ganguly, Benita Parry, Neil Lazarus, and Joe Cleary. More recently, commentaries and translations by scholars such as Nicholas Brown, Emilio Sauri, and Ericka Beckman deserve mention.

37. The later Frank sees Wallerstein as conflating the West with capitalist modernity. What is more relevant nonetheless is to see "universal history" (Frank's preferred term) as intertwined with capitalism's uneven expansion as a world-system. In fact, such an emphasis marks Frank's own early interventions.

38. The materialist critique of Eurocentrism differs substantially from the later postmodern and postcolonial uses of the term. For a conceptual account of the former, see Samir Amin, *Eurocentrism*. The same difference of emphasis also applies to "discourse," a term theorized by Mikhail Bakhtin but today generally associated with Michel Foucault.

39. The relation between Jamesonian national allegory and current debates of world literature has been well explored by the Warwick Research Collective's *Combined and Uneven Development*, see especially chap. 1. For a related discussion, see chap. 2 of Neil Lazarus's *The Postcolonial Unconscious*.

40. The persistence of imperialism in the twenty-first century, albeit under significantly changed circumstances, contradicts the claims put forward by pro-globalization theorists. See John Smith, *Imperialism in the Twenty-First Century* and Utsa and Prabhat Patnaik, *A Theory of Imperialism*, among others.

41. Lukács's discussion of Dante in *The Theory of the Novel* is also noteworthy in this regard. As I understand it, for Lukács and Jameson afterward, the *Divine Comedy* formally registers the discontinuous sensibilities of social transition in Europe.

42. Gramsci's formulation of the distinct social types of intellectuals would undoubtedly resonate with the Bengali writers and critics I discuss in this book. However, unlike his Latin American reception, for example, Gramsci was little known in these circles well into the 1970s. When Bengali radicals spoke in similar terms, they relied on other figures such as Lenin and Mao. The exceptions to this trend are also remarkable: shortly after 1957, Bhabani Sen wrote a favorable review of Gramsci's *The Modern Prince* in the journal *Parichay*, and in 1968, Sushobhan Sarkar published a significant review essay, "Thought of

Gramsci" in *Mainstream* magazine. In short, the intellectuals ranged on opposite sides of the Tagore debate of 1949–1950 were pioneers in introducing Gramsci to Bengali Indian audiences. Others to write on Gramsci were Sobhanlal Datta Gupta in 1973 and Mohit Sen in 1974 (these details are from Datta Gupta, "Gramsci's Presence in India"). For additional examples of M.N. Roy's and Mahasweta Devi's "engagements" with Gramsci and Gramscian refractions in the work of the Subaltern Studies collective, see Chapters 2 and 4. On the other hand, scholars such as Brennan, *Wars of Position*, and Thomas, *The Gramscian Moment*, argue that the Communist basis of Gramsci's thought is obscured and/or selectively elided in Anglo-American reception.

43. Kang bemoans, in this regard, the "ahistorical and idealist tendencies of certain Western Left academicians or anarcho-liberalist 'post-Marxists.'" His commentary is concise: "In China studies, the postcolonialist paradoxical debunking of a radical revolutionary legacy from which s/he finds a mirror image of her/himself, only obfuscates the real question of coming to grips with the complex legacy of Chinese revolution and revolutionary hegemony" (*Aesthetics and Marxism* xiv–xv).

44. For a distinctive and critical approach to the Cultural Revolution, see Yiching Wu, *The Cultural Revolution at the Margins*. The works of prominent Chinese New Left figures deserve mention, such as Mobo Gao, *The Battle for China's Past*, and Wang Hui, *China's Twentieth Century*, among others. Wolin, *The Wind from the East* provides a nuanced evaluation of French intellectuals' relation to Maoist China.

45. In her careful survey of Woolf's fiction and writings on Russia, such as the novels *Orlando* and *The Voyage Out* and the essay "The Russian Point of View," Darya Protopopova finds that Russia alternatively serves either as a "savage" ahistorical space inhabited by "mysterious natives," or as the projected "symbol" of Woolf's own psychologized "modernist sensibilities" ("Virginia Woolf's Versions"). Either way, the contemporary events after the Bolshevik Revolution, of which Woolf was hardly unaware, are seldom given much significance.

46. I draw from the Italian intellectual historian Domenico Losurdo, who illuminates this point with great rigor in *Liberalism: A Counter History*. From Locke to Edmund Burke to Tocqueville, successive generations of progressive and conservative thinkers in England, France, and the United States articulated the self-consciousness of property-owning free men, constituting a "master race democracy," as compared to the illiberal and unfree working classes, women, and colonial peoples.

47. I have in mind Carpentier's essay on the "Marvelous Real" (1949) and Césaire's *Discourse on Colonialism* (1950), which are sharply critical of Nietzsche's influence on contemporary Latin American intellectuals. Contemporaneous to these accounts is Lukács's magisterial polemic against Nietzschean irrationalism, *The Destruction of Reason*, published in 1952, which he started writing during the mid-1930s.

CHAPTER 2

The Memoir and Anticolonial Internationalism in M.N. Roy

In a chapter titled "The New Science," tracing the thought of Giambattista Vico, Manabendra Nath (M.N.) Roy proclaimed: "the truths discovered by Vico were not left to be perverted by Marxist dogmatism and subsequently to be vulgarized by the regimented fascist dictatorship" (*Reason* 220). This was the objective assessment of a self-taught philosopher, as much as the subjective experience of an activist. Roy's magnum opus, *Reason Romanticism and Revolution*, from which I take this quote, delineated a philosophical genealogy of "humanist reason," with Vico and Marx as its two key figures. It was drafted during Roy's years in a British Indian prison in the 1930s, where he had been sent on the charge of conspiracy against the colonial government. Marx's appeal is understandable in this milieu, but *why Vico*? What made an Indian anticolonial activist claim an eighteenth-century Italian thinker and the latter's concept of non-hierarchical and non-coercive humanist reason?

A singular if little-remembered figure, M.N. Roy participated not in one, or two, but four major revolutions of the twentieth century: the Mexican, the Soviet, the Chinese, and the Indian. He co-founded two of the earliest Communist parties outside Russia, the Mexican party established in 1919, and the Indian party in 1920. Throughout the 1920s, with the patronage of first Vladimir Lenin and subsequently Josef Stalin, Roy enjoyed international prominence as a Marxist authority on the East. He presented, as an invitee to the newly instituted Comintern, a "Supplementary Theses on National and Colonial Questions" that challenged Lenin's views on the subject. Thereafter, Roy served as a military commander in Central Asia and traveled to China as a Soviet emissary. In addition, Roy authored widely circulated tomes on different revolutionary contexts: *India in Transition* (1922) and *Revolution and Counterrevolution in China* (1930). However, he could not survive the Third Period: in 1928, Roy was expelled from the Comintern, apparently for his differences with Stalin on the aborted Chinese Revolution. Later on, Roy turned sharply anti-Stalinist and anti-Communist.

Such twists and turns were no worse than those experienced by many activists of the period. For example, Roy's Comintern colleague and sometimes rival, the fellow Bengali Virendranath Chattopadhyaya, was executed during the Great Purge of 1937–1938, as was another Bengali Communist, Golam Ambia Khan Lohani. The reversals of Roy's fortunes nonetheless are not without their distinctive ironies. Over the course of a storied career, Roy received remarkable honors and dubious calumnies in equal measure. Leon Trotsky excoriated him as a Stalinist lackey at one time, and at another Stalin's followers hounded him as a Trotskyist collaborator. In the 1930s, Roy was tailed by British intelligence as the most dangerous Communist operative in India. He was captured and sentenced to a twelve-year imprisonment. Upon his release – on medical grounds – after five years, the congressman and future prime minister Jawaharlal Nehru welcomed him as a comrade. Yet, by the 1940s, Indian Communists and the party he helped establish, the Communist Party of India (CPI), were denouncing Roy as an agent of British imperialism.

These varied receptions gesture to but nonetheless bracket the most significant of Roy's failures. In the years leading up to independence in 1947, Roy and the various Communist groups articulated distinctive positions emphasizing the emancipation of the workers and the peasants, compared to the Gandhi-led Congress or Jinnah's Muslim League. But the Communist groups were unable "to produce a consistent strategy by which they could compete for hegemony against Gandhi and mobilize revolutionary classes at the same time" (Shingavi, *The Mahatma Misunderstood* 190). Thus marginalized, Roy turned to writing and preaching the philosophy of "radical humanism" to a motley group of followers. In this untimely and unfinished body of work, he explored the many crises of the previous half century: not only the depredations of imperialism and fascism but also the atrophy of Communism and anticolonial nationalism. A consideration of his thought, as much as if not more than his activism, provides a remarkable counterpoint to the polyphonic *Geist* of the era.[1]

Roy's recuperation of Vico, as I contend later, militated against the gradual degeneration of the Bolshevik Revolution in Russia. Philosophically and politically, Roy's resistance to dogma was inseparable from his commitment to humanism. In philosophical terms, he emphasized not only the human ability to articulate itself in freedom but also the centrality of humanist agency to social transformation, just as much as he resisted the individual's erasure under the determinist rubric of the socialist and/or nationalist collective. Roy's advocacy of an encounter between subjective reason and the objective world of global politics finds its clearest narrative expression in his *Memoirs*, published posthumously in 1964.

In this chapter, I turn to *Memoirs* to reconstruct a neglected yet vital conjuncture of peripheral internationalism, recalling Roy's activities within diverse and overlapping networks of the interwar period: Indian and Black American activism in the United States, socialist militants in Mexico, and "Afro-Asian" solidarity at the Soviet-led Comintern. The *Memoirs* not only focalizes the unrealized solidarities of the anticolonial era, but also posits them as sources of future resistance. Indeed, Roy's passionate denunciations of the Soviet Union did not imply a repudiation of materialism. Rather, at the precise moment when Soviet Communism was assuming quasi-hegemonic form (alongside its rival, the US-led Western bloc), Roy's *Memoirs* laid claim to its counter-hegemonic and demotic elements. My reading of *Memoirs* draws attention to aspects that have received little attention: namely, the synergy between Indian, Pan-African, and Black American radicals; Roy's non-European theorization of class; and the imbrication of nationalism with race and caste. Roy's final work, *Memoirs*, was left unfinished by his death a year before the Bandung Conference (1955), a platform of newly independent Asian and African countries: as we will see, he was one of the unheralded predecessors and prescient critics of the emancipatory possibilities of Bandung.[2]

Clearly, the Soviet – and specifically the Marxist-Leninist – critique of Western imperialism played an important role in Roy's theorization of *anticolonial solidarity*, or what one might today term, anachronistically, as "South-South" alliances. It needs underscoring that in the subsequent discussion, anticolonial nationalism and solidaristic internationalism were, and are, never posed as mutually antithetical categories. Rather, Roy warned against the tendency of some nationalists, including but not limited to his onetime antagonist Mohandas Gandhi, to affirm what a later scholar terms "creative" postcolonial nationalism as modalities of "difference" from the West (Chatterjee, *Nation* 5). Nationalism based on binary notions of difference, Roy advanced, no matter how nuanced inevitably end up mimicking the "murderous nationalisms" of imperial Europe.[3] Roy explored the staggering achievements as well as the catastrophic failures of Indian anticolonial nationalism *in movement*: the immanent and immediate contradiction between, say, the humanist landmarks of universal suffrage and Dr. Ambedkar's drafting of the Indian Constitution and the trauma of partition and Gandhi's assassination by religious nationalist zealots. These agonistic movements variously flowed into, strengthened, or undercut the burgeoning antinomies of the postwar terrain marked by the Soviet-American Cold War.

The second half of the chapter demonstrates the continuities – and evolution – between Roy's Marxist and radical humanist critiques of nationalism-by-difference by exploring two earlier and overshadowed documents: the "Indian Communist Manifesto" of 1920 and *India in Transition* of 1922. These texts illustrate the fraught conceptual negotiations, at that period quite novel but not unprecedented, between Marxian analytic categories and the particular social forms of the periphery. *India in Transition* articulated an analysis of peripheral form that anticipates later discussions of subalternity, caste-class, and dependency and posed the resistance of multiply marginalized groups, such as the peasantry, to the capitalist world-system. Alongside his better-known peers, Antonio Gramsci, Leon Trotsky, and Rosa Luxemburg, Roy too extends and reconfigures "classical" Marxist frameworks in the interwar period, as do – in separate contexts – Mirsaid Sultan Galiev, Aimé Césaire, and José Carlos Mariátegui.

Similar to Tagore and Mao as noted in the previous chapter, our discussion of M.N. Roy foregrounds a constellation that is still not adequately registered in Anglo-American theory: namely, the non-Western conceptualization of universalism and humanism. These concepts suffer from "the generalized aversion toward Enlightenment categories within ... postcolonial inquiry," casting away important thinkers from the field, as Aishwary Kumar recently suggests for B.R. Ambedkar (*Radical Equality* 22). My elaboration of this intellectual history complicates both liberal historicist teleology as well as the anti-historicist framework of difference and multiple modernities: by reading *Memoirs* alongside *India in Transition*, I adduce Roy to a materialist theorization of caste-class and a singular if uneven modernity. As a growing body of scholarship demonstrates, anti-caste, anti-race, and demotic equality were and continue to be interconnected rather than isolated conversations involving diverse figures such as Savitri and Jyotirao Phule, W.E.B. Du Bois, Ambedkar, and Gramsci. What this interlocking dialogue implies for a *theory* – and intellectual history – of the concepts of universalism and humanism is far less obvious but nonetheless relevant.[4]

I conclude with the Jamaican-American writer Claude McKay, whose autobiographical *A Long Way from Home* (1937) recounts his brief interactions with Roy in interwar Moscow. The significance of such meetings for what Joel Nickels terms the lineages of "dissident internationalism" in world literature is manifold. First, they indicate – in discontinuous and inchoate form – the vital constellation of Afro-Asian militants that interacted, not exclusively through the Comintern, with varying and uneven degrees of success. Second, as Kate Baldwin reminds us in her pioneering work on Black American radicals and Bolshevism, the neglect of the Soviet Union – and especially the Comintern – in Anglo-American postcolonial and critical race studies scholarship is an ideological function of the Cold War. The neglect is compounded, Baldwin adds, by the "prolongation of a 'Red Scare' mentality," as well as the difficulties of "translation" and "differential access ... in the retrieval of sources in which those differences are themselves housed" (19). Such problems of recognition – of unwieldy sources, multiple languages, scarce translation, and so on – arguably make *literature*, including the memoir and the autobiography, one of the key sites of exploration and recovery of peripheral encounters. In this respect, I adapt Nickels's characterization of McKay as "an anti-Communist communist," for our discussion that delineates a Left anti-Stalinist position not reducible to the Cold War ("Claude McKay" 5; see also Nickels, *World Literature*). As the key Indian figure shaping the policies of the Comintern with respect to intellectuals, writers, and activists from the non-Western periphery, M.N. Roy not only identified with but also played a decisive role in forging the futures of "anti-Communist communism."

The *Memoirs* as Literary Internationalism

The unevenness of the Soviet archive – to paraphrase Baldwin – necessitates that we look to non-archival sources, such as the memoir, to fill the gaps of the historical record. This is where M.N. Roy has important things to say. Of course, Roy is not a literary writer; his *Memoirs*, however, is vital for illuminating – and narrativizing – a key transitional moment between interwar and postwar periods. My reading of *Memoirs*, alongside Roy's other texts, shows how literary form articulates the productive contradictions of internationalism. In seeking to constellate memoir with political history, narrative with archival record, I do not suggest a binary relation between fiction and fact. Rather, I explore how a supposedly minor form, the memoir, nuances historiography and its relation to the shifting solidaristic landscapes of the Soviet Union. Roy's *Memoirs* ventriloquizes diverse and contradictory forces through the individual participant. Such positioning involves a number of factors: for instance, how does the memoir address "the discontinuities and disjunctures" of translation (Brent Edwards 22) inherent in an internationalist project? What formal attributes are deployed to achieve this purpose, and how does the narrative form of the memoir articulate, deflect, or otherwise express the tensions between individual subjectivity and collective institutionalization?

In literary theory, the memoir "has been treated as a minor form of autobiography" (Rak 305). Autobiography in this privileged sense presupposes a subject capable of articulating her unique interiority. As Gusdorf remarks in his classic study, "the appearance of autobiography implies a new spiritual revolution: the artist and the model coincide, the historian tackles himself as object" (31). The emphasis on the coherent self that such a description implies has been modified in recent times by the influences of critical theory and its focus on the fragmented human subject.[5] As Rak further notes, "the changing relationship between ideas of selfhood and the role of public and private spheres in late capitalism" (324) brings new attention to the memoir as a form of life writing, a "Derridean dangerous supplement" to autobiography that incorporates the perspectives of women, people of color, and other marginal subjects.

My own discussion of the memoir takes a different route. I seek to locate the memoir in relation to the Latin American *testimonio* as two distinct examples of peripheral political writing. To this end, I draw on as well as depart from John Beverley's well-known account of the *testimonio*. Beverley's study defines the *testimonio* as "a novel or novella-length narrative in book or pamphlet (that is printed as opposed to acoustic form), told in the first person by a narrator who is also the real protagonist or witness of the events he or she recounts" (12–13). Incorporating a number of other genres, the *testimonio* is nevertheless a distinct genre in itself.[6] *Testimonio* directly ties the idea of literary representation to political participation. It is, "the sort of direct participant account, usually presented without any literary or academic aspirations whatever (although often with political ones), represented by Che Guevara's *Reminiscences of the Cuban Revolutionary War* (1959)" (14). Such a description resonates with my discussion of M.N. Roy's *Memoirs*, not least because of Roy's own connections to Mexico and Latin American socialism that take place in an earlier period than Guevara's *Reminiscences*. But my discussion takes note of the literary aspect – narration rather than description – of the memoir as well.

Nonetheless, it is unwise to conflate the *testimonio* and the memoir, thus denying the cultural specificities of their narrative forms. I nuance Beverley's thesis that "the narrator in *testimonio* ... speaks for, or in the name of, a community or group, approximating in this way the symbolic function of the epic hero, without at the same time assuming his hierarchical and patriarchal status" (16). In distinction to the *testimonio*, I submit that the memoir in M.N. Roy provides the imperative to translate freely *across* diversely located anticolonial communities or groups. The narrativization of Roy's *Memoirs* testifies less to the tribulations of the "epic hero" and more to the formation of a collective internationalism. I will return to these points.[7] But given the unremarked scope of our subject, especially for literary studies, first some contextualization is in order.

M.N. Roy started his revolutionary career as an associate of the firebrand nationalist Jatin Mukherjee. In the first decade of the twentieth century, the "extremist" nationalists of Bengal were defined by their ideological affiliations to international anti-imperialist currents. What Maia Ramnath terms their "Kropotkinism," namely, the influence of the Russian anarchist Peter Kropotkin, extended to solidarities with the Japanese resistance to Tsarist Russia, as well as the Irish armed struggle against the English (*Decolonizing Anarchism* 45–77). These affiliations and a decided preference for armed struggle were not the only distinguishing aspects that separated the extremist nationalists from their mainstream counterparts. As early as 1870, requests had gone out from Calcutta to the International Working Men's Association, or the "First International," for the establishment of a local chapter. Under the influence of Aurobindo Ghose, the Bengali nationalists incorporated a popular "socialism" in their 1907 charter, including among other things a demand for land reforms and the redistribution of land. Notwithstanding such aspects, extremist nationalism was also marked by a strong undertone of majoritarian ethos and ambiguous nativist philosophies (particularly in Bengal, those of Bankim Chandra Chattopadhyay and Swami Vivekananda, and Dayananda Saraswati and Bal Gangadhar Tilak in Bombay). Its mostly male and upper-caste constituents were – to one degree or another – at times isolated from, drawing on, and even dismissive of the labor movement and the broad "popular classes," to borrow Gramsci's resonant phrase.[8]

These nationalists suffered a decisive blow in 1914 with the foiling of a planned insurrection coordinated from Germany. The Berlin Committee of Indian Revolutionaries, a platform accommodating a large number of radicals spread all over the world, sent supplies of munitions to Bengal, where these were apprehended. Roy, a key figure in the plan, left India soon after. He traveled to Japan and then on to the United States, first to San Francisco and onward to New York City. Both San Francisco and New York, but especially the former, were key cities of organizing for the Ghadar Party, formed by exiled Indian radicals. In turn, New York served, as Minkah Makalani has shown, to facilitate the interaction of Indians with other Asian and Black revolutionaries: African, Caribbean, and African American (*In the Cause*). Thus M.N. Roy's political activities in the United

States were shaped by activist circles that not only included Ghadar Party radicals but also members of Black revolutionary groups such as Marcus Garvey's Universal Negro Improvement Association (UNIA) and Cyril Briggs's African Blood Brotherhood for African Liberation and Redemption (ABB). Other Asian radicals present in the United States at the time, such as the Japanese Sen Katayama who worked with the ABB, the Vietnamese Ho Chi Minh who attended UNIA's meetings, as well as exiled Chinese Communists, played key roles in linking their specific anticolonial visions to a larger international project. Thus, Cyril Briggs's iconic journal, *Crusader*, devoted "considerable space ... to movements in China, Japan and India" (Makalani 58), while a young Nguyen Sinh Cung (Ho Chi Minh) wrote of Black oppression and lynching in the American South.

In 1917, Roy was arrested in New York, after yet another attempt by Ghadar radicals to secure weapons from Germany. Roy moved to Mexico soon after this event. In Mexico City, he associated with socialists, becoming editor of the Socialist Party newspaper *La Lucha* (The Struggle). Shortly thereafter, he met the Bolshevik agent Mikhail Borodin. In 1919, Roy, Borodin, and Charles R. Phillips co-founded the Mexican Communist Party (*Partido Comunista Mexicano* or PCM). Soon, Roy was on his way from Mexico City to Moscow to attend the Second Congress of the Comintern as an official representative of the PCM. Two important events took place in 1920, the year of Roy's travel to Moscow: first, Roy co-founded the Communist Party of India in Tashkent, Uzbekistan; second, the "Indian Communist Manifesto" was published, as I discuss later. Other members of this group were Roy's wife and fellow-activist Evelyn Trent, Abani Mukherjee, Mohammed Shafiq, and M.P.T. Acharya. This was a motley group, including a Hindu, Muslim, Sikh, all men except for a white American woman, with disparate political backgrounds. The gathering at Tashkent was preceded by a previous event, the drafting of the "Indian Communist Manifesto" in Berlin. Thus, between the years 1914 and 1920, these diverse "intercolonial" networks – the term is from Brent Edwards – enabled Roy's political shift from cultural nationalism to Marxism, to use his own description.

The *Memoirs*, covering the period from 1914 to 1926, offers a unique if little explored "documentary" perspective on these developments. The text charts the protagonist's growing awareness of diverse forms of anticolonialism: in the United States and Mexico; in Germany, France, and the United Kingdom; and last but not least, the Soviet Comintern and its platform of anti-capitalist world revolution. *Memoirs* appeared serially in the late 1940s and early 1950s in the magazine *Independent India* – set up by Roy and his second wife Ellen Gottschalk – whose name later changed to *The Radical Humanist*. The text bears the mark of its form of publication, serialization, which results in an episodic structure, just as much as it reflects the benefits of hindsight. In the words of Roy's recent biographer Kris Manjapra, *Memoirs* does not produce "a *Bildungsroman* of stadial change reaching ultimate culmination, but rather a discontinuous and fragmentary narrative ... [with] a continual explosive encounter with the new" (*M.N. Roy* 1). Manjapra further muses that "as a piece of expressionist art," the text "recounts repeated breakages of time flow, in which new ideas and new time intrude" (1). Given Roy's familiarity with the European avant-garde, the influence of continental expressionism is understandable. Yet, I would advance that the "discontinuous and fragmentary" nature of the narrative gestures to something more: it looks back on the development of an internationalism that spanned four continents and involved heterogeneous and contradictory processes.[9] In other words, the text has an imaginative and aesthetic element – as much as a documentary one – of *reconstruction*. This is manifested at the level of narrative details.

Recounting his escape from India to the United States via the Pacific, Roy observes, "Wandering through Malay, Indonesia, Indo-China, in summer of 1916, I landed in San Francisco" (22). As a self-conscious literary narrative, *Memoirs* is marked by the interplay of experiences, alternating between emotion and reason as the protagonist undergoes several fundamental transformations of selfhood, or in Roy's phrasing, "rebirths": "[A]fter a couple of months on the West Coast, I crossed the continent, to celebrate my rebirth, spiritually as well as politically, in the City of New York" (22). The trope of "rebirth," with its cunning association between the spiritual and the political, is repeated at several points in Roy's journey, first in San Francisco and New York but also later in Mexico, "[again] the land of my rebirth" (217). In Mexico, he is initiated into the Marxist "faith," with "a new god and a new religion": "I joined the ranks of the faithful in quest of the utopia" (145). The quest for personal transformation in each of these instances is tied to the changing contours of political vision.

Subtly, the narrator underscores the dynamics of this shift. Once, at a New York meeting with Roy's then-mentor, the Indian anticolonialist Lala Lajpat Rai, an audience member from "the extreme left-wingers of [the] American labor movement," raises the question: "what difference would it make to the Indian masses if they were exploited by native capitalists instead of foreign capitalists?" Roy is left dissatisfied at his mentor, Rai's, answer: "it does make a great difference whether one is kicked by his brother or by a foreign robber." No longer comfortable with the nationalist rhetoric of "brotherly" unity, Roy believes that "there was something wrong in our case. Suddenly, a light flashed through my mind; it was a new light" (28). These encounters and the sense of dissatisfaction they provoke lead to the search for more comprehensive political positions, and "a different sense of freedom" (28). Roy contrasts the emotional appeal of nationalism, of "loyalty to old comrades," to "an intelligent choice of a new ideal" (35). This is not a question of simply preferring internationalism to nationalism, or intelligence to emotion; Roy speaks of "a philosophical revolution, which knew no finality" (217), which leads to a capacious reformulation of the concept of "freedom." Thus, he ponders: "I no longer believed in political freedom without the content of economic liberation and social justice. But I had also realized that intellectual freedom – freedom from the bondage of all tradition and authority – was the effective condition for any effective struggle for social emancipation" (219–220). In this expansive definition, the "nation" ceases to be an adequate arena of either political or philosophical struggle. He further muses, "The new ideal of freedom was not to be attained within national or geographical boundaries. The struggle for its attainment must take place throughout the world, the entire civilized mankind participating in it" (217–218). While the Hegelian emphasis on "civilized mankind" might strike the present-day reader as problematical if not racist, it is worth underscoring that Roy rejects imperialist and nationalist hierarchy; his emphasis is squarely on a new humanity that deems conceptual and corporeal emancipation to be inseparable from each other and indeed coeval.

The structure of *Memoirs* formally reflects the transformations of its protagonist. The narrative is divided into sections, beginning with "In Search of an Ideal" that briefly recounts Roy's departure from India and travels through East Asia in search of weapons for waging nationalist struggle back home. It also illustrates Roy's encounters in the United States and Mexico and his rejection of essentialist nationalism. The next two sections, titled "The New Faith" and "In the Holy Land," deal respectively with post-1918 Europe, especially the Spartacist uprising in Germany, and Roy's subsequent journey to attend the Comintern in the Soviet Union. These section headings alert us to the different locales where "new ideas and new time" intrude into the life of the protagonist. As well, they perform a related if somewhat different function. By drawing attention to faith and the Holy Land, these headings set up a productive dissonance with the text's content, which in fact narrates the protagonist's critical interrogation of faith. This is a double displacement: on the one hand, it marks Roy's disaffiliation from the old certainties of cultural nationalism, itself predicated on the idea of Indian (read Hindu Brahminical) spiritual superiority and exceptional status. On the other hand, it self-consciously questions the new credo of Marxism. Roy's reference to the latter is accompanied by an illustration of fellow sectators who embrace it uncritically. His linking of the Marxist project with intellectual freedom is interesting in this regard; the explicit basis for emancipatory politics is "freedom from the bondage of all tradition and authority" (220). Far from being an avant-garde formation as in the 1920s, the problems of Marxism as an arbiter of authority had become patently obvious by a later period.

Although *Memoirs* does not admit it as such, this is clearly a *post facto* sentiment, indexing later events and developments beyond the epochal moment of 1917. As noted earlier, Roy came to pit a humanist Marx against Communist orthodoxy. One must note here, if only in passing, his resonance with other humanist Marxist, and Trotskyist, thinkers in the anti-Stalin tradition, such as Raya Dunayevskaya, C.L.R. James, Walter Rodney, and others.[10] "The habit of identifying Marxism with Communism is erroneous," he avers elsewhere, "Marxism is not a dogma ... [but] a philosophy of life" (*Heresies* 145, 146). Specifically, Roy questions the dogmatic ideology that relegated human agency to secondary importance – not only as a matter of expediency but also, far more gravely, as a philosophical conception. Marx, Roy continues, is a radical theorist of the "science of humanism," balancing in a productive tension two seemingly opposite attributes of material process and human consciousness. While physical matter obeys the laws of nature, ideas have their own laws that are neither identical to nor reducible to the former. The evolution of humanist reason is characterized by "the rejection of all faith, even in Marxism" (*Heresies* 155). At the same time, Roy further emphasizes the *relative autonomy* of ideas not excluding those of religious faith. He says: "Philosophically, the materialist conception of history must recognize the creative role of intelligence" (*Reason* 11).[11] Perhaps, it bears repeating that Roy is not a "new atheism" style advocate of reason over religion; he ties humanist imaginative reason to (Vico's notion of) poetic history, subjected to constant contestations and reconfigurations, rather than inevitable and linear progress.

The inspiration of poetic history is manifested in *Memoirs* at the level of *form*. The narrative repeatedly ties the rebirth of the individual to cycles of social and political change. At one level, the framing device of birth is a reference to the protagonist's Brahmin background, where the Brahmin is born "twice" (*dwija*, twice-born, is another word for Brahmin). At another level, Roy's subsequent rejection of his birth identity is tied to his repudiation of cultural nationalism as a collective entity. More prosaically, the rebirths are necessitated by the contingencies of revolutionary life. As he travels from one place to another, Roy adopts various guises to avoid the attention of the law. "Father Martin," the first of Roy's many personas, is "a novice from Pondicherry going [by sea] to study theology in Paris – duly armed with a copy of the Bible and the golden cross dangling from the watch chain" (22). While the docile Christian missionary is the very opposite of a Hindu radical – and thus effective as a disguise – this once again highlights the interplay between faith and reason. Roy shuffles multiple such personas in his travels: he is originally Narendranath Bhattacharya, his birth name; he flees from India via China as Father Martin with a "French-Indian passport" (18); once in the United States, Father Martin gives way to "M.N. Roy," the proper name by which he would be known for the rest of his life. In addition, he embarks on the trans-Atlantic journey from Mexico to Spain as a mixed-race hybrid, a child of an interracial marriage between "an eccentric Englishman" and "an aristocratic Mexican lady" – "the mixed parentage came in handy because it explained the flaws in my Spanish" (223). And in the files of the Comintern, Roy becomes "Robert" just as Claude McKay was given the name of "Sasha" (Holcomb, *Claude McKay*). Shifting names, born of the desire to change, and material circumstance or the *limits* to change, serve as oblique indicators of Roy's transformation.[12]

The growing awareness of a racial perspective is an important feature in these alterations. While race and racial oppression undoubtedly featured in Indian cultural nationalist thought, such a perception was muddled by the vaunted claims of spiritual superiority, exceptionalism, and caste. In contrast to the usual claims of Indian nationalism, *Memoirs* offers a nuanced if not entirely worked out perspective on race and religion. We will return to this point. Roy's first encounter with white American missionaries is instructive: disguised as Father Martin, he befriends the adopted daughter of an evangelical couple. This is met with suspicion – "as good Americans, they evidently did not like their ward getting too familiar with a colored man" (21). In that same journey, he notices, "the Japanese also behaved like members of a superior race" (21). Such instances, early on, unsettle the nationalist belief in racial exclusivity. But it is in the United States, through subsequent experiences with other "good Americans" as Roy sarcastically calls them, that his racial sensibilities are particularly developed. He is arrested in New York and taken for interrogation at the "sanctum of American criminal justice ... the frightful 'Tomb,' the medieval prison of super-modern New York" (38). His interrogator, the district attorney, tries to disarm him at first "with the typical American joviality": he assures Roy that "a wise man from the East" would not be treated badly if he disclosed information on his political activities and ratted on his comrades. When that fails, Roy is taken to the "underground" interrogation chambers, "a damned colored man." On his way down, he discovers another person from his group, a "Dr. Chakravarty" who has also been arrested and, obviously, tortured. The guards jeeringly refer to the Indian Chakravarty as "the oily leader of the oily revolution" (38). Roy is given insight into the prison's activities by the guards who describe the torture of prisoners in starkly racial terms – "We have caught other birds – black, brown and pink. They are all safe here." (39) The narrative does not get into the details of other prisoners, but the phrase "black, brown and pink" alerts us to the (multi) racial politics of incarceration, just as much as the "medieval prison" provides a stark contrast to "super-modern" New York City in the late 1910s. As Huey Newton would remark several decades later, the systemic anti-Black politics of race in America means that the imprisoned, irrespective of race, are all political prisoners of the US racial system.

Roy carries this awareness of US racial politics in his journey to Mexico. His encounter in the capital city with the Black American pugilist Jack Johnson is notable in this regard. Johnson, a celebrity athlete of his time, had fled to Mexico to avoid the Mann Act, which punished offenders for "transporting women across state lines for immoral purposes." Johnson, who was married to a white woman, Lucille Cameron, had been falsely charged under that act. Roy's encounter with Johnson in Mexico is significant for a number of reasons: both are escapees from the law, and Johnson's "immoral" relation with a white female is parallel to M.N. Roy's own marriage to his then-wife, Evelyn Trent, who accompanied him on the trip. Roy and Trent see the couple, Johnson and Cameron, at a restaurant in Mexico City in "the fashionable Avenida de Madero ... [where] none came to serve them" (116). After witnessing some tense exchanges between the couple and the restaurant staff, Roy notes:

> I knew that Negroes (*sic*) were not served in American restaurants, not even admitted to barber shops kept by white men. But we were not in America, and the Mexicans, with mixed blood running in their veins, were well known for racial catholicism ... my sympathy warmed up to indignation when I noticed the supercilious smile and sly giggling all around. (116)

One does not know, for lack of further details in the *Memoirs,* how this lapse of "racial catholicism" affects his perception of race relations in Mexico, but what is evident from the quoted passage is the clear impact of race oppression in the United States on Roy's personal and political sensibility. His caustic observation, "we were not in America," and his determination "never to come to the place again," bear testimony to this fact. The narrative's portrayal of Johnson makes him almost a mirror image of Roy's personal situation, in terms of racialized masculinity. *Memoirs* further mentions, as point of fact, the political impact of this event on Johnson. Later, Roy and another associate run into him again, while "collecting money to publish a Spanish translation of the Soviet Constitution" (117). They tell Johnson of the "Bolshevik" cause and ask him if he has "anything against the Bolsheviks." Not only does Johnson reply in the negative, he donates ten dollars, "with a broad grin, and wishes the Bolsheviks luck" (117).

However, the story is a little more complex. In a telling act of silencing, Roy omits any mention of his fellow militant, Evelyn Trent, either in this episode or elsewhere in the *Memoirs*. As Isabel Huacuja Alonso has recently shown, Trent was an important presence in the activist circles of Mexico City and no less influential in the Mexican Left's critique of racial and national chauvinisms ("M.N. Roy and the Mexican Revolution"). The picture we get from *Memoirs* is incomplete and marked by narrative biases and obviously in need of further exploration. Roy himself warns us against taking *Memoirs* too literally. He claims at one point: "I consider autobiography very unreliable as a source of objective truth ... [i]t is not a question of honesty or integrity [of the writer]. It is the great 'Unconscious'" (566). It is possible to discern though not endorse several such unconscious patterns.

Another episode is Roy's decision, while in Mexico City, to write a primer titled *La India: Su Pasado, Su Presente y Su Porvenir* [India: Her Past, Present, and Future] that went against the sentimental "view about ancient Indian culture" (549). Published in 1918, Roy's Mexican treatise vigorously disagreed with the "mythical" past of India and its Aryan origins. By contrast, Roy advanced the notion of a pre-Aryan, Dravidian civilization in India. Such a thesis, flying against nationalist claims of racial exclusivity, "could not [be] substantiate[d] with factual evidence ... in those days" (550). He writes in the *Memoirs,* "The eagerness of the average Indian to claim Aryan ancestry was, and still is, very widespread. As a reaction to the American prejudice against the colored races, the Indians in the United States laid emphasis on their descent from the white Aryan race" (550). Roy's rejection of the Aryan thesis is a repudiation of diasporic Indian aspirations to whiteness. Instead he advocates solidarity among "colored races" (*sic*) against "American prejudice." Lacking in "factual evidence," Roy's treatise on the forced Aryan supremacy over Dravidian ethnicities represented – for him – a translation of US anti-race politics. What Roy fails to mention, though this could hardly be unknown to him by the 1950s if not in 1918, is that the critique of Aryanism-Brahminism was also a commonplace to the likes of E.V. Ramaswamy or "Periyar," the leading anti-caste intellectual and proponent of Dravidianism in southern India.[13] The *Memoirs'* narration, as noted, is not without its significant gaps.

Similar processes of translation and elision mark Roy's embrace of Marxism. He learns of the works of Karl Marx at the New York Public Library and "discover[s] a new meaning in them" (29). The news of the Bolshevik Revolution, while Roy is in Mexico, "fires the imagination" of "a utopia" among the radicals, as "the idea that to be actually in possession of political power might be within the realm of political possibility shook the preconceived anarcho-syndicalist theoretical antipathy for the State" (131–132). Such transformations of "theoretical antipathy" are achieved through the literal groundwork of translation; as the Soviet Constitution is translated to Spanish for circulation, Roy is entrusted with the "English section of *El Heraldo*" (131), the Socialist Party organ. Such translation across languages and cultures also results in mistranslations. Roy notes with evident amusement – and perhaps more than a touch of condescension – the case of a "jovial ... Indian [indigenous] military commander." This "unexpected follower of Lenin," fired by anti-US sentiments embraces Bolshevism and declares with impeccable logic that "I don't know what is Socialism ... [t]he Yankees (*sic*) do not like the Bolsheviks, they are our enemies; therefore, the Bolsheviks must be our friends, and we must be their friends. We are all Bolsheviks" (153–154). While such anecdotes are recounted to show the problems of "disproportionate passion," they also illustrate the multiracial appeal of Bolshevik utopia for many stripes of "Indians" – Eastern and indigenous American, even if these are not all equal.[14]

Roy's internationalism develops through such diverse experiences and complex prisms of cultural history. The dialectical flow between adoption and rejection is crucial to the *Memoirs*. On the one hand, the Marxist critique of imperialism enables him to crystallize these fragmentary positions into a coherent world view. The primacy of anticolonial politics for Roy, on the other hand, resists the Eurocentric tendencies of official Soviet

Marxism. As he departs for the Soviet Union in 1920, Roy's description of his trans-Atlantic voyage powerfully illuminates the dialogues coursing through, and animating, his self-transformation:

> Only four years ago, I had made the longer voyage across the Pacific.... [I]n the intervening period, I had lived through a couple of centuries of cultural history.... [T]he trans-Atlantic journey was enjoyable, and the perspective exciting, whereas the voyage from Asia to America had been depressing. Then I was going from the known to an unknown world. Now it was a pilgrimage; on the way, I would have the privilege to witness capitalist Europe collapsing, and, like, Prometheus unbound, the revolutionary proletariat rising to build a new world out of the ruins. (225)

The knowledge gained in the United States and Mexico transforms Roy's thinking away from the known certainties of nationalism. These new knowledges in turn meant that for Roy, the "revolutionary proletariat rising" in Europe could no longer be seen in exclusively European but in world-historical terms, "a new world." Roy's support for the "revolutionary proletariat" in Europe is accompanied by a sharp critique of metropolitan *chauvinism*, connected to Lenin's well-known criticism of the "labor aristocracy." He comes to realize "during my several months' stay in Germany ... that the proletariat in the metropolitan countries would not ... capture power *unless* Imperialism was weakened by the revolt of the colonial peoples" (306, emphasis added). Roy "suspect[s] nationalist atavism" in his "feeling," but at the same time claims to be "exasperated by the insularism of the average proletarian revolutionary who sympathized ... but did not believe that it [colonial liberation] would succeed *before* socialism was established in Europe" (306, emphasis added). Indeed, Roy's contrarian views amounted to contesting the teleology of revolution.

Certainly by the 1950s, Roy would have been convinced of the need to rethink the standard Marxist notions of progress. Alongside Vico and Hegel, he came to emphasize the importance of non-European philosophical systems such as the Indian and the Chinese materialist traditions in this regard.[15] The *Memoirs* projects these convictions to an earlier period. Residing in Berlin in 1919, he notes that the suppression of the Spartacist uprising, led by Rosa Luxemburg and Karl Liebknecht, had a devastating impact on Communist plans for a worldwide uprising. For many, the success of the working class in Germany, with its long history of socialist organization, would be key for sustaining the revolution elsewhere. In the *Memoirs*, Roy ascribes such a perception to the faith in "'inevitability', the magic conception of Marxism" (251). His critique of this magical Eurocentric model is extended, in vein, to the "major European delegates [at the Comintern] ... who took little interest" in Lenin's theses on the "National and Colonial Questions."

Roy's affinity with the later Bandung articulation of anti-imperialist South-South solidarity emerges most clearly in the interactions at the Comintern. Recalling, for instance, Tom Quelch, the head of the British delegation in Moscow, Roy piquantly observes, "[Quelch] vaguely felt that Lenin's thesis would transfer the proverbial 'White Man's Burden' on the working class in the imperialist countries. The sense of responsibility [sic] induced him to befriend the delegates from the colonial and semi-colonial countries" (365). Roy's interactions at the Second Congress of 1920 were shaped by many such dissonances and contestations between the official Comintern position on internationalism, what he terms "Lenin's broad vision" (365) and the "insular" disregard of the major Communist representatives of Germany, France, and the United Kingdom.[16] This was accentuated by the supposed weakness in Lenin's own position about the role of the democratic-bourgeois elite in anticolonial struggles.

In *Memoirs*, Roy recounts receiving Lenin's theses in an "English translation" (339). Lenin claimed, "the colonial countries must have their bourgeois democratic revolution *before* they could enter the stage of the proletarian revolution" (379, emphasis added). Lenin's theses stressed the need to "achieve the closest alliance, with Soviet Russia, of all the national and colonial liberation movements." Roy's intervention on this issue, his "Supplementary Theses," was tabled alongside Lenin's for discussion at the Second Congress. It consisted among other things of two major rebuttals: one, a rejection of revolutionary teleology that assumed the primacy of revolution in Europe, and second, a critique – not entirely unsympathetic – of bourgeois nationalism in the colonies. Filtered through his previous experience of the failed uprising in Germany, the "Supplementary Theses" maintained the following:

> Superprofits gained in the colonies is the mainstay of modern capitalism, and so long as the latter is not deprived of this source of profit, it will not be easy for the European working class to overthrow the capitalist order .... Without the breaking up of the colonial Empire, the overthrow of the capitalist system in Europe does not appear possible. (Point 3 of "Supplementary Theses," in Roy, *Selected Works I*, 124)

The response in the Comintern to such heterodox formulations was significant: agreement was reached at the end of the debates that one, capitalist development was not "inevitable in the backward countries,"[17] and second, that the Comintern was to extend support to "the bourgeois movements for liberation in the colonies only in cases when they are really revolutionary."[18]

Yet it is precisely at the point of these dramatic transactions, involving the translation of Leninism into an anticolonial political position that insisted on its own autonomy, that we reach the narrative limits of the memoir. Unlike the historical records of these debates, *Memoirs* does not go into the details; perhaps, literary representation fails at the juncture of radical heterodoxy.[19] Significantly, *Memoirs* is wholly silent on the final forms in which Roy's and Lenin's theses were adapted. Roy's observation on the central role of anticolonial revolution was dropped, and his draft was modified to imply that anticolonial struggles would be defined in a relation of tutelage directed from the center, that is, by the Soviet Union. Inverting the hierarchy suggested by Roy's theses, Lenin's adapted final theses stated as follows:

> The victorious proletarian Soviet Republics will lend a helping hand to these masses [in the colonial countries] .... [T]he Communist International must declare on theoretical grounds that *with the assistance of* the proletariat of the advanced countries the backward nations can arrive to the Soviet form of organization. (*Selected Works I*, 126, emphases added; see also Makalani 77–81; Manjapra 59–62)

This shift in focus, from "without the breaking up of the colonial Empire, the overthrow of the capitalist system in Europe does not appear possible" in Roy to Lenin's emphasis on "the assistance of the proletariat of the advanced countries," deserves our attention. These alterations – at the level of the text(s) – marked the negotiation of contending visions of revolutionary praxis. Certainly, these positional differences indicate the still-supple nature of Soviet theoretical debates at the time (1920), with scope for a certain degree of debate and dissent. Equally, on the other hand, they provide an early indication of the long drawn out transformation of Soviet internationalism from Lenin to Stalin's much more inflexible and authoritarian approach. Of course, as one of many texts involved, so to speak, the "Supplementary Thesis" is unable to resist such transformations single-handedly. Nonetheless, Roy's work can be read as gesturing to an alternative complex of actors and consciousness – in articulation as much as in silence.

This is a good place to comment on the literary politics of genre. The *Memoirs* connects the subjective realm of the imagination to the objective terrain of politics: Roy's personal experiences and his uneven, conscious and unconscious, reflections on the former provide the basis for his broader affiliations and counterfactual speculations. Contrary to Misch's canonical description of the memoir as a passive genre, Roy's role in the narrative is certainly not lacking in agency. Nor is his keenly humanist narrative persona reliant, as Julie Rak suggests for the memoir, on postmodern fragmented subjectivity. If anything, the narrator's utopian looking forward to "Prometheus Unbound" (*Memoirs* 225) is a far cry from postmodern skepticism. Our reading of the *Memoirs* further nuances Beverley's concept of the *testimonio*. Beverley suggests that the *testimonio* is an objective literary form for the political imperative of national liberation in the periphery. I wholeheartedly concur, but with one proviso. While the personal trajectory of the protagonist in the *Memoirs* parallels his evolving political negotiations, the narrative makes it clear that such articulations cannot take place only for "*a* community or group" (Beverley 16, emphasis added). Roy's *Memoirs* persuasively demonstrates that such national expressions – or national allegories, as I argued in the previous chapter – have to accommodate a dialectical understanding of collectivity as well as difference and establish dialogue among multiple emancipatory projects with distinctive and even different goals and ends. Indeed, *Memoirs* registers the imagining of amorphous but grand transformations. We now invert Roy's reflective method of narrating the past from the vantage point of the present and consider how his later convictions measure up to his own earlier writings. I turn to Roy's critique of the exclusionary registers of bourgeois nationalist thought, one that he maintained since the early 1920s.

India in Transition

Appearing some three decades before the serialized *Memoirs*, the "Indian Communist Manifesto" was written in Berlin and published in *The Glasgow Register* in the middle of the year 1920. M.N. Roy, Evelyn Trent, and Abani Mukherjee were the cosigners. This text helps us understand the unremarked overlaps between Roy's Bolshevik and radical humanist phases, his divergence from cultural nationalism including both the moderate and extremist varieties and his developing interest in a materialist analysis of the periphery. The 1920s was a revolutionary decade not only for the eastern peripheries of imperial Europe (the Soviet Union) but also colonies and semi-colonies everywhere, from Mexico to Ireland to China. The 1920s was when nationalism became, in the South Asian subcontinent, a truly mainstream phenomenon, away from the restricted domain of elite social groups and avant-garde circles of radicals: at the same time, the convergence between elite and popular classes, the latter with a much older history of radical struggle, created the historic conditions as well as contradictions of postcolonial nationalisms.

Some portions of this document are worth highlighting to illustrate this point. First, the "Manifesto" notes, "the nationalist revolutionary movement, recruited from educated youths of the middle classes ... did not inspire the masses with lasting enthusiasm." This is the result of the nationalists' lack of a comprehensive conceptualization of the liberation struggle, where "the leaders failed to prescribe remedies for the social and economic evils from which the workers suffer." Alongside the emphasis on "workers," the Manifesto brings back the question of the "peasants." This had been part of the Bengali extremists' program, as I noted, but this time a new focus emerges: "the real revolutionary movement stands for the economic emancipation of the workers and rests on the growing strength of a class-conscious industrial proletariat and landless peasantry." Such statements clearly distinguished the "Indian Communist Manifesto" from the politics of mainstream Indian nationalism at that time. The "Manifesto" highlighted the working classes – the workers and the peasants – and posited their liberation to be antagonistic to not only British imperialism *but also* to the Indian nationalist elite. This last point was stated without ambiguity – "we want the world to know that nationalism is confined to the bourgeois ... the working class in any country must always be indifferent to purely nationalist aspirations" (all quotations from "Indian Communist Manifesto," in *Selected Works I*, 162).

The specific form of address in the statement "we want the world to know" is interesting to note. In addition to performing the rhetorical function demanded of a manifesto, the proclamation also gestures to the appropriate international networks: its context of production (Berlin), publication (Glasgow), and multiple outlets of dissemination through translation.[20] Such sites included the metropolises of New York, San Francisco, and Berlin but also the relatively peripheral locations of Calcutta, Mexico City, Tashkent, and Moscow. Anarchism, national liberation, and socialism are some of the identifiable ideological strands in the document.

The effort to place anticolonial liberation at the heart of the project of anti-capitalist revolution, and vice versa, finds its most succinct expression in what is one of Roy's most significant theoretical works, *India in Transition*, published in 1922. His attempt to guide Comintern policy (as a functionary) was complemented by his writings. Written in the aftermath of the Lenin-Roy debate, *India in Transition* secured Roy's reputation – which was not meant to last – as one of the Comintern's foremost intellectuals on the colonial question. The book provides a Marxist case study of British India including the territories of present-day Bangladesh and Pakistan, possibly the earliest and undoubtedly one of the finest examples of its kind.

As in the multi-authored "Indian Communist Manifesto," here too Roy argues that the interests of the landed and industrial elite on the one hand and the working class and peasantry on the other are incommensurable to each other in the last instance. Many of the specific claims and details of the book, such as the growing strength of the industrial working class at the beginning of the 1920s, are admittedly less relevant today. The wide array of thinkers that *India in Transition* draws upon and in turn speaks to, as well, suffers from varying degrees of neglect and oversight. These include Vladimir Lenin's discussion of agrarian capitalism in Russia, Leon Trotsky's closely related "Law of Uneven and Combined Development," José Carlos Mariátegui's analysis of "semi-colonial, semi-feudal" formations in Peru (taken up by Mao in China), and Dadabhai Naoroji's "drain theory of poverty."[21] These provide Roy with the methodological and conceptual tools of analysis, "the searchlight of Historical Materialism" as he terms it (*India in Transition* 17). However, the text's persistent relevance lies in its illustration of the combined and uneven forms of colonial-capitalist development in India, one that necessitates engagement with and simultaneous distancing from bourgeois cultural nationalism.

If Roy's activist career marked a move from cultural nationalism to Marxist internationalism and beyond, *India in Transition* might be said to index an opposite trajectory, reorienting Marxist and anticolonial nationalist theory to account for the distinctive forces of emancipation in the struggles of his natal land. Among recent scholars, Vivek Chibber points to Roy as a "pioneer in the political analysis of Indian nationalism," as well as the early importance of *India in Transition* alongside works by R.P. Dutt, *India Today* and A.R. Desai, *Social Background of Indian Nationalism* (*Postcolonial Theory* 253 n). At the very outset, *India in Transition* highlights the unreliability of the "archive": to put it in recognizable idiom, the book's opening illuminates the complicity of knowledge with colonialist-nationalist power:

> We are obliged to learn about the past of the Indian people from two sources, namely the imperial historians, who write more about the civilizing

mission of their illustrious countrymen than about the life and conditions of the conquered people, and Indian authors, who are very apt to sacrifice historical facts at the altar of patriotism. (17)

Thus constructed, the archive provides "little information as to the economic condition of the toiling masses." In addition to economic life, Roy's text seeks to account for the specificity of India's social formation and the impact of socioeconomic forces on the development of subjective consciousness. These are the areas where Roy's work anticipates if in a limited sense the Subaltern Studies (SS) scholars such as Ranajit Guha.[22] There have been two sets of notable differences – related but distinct – in the reception of Subaltern Studies: first, a continuing debate on the relative importance of Marxist and post-Marxist Foucauldian methodologies for history writing, and second, a sharper set of criticisms against the "Orientalist" assumptions of SS practitioners such as Guha, Partha Chatterjee, and Dipesh Chakrabarty. Roy's discussion of caste and colonial underdevelopment, I think, provides an unexpected – interwar and Indo-Soviet – genealogy of this divergence.[23]

In *India in Transition*, Roy takes issue with the notion that caste hierarchies result from the "uniqueness" of Indian civilization, that "Indian culture has been a unique thing" (95). He objects that such culturalist approaches "preach that class-struggle is the peculiar outcome ... of the West and is not possible in Indian society" (95). By contrast, his exploration of the "economic basis of caste" shows that "coming down to the origin of it [caste], one discovers slavery" (95). This is not a mechanical analysis that crudely reduces social phenomena to economics; rather, the economic function of caste hierarchy is complicated by "the [cultural] distinction made by color." Parallel to the *Memoirs*' discussion of Indo-European Aryanism, Roy contends, "the caste-line was first between the Aryan conquerors and the conquered aborigines. The distinction was made by color, the conqueror being fair and the conquered dark" (96).

Additionally, the scriptural sanctions behind caste encourage a passive subjectivity, which means accepting one's enslaved status as ordained not by human-made society but supra-human considerations of divinity. This was precisely the essence of the *Vichian* intervention, one that Roy adapts to his own analysis: as he argues elsewhere, the otherworldly notion of acceptance in the "spiritualist" reading of Vico forms the socialized basis of European fascism.[24] Yet, caste did not rest simply on foundational narratives of origin or uncontested ideas of divinity. Roy goes on to illustrate the manifestations of caste in diverse formations of socialized labor. Thus, the early "village community" that relied on "the hereditary division of labor stereotyped into the caste system," forming "guilds" similar to the trade and manufacture guilds in Europe. He reasons, "Caste was the basis of socio-economic organized production ... the class-line ran through the caste-system" (96). Gender is largely absent from Roy's analysis at this stage, only to develop in later writings of the 1930s.[25]

Roy's explanation of the persistence of precapitalist forms of caste in the colonial-capitalist periphery is striking and bears repetition. He avers, "since the capitalist exploitation was carried on by a foreign imperialist bourgeoisie, the outward effects of the capitalist mode of production [namely the formal *freedom of labor*] were not clearly felt on the Indian society" (97). Yet, he notes in the same passage, "the fundamental social transformations that result from the capitalist control of the national economy have already taken place." The peculiar structure of colonized Indian society is determined by these two contradictory determinations. Colonial-capitalist penetration on the one hand causes "fundamental social transformations," but on the other hand these changes occur unevenly, "without causing serious disequilibrium on the surface" (97). This is, to tweak Marx's famous formulation, real incorporation *without* formal emancipation. The precapitalist social forms – such as patriarchal gender and caste relations – continue to coexist with and impinge on formal and juridical notions of equality. The latter are, at any rate, unevenly formalized. Far from emancipating the laborer, even nominally, caste in an unevenly capitalist society dehumanizes her entirely. The intersectional aspect was not lost on the later Roy, who claimed: "In the social organization of India, *women* occupy, and have always occupied, the position of chattel" (qtd. in Loomba, *Revolutionary Desires* 116, emphasis added).[26]

Roy's comments on the relation between texts of caste law and the division of labor in the village community, it should be underscored, combine the insights of the previous century's radical thinkers. In the nineteenth-century tract *Ghulamgiri* (Slavery), Jyotirao Phule, the Marathi anti-caste reformer and social theorist, traced a similar relation between textuality and Brahminical caste power:

> Writers with their selfsame objects as those of Manu [the law giver] and others of his class, added from time to time to the existing mass of legends, the idle fantasies of their own brains and palmed them off upon the ignorant masses as Divine Inspiration [caste law], or as the acts of the Deity himself. (*Selected Writings* 31)

When *Ghulamgiri* was published in 1873, Phule was already comparing Dalit slavery in India to the situation of African American slaves in the United States. Earlier in 1845, Marx and Engels had theorized the interaction between forms of social production, law, and ideologies of caste thus:

> The "idea," the "conception" of the people in question about their real practice, is transformed into the sole determining, active force, which controls and determines their practice ... [This is] the crude form in which the division of labor appears with the Indians and Egyptians [and] calls forth the caste-system in their State and religion. (*The German Ideology* 60)

Marx would go on to explore caste-class later, in relation to capitalist production and the social division of labor, in Volume I of *Capital*. Among Roy's contemporaries, Ambedkar, proceeding from a different direction, went the furthest in theorizing labor and the specific social form of caste-class. For diverse thinkers such as Phule and Marx, Ambedkar and Roy, and many more, as I have argued elsewhere, "caste" and "class" were neither equivalent nor irreducible categories, but comparable and intertwined aspects of a singular and uneven modernity (see Majumder "Caste, Race, and Intellectual History").[27]

This is made evident in Roy's explanation of colonized formations (in a diachronic conversation with Naoroji, Lenin, Trotsky, Mariátegui, Mao et al.) that articulates an early version of the dependency school associated with Latin American economic theory. Thus he notes: "the forcible export of more than 70 per cent of the accumulated wealth of India by the East India Company ... [and] the deliberate destruction of the craft industries and the consequent forcing of the artisan class back to the land" (21) were all factors that prevented the growth of industrial capitalism and stunted the native classes of the bourgeoisie and the proletariat in colonial India. What distinguishes Roy from standard-issue economic nationalism is his emphasis not only on national impoverishment due to deindustrialization, which was commonplace, but also its crippling effect particularly on workers and peasants, which was not. As *India in Transition* suggests, the introduction of "capitalist exploitation" created a distinctive situation in the colonial periphery as compared to the imperial metropole: "The Indian artisans, after having lost their independent means of production, were not absorbed into large industrial centers.... [I]n India, the social expression of machine production did not take the form of a city proletariat, but that of a vast mass of land-workers and pauperized peasantry" (94, 55). This is distinct from the "classical" – and "exceptional" – path that Marx and Trotsky had described with respect to capitalism in England, of the peasantry's expropriation from the land and absorption into the industrial and urban proletariat: in the face of the relative insignificance of the city-based working class, the task of Marxist analysis in the periphery, directly colonized as in India but also non-colonial yet peripheralized such as in Russia, China, Italy, or Peru, involved a global, comparative redefinition of the proletariat.[28] This was the basis of peripheral Marxism so to speak; once again, the specifics of Roy's formulation are interesting to note.

The significance of this task is made evident in the section titles of the text. After an opening section on "The Growth of the Bourgeoisie" (or more precisely, the weakness thereof in colonial India), the following section relates it to its logical correlate; the next section is titled "The Condition of the Rural Population." This is followed by three sections that comprise the bulk of the text, titled "The Proletariat I, II and III," exploring and illuminating a historically specific, materialist analysis of colonial underdevelopment. The large masses of "land-workers and pauperized peasantry," numerically the most significant and economically dispossessed among the Indian populace, are key to Roy's vision of anticolonial liberation. He calls them a "floating population" (47). Their nontraditional relation to capitalist commodity production is described thus:

> The social production and economic life of India today are inseparably woven with the structure of world capitalism. The agricultural industry in India is an adjunct of the British industrial system, and for this reason, 72 per cent of her population engaged in the cultivation of the earth, *to all interests and purposes*, occupy the social position of the proletariat in the wide scheme of capitalist exploitation. (101, emphases added)

This agricultural proletariat is distinct from the traditional proletariat (if the latter exists beyond an ideal concept), not only in economic but also in terms of "social position." While both are antagonistically placed against "world capitalism," the former bears a relation of multiple antagonisms: capitalist-imperialist exploitation along with localized pre- and non-capitalist coercion and dehumanization. All of these in combination, capitalist, pre-capitalist, and non-capitalist forms, contribute to the "social production and economic life" in India as per Roy's analysis.

As Roy argued at the Comintern, proletarian desires in the periphery are not identical to the proclivities of the national elite. Roy's emphasis on the "land-workers and pauperized peasantry" as the "adjunct of the British industrial system" is contemporaneous to Mariátegui and Mao Zedong, as noted, and precedes the better-known examples of Fanon, Cabral, and others in historically different but comparable circumstances. It is worth pointing out, however, that Roy took a less than stellar view of Mao, especially the latter's position on the peasantry and role in aligning the Chinese Communists with the nationalist Kuomintang forces during and after the failed revolution of 1927. Roy's critique of the missteps of the Mao-led faction and his assertion that "Mao Tse-Tung, in the critical days of 1927, represented the *extreme right-wing view* in the leadership of the [Chinese] Communist Party" (*Revolution and Counter-Revolution* 615, emphases added) align if somewhat uneasily with recent scholarship on the subject.[29]

On the other hand, *India in Transition*'s braiding of capitalist, pre- and non-capitalist forms in colonial India bore unrealized parallels to Antonio Gramsci's exposition of Italian underdevelopment and state formation in imperial Europe. Roy recalls that Gramsci, whom he met in Moscow in the early 1920s,

> came to the conclusion that the philosophical aspect of Marxism should be revised so that it could give the idealistically inclined all that Croce gave and much more. [At the time of his death in 1937] Gramsci had left behind 2000 pages of manuscript as the result of a profound study in prison. It may turn out to be the greatest contribution to philosophical thought hitherto made by any Marxist. (*Memoirs* 275)

Sadly, he does not elaborate further. In this respect, Roy's – proto-Gramscian – linkage between combined and uneven social form in the periphery and the expressions of religious, caste, and gendered forms of hegemonic subjectivity deserves further exploration. His notable concept, the articulation of a "floating population" that is only partially absorbed among the "city proletariat," complicated homogenous and economistic notions of the working classes.[30]

In many respects, Roy's practical program collided – at crucial moments and in productive tension – with that of M.K. Gandhi, the chief ideologue and leader of Indian decolonization. Though a full discussion is outside our scope, certain aspects may be mentioned in passing. Roy recognized that among all the nationalists, it was Gandhi who successfully incorporated the laboring and marginal classes as part of a broad program of emancipation. Arguably, the latter transformed anticolonial nationalism from an elite affair to a mass upsurge; this was all the more reason to deeply engage with Gandhi's blind spots. Among other things, Gandhi's strategic opposition to the independent action of industrial and agricultural workers drew the severest condemnation from Roy (and those on the Communist and socialist Left in general). Just as much, Roy saw Gandhian philosophy as articulating contradictory and competing tendencies: a broad prospect of humanist emancipation from below and archaic forms of conservatism and patriarchy, as prevalent in India as in Europe. In an article, "Mahatma and Bolshevism," Roy declaimed (in 1924) that Bolshevism "forged ahead, breaking one link after another in the mighty chain of time-honored servitude ... while [Gandhism] gropes in the dark, spinning out ethical and religious dogmas."[31] Interestingly, the sardonic contrast did not sit well with Lenin, who viewed Gandhi as a revolutionary.[32] The relation between Roy and Gandhi became less acrimonious possibly on account of their mutual abhorrence of muscular nationalism but remained uncomfortable over the years, all the way to the latter's assassination in 1948. It is possible to speculate, with the due qualifications, that Roy's trenchant yet prescient critique of the "Mahatma" (Great Soul, the name given to Gandhi by Tagore) – like that of Ambedkar in a comparable vein – illustrated aspects of Gandhianism that he, Gandhi, was not fully aware of. But such neglect had unintended and deadly consequences. For it was not Gandhi or the party he led, the Congress, but his political opponents to the Right, the Hindu supremacists inspired by Italian fascism, that came to aggressively embody the worst "dogmas" of cultural nationalism.[33] Of course, cultural nationalism itself underwent several important mutations during the intervening period as well.

Roy, McKay, and Afro-Asian Internationalism

I have tried to show that Roy's internationalist solidarity developed both within and against the framework of Soviet Communism. These were not self-contained but, rather, evolving constellations. Over the years, dominant Soviet Marxism (Stalinism) was subjected to dynamic pressures and contestations from various directions, some realized and many more unrealized. We know that Roy and the Jamaican American writer Claude McKay crossed paths in these decades. While Roy's *Memoirs* does not mention McKay, the latter's *A Long Way From Home* (1937) brings up two such encounters. In Moscow in 1922, McKay recalls being "photographed with the popular leaders of international Communism" that included "Zinoviev, Bukharin, Radek, Clara Zetkin, Sen Katayama, Roy" (*A Long Way* 134). Then again in Berlin in 1923, he runs into Roy, who asks McKay to "contribute an article to his paper about Communism and the Negro (*sic*)." (187) In a significant slippage that mixes up the two contexts of African American and Indian anticolonial liberation, McKay informs the reader that he does not write the said article, being advised by an English friend to "keep away from the *Indian* movement because it is too 'complicated'" (187, emphasis added). McKay's autobiography is silent on the possibilities, or contours, of such internationalist conversations taking shape in the networks connecting Moscow and Berlin.

It is a matter of speculation if either was familiar with the other's writings. In spite of the lack of such evidence, it is still possible to visualize these two figures as standing at the crossroads of – and embodying – a vital juncture of "Afro-Asian" radical thought. As I have argued in these pages, Roy's inchoate and no doubt incomplete analysis of caste was, nevertheless, informed by his experience of American race politics and the Soviet critique of imperialism. On the other hand, McKay's critiques of Black cultural nationalism (from the Left) and the chauvinism of white American socialists resonate with Roy's sharp denunciations of elite Hindu nationalism, and the dominant trends of European and Soviet Communism. For Roy and McKay, these remain restricted to the plane of imagined affiliations. However, such interactions among radicals also led to real-life collaborations, as we learn from Harry Haywood, one of the leading African American activists of the Communist Party USA (CPUSA).

In his autobiography *Black Bolshevik*, Haywood recounts meeting a diverse group of Indian students at the University of the Toilers of the East (KUTVA). This was a significant institution, attended by other notable Asian activists such as Ho Chi Minh and Liu Shaoqi, future leaders of the Vietnamese and Chinese Communists, respectively. The Indian coterie included activists belonging to the Ghadar Party in California and Ghadarite soldiers previously escaped from Hong Kong, "to Shanghai where they were taken in charge by M.N. Roy, an Indian and then Comintern representative to China. Roy [then] sent them to Moscow" (165). Particularly, Haywood comments on another member of the Indian group, "Sakorov," Dada Amir Haider Khan, who went on to play a leading role in the Communist Party of Pakistan. The meeting between Haywood and "Sakorov" in Moscow in 1926, as *Black Bolshevik* recounts in great detail, was the beginning of a decades-long friendship.[34]

These interactions, occurring on the sidelines of mainstream Communist activity, nonetheless came to sharply inflect Soviet policy. The Comintern adopted the Black Belt thesis in 1928, which recognized African Americans in the southern United States as an "oppressed nation" and "national minority" in the north of the country. These perspectives also positively shaped the CPUSA's participation, led by Haywood and others, in one of the most notorious controversies of interwar American history, the Scottsboro trials in Alabama in 1931. In Chapter 4, I discuss one peculiar case of traveling cultural form: how the Scottsboro case is adapted, unexpectedly and ingeniously, to Bengali Indian people's theater by Utpal Dutt. African American and Indian interactions reached a crescendo in the period of the 1960s and 1970s, within and against the competing Cold War and Bandung frameworks of nationalism. The anti-imperialist resistance in Vietnam, Cuba, and elsewhere galvanized this later exchange, yet it was no doubt informed by these earlier interactions.

A key intervention of the Afro-Asian intellectuals at the Comintern, I would suggest, is the renewed understanding of proletarian politics. This was fostered through the focus on race, caste, and anticolonial liberation. The notion of a nontraditional proletariat is articulated in Roy's analysis of the "agricultural proletariat" of the periphery. In McKay's literary work, such as the novels *Banjo* or *Banana Bottom*, one finds similar though not identical invocations of a "Black lumpen proletariat" (see Edwards, Holcomb, and Nickels for McKay). The succeeding chapters of the present book further elucidate the notions of the lumpen and the agricultural proletariat. Indeed, such formulations represented not rejections but rather creative reconstructions of the Marxist project from a non-Western perspective. As would be apt, the majority world of the periphery came to occupy the center.

The terrain of "dissident internationalism" – the phrase is from Joel Nickels – that figures such as M.N. Roy and McKay map out is significant. The term "dissident" is of postwar provenance and carries with it the ideological baggage of Cold War anti-Communism: it is useful nonetheless. Such lineages would include not only male figures such as Ho Chi Minh, Sen Katayama, Otto Huiswoud but also female activists such as Clara Zetkin, Agnes Smedley, Kamaladevi Chattopadhyay, Una Marson, Dolores Ibárruri, and many more. In the interwar period, these figures and the formations they represent problematize – if only as a trace – the triumphant narrative of a Soviet orthodoxy. In the post-Stalin era, the Soviet Union extended support to elite-led as well as popular nationalisms with mixed results and often guided by its own pragmatic interests. By contrast, dissident internationalism allows us to see that the Soviet Union enabled, but could not entirely dictate, the exchange of anticolonial ideas.

M.N. Roy's remarkably frank debate with Vladimir Lenin on the primacy of the periphery to a post-capitalist world is a pioneering event in this regard, as is his original though not unique contribution to a materialist theory of combined and uneven development. Roy, perhaps more than any other among his contemporaries, identified the key contradiction unfolding through the various sites of anticolonial struggle, namely, the emergence and consolidation of a strikingly paradoxical ideology – nationalism – that spoke on behalf of and yet worked against the emancipation of the masses. His vehement critique anticipates the conflict, which only takes full shape after formal decolonization, between the native bourgeoisies on the one hand and those subaltern groups on the other hand, dispossessed along the various axes of location, gender, caste, race, and class. Even as Roy's own influence – quite unlike Tagore in this case – largely declined after his death, the ideas traced by him found other proponents especially in the fields of literature and culture. As we see next, the urban lumpen and the agricultural proletariat articulate a radical conception – or a counter-history – of Bandung that went far beyond the latter's dominant interpretations.

Notes

1. M.N. Roy's biographer Samaren Roy (no relation) argues that "[Roy] differed from all those before him ... in holding that revolution in the colonies would liberate the proletarians in the metropolitan countries" (Samaren Roy, *Twice-Born Heretic* xiii–xiv). A recent and more tempered biography still terms him as "an anti-colonial thinker of tremendous clout," situating Roy alongside the likes of Aimé Césaire, Frantz Fanon, and Albert Memmi (Manjapra, *M.N. Roy* xiv). For the interactions between internationalism and nationalism in interwar South Asia, see Seth, *Marxist Theory and Nationalist Politics*; Raza, Roy, and Zachariah, *The Internationalist Moment*; Prashad, *Communist Histories*; and Louro, *Comrades Against Imperialism*.
2. For Communism and anticolonialism in the aftermath of the Bandung Conference, see Popescu, *South African Literature Beyond the Cold War*; Frazier, *The East Is Black: China in the Black Radical Imagination*; Prashad, *The Darker Nations*; and Lee, *Making a World After Empire*. While different in scope, Ahmad's *In Theory* to my mind remains the outstanding theoretical work on the topic.
3. The phrase "murderous nationalism" is from Eric Hobsbawm's magisterial study of modern Europe. The First World War (WWI), he notes, "creat[ed] coherent territorial states each inhabited by a separate ethnically and linguistically homogenous population," whose "logical implication ... [was] the mass expulsion or extermination of minorities"; such, Hobsbawm concludes, "was and is the murderous *reductio ad absurdum* of nationalism" (*Nations and Nationalism* 133). He thereby justifies Partha Chatterjee's rebuttal: "If nationalisms in the rest of the world have to choose their imagined community from certain 'modular forms' already made available to them by Europe and the Americas,

what do they have left to imagine?" (*Nation and Its Fragments* 5). Chatterjee's counterstatement claims, "the most powerful as well as the most creative results of the nationalist imagination in Asia and Africa are posited not on an identity but rather on a *difference* with the modular forms of the national society propagated by the modern West" (5, original emphasis). More on this later.
4. See among others Rao, *The Caste Question*; Zene, *Gramsci and Ambedkar*; Viswanath, *The Pariah Problem*; Kumar, *Radical Equality*; and Slate, *Colored Cosmopolitanisms*.
5. Georg Misch's early work, *A History of Autobiography in Classical Antiquity* (*Geschichte der Autobiographie*, 1907) distinguishes between the autobiography and the memoir based on varying levels of subjective agency. As he states, "Man's relation to the world may be conceived actively or passively. From this consideration comes the distinction between autobiographies and 'memoirs'. In memoirs that relation is passive in so far as the writers of memoirs … introduce themselves in the main as merely observers of the events and activities of which they write, and if they join the active participants it is only in minor parts" (15).
6. According to Beverley, the *testimonio* "may include but is not subsumed under, any of the following textual categories, some of which are conventionally considered literature, others not: autobiography, autobiographical novel, oral history, memoir, confession, diary, interview, eye-witness report, life-history, *novella-testimonio*, nonfiction novel or 'factographic literature'" (13). In the same passage, he further claims, "*testimonio* coalesces as a new narrative genre in the 1960s and further develops in close relation to the movements for national liberation and the generalized cultural radicalism of the decade" (13).
7. For Beverley, "*Testimonio* is not so much concerned with the life of a 'problematic hero' – the term Lukács used to describe the nature of the hero of the bourgeois novel – as with a problematic collective social situation that the narrator lives with or alongside others" (15). Beverley's connection of *testimonio* to larger social contexts is similar if less rigorously theorized to Roberto Schwarz's notion of objective literary form and Fredric Jameson's national allegory, as discussed in the previous chapter.
8. Sarkar, *The Swadeshi Movement in Bengal*, is the classic study of the early phase of Bengali Hindu nationalism. Ramnath, *Decolonizing Anarchism* and *Haj to Utopia* illustrate the transnational networks of Swadeshi and Ghadar activists. Suchetana Chattopadhyay's *An Early Communist*, a biography of the Communist leader Muzaffar Ahmad illuminates a third trajectory to dominant Hindu nationalism and emergent pan-Islamism: the interactions between Bengali Muslim intellectuals such as Ahmad and Kazi Nazrul Islam, working class movements, and international socialism.
9. In its preference for a discontinuous and fragmentary form, *Memoirs* aligns with the late-modern *bildungsroman* from the colonial peripheries. See Esty, *Unseasonable Youth* on the latter. However, the politics that marks the text's attempt to synthesize its multiple component parts distinguishes it from purely formal experiments of fragmentation.

10. An unremarked classic of American Marxism, Dunayevskaya's *Marxism and Freedom* (1958) charts an analysis of Marxism and the Black radical tradition that still has few parallels. James's *Notes on Dialectics* (1969), perhaps the most cogent summary of the great thinker's oeuvre, focuses on the legacies of Hegel in Marx and Lenin. Contemporaneous to James's study, Rodney's *How Europe Underdeveloped Africa* (1972) and *The Russian Revolution*, a collection of lectures at the University of Dar es Salaam, explore the colonial world in terms of universal history. One wonders if these figures found Hegelianism to be entirely Eurocentric: in Chapter 4, I outline the feminist reconfiguration of universal history by writers little known in the Anglo-American academy.
11. The full passage on consciousness versus matter reads: "Materialism cannot deny the objective role of ideas. They are not sui generis; they are biologically determined; priority belongs to the physical being, to matter, if the old-fashioned term may still be used. But once the biologically determined process of ideation is complete, ideas are formed; they continue to have an autonomous existence, an evolutionary process of their own, which runs parallel to the physical process of social evolution. The two parallel processes, ideal and physical, compose history" (Roy, *Reason* 11).
12. On the philosophy and politics of naming, see Badiou, *Metapolitics*, chap. 2, and Sylvain Lazarus, *Anthropology of the Name*.
13. From the 1920s onward, the Justice Party and the Self-Respect Movement steadily advocated opposition to Brahminical domination, which these groups saw as the consequence of Aryan invasion from the north. They further emphasized the distinctiveness of Dravidian languages, which were held to be fundamentally different from and in fact predating Sanskrit. Ramaswamy, *Passion of the Tongue*, provides an overview.
14. The changing conception of the state among the various constituents of the Mexican Revolution is explored in Gilly's classic study, *The Mexican Revolution*, and more recently, Easterling, *The Mexican Revolution: A Short History*. Based on Soviet sources, Spenser, *Stumbling Its Way*, discusses the early Comintern's activities in Mexico.
15. Roy emphasized that Eastern philosophical traditions were co-constitutive of a political philosophy of anticolonialism, and that Marx's European provenance meant the German thinker could not be dogmatically copied elsewhere. In "What Is Marxism?" an essay published in 1940, he maintains: "The analysis of Chinese or Indian systems did not enter into Marx's writing simply because they were not known in Europe at his time . . . . Even the present events in Europe tend to show that things do not always develop straightly and exactly as Marx visualized. New factors have arisen which he could not foresee . . . . If you study the history of Indian philosophy, you will find the analogous origin of materialist thought in our country" (*Heresies* 148, 149, 152).
16. Henk Sleevliet alias Maring, the Dutch secretary of the Commission on the National and Colonial Questions, commented, "I have the impression that,

with a few exceptions, even this Congress of the Communist International has not fully understood the significance of the oriental question" (qtd. in Manjapra 59). According to another account by Sibnarayan Ray, M.N. Roy "had to remonstrate openly at the closing session [of the Third Congress] that the Eastern Question had been grossly neglected by the Executive" (*Selected Works I*, 26).

17. Lenin noted, "This question aroused quite a lively discussion in the Committee, not only in connection with the theses advanced by myself, but much more in connection with those of Comrade Roy . . . [t]he question was whether it is correct to assume that the development of capitalist economy is inevitable in those backward countries which are now liberating themselves, and in which progressive movements have started since the war; and we came to the conclusion that it is not inevitable" (qtd. in *Selected Works I*, 173).

18. In summarizing this discussion, M.N. Roy concludes, "The result of the discussion was that we came to the unanimous conclusion that we should not deal with bourgeois democratic movements but with revolutionary nationalist movements. There is no doubt that every nationalist movement can only be a bourgeois democratic movement, for the great mass in the backward countries consist of peasants" (*Selected Works I*, 172).

19. See the proceedings, painstakingly compiled by John Riddell, *Workers of the World*, of the Communist International's Second Congress of 1920.

20. The text in this volume (*Selected Works I*, 162) is from the weekly report of the director, Central Intelligence, Shimla, and dated August 2, 1920. It mentions Abani Mukherjee and Shanti Devi (pseudonym of Evelyn Trent, Roy's wife) as cosignatories. Roy was in Berlin at the time of writing, so we can assume it was written a little before the Comintern's Second Congress in July, and definitely before the founding of the CPI in Tashkent in August.

21. Roy's *India in Transition* (1922) is broadly contemporaneous with Mariátegui's *Seven Interpretive Essays on Peruvian Reality* (1928) and Trotsky's *History of the Russian Revolution* (1930). My point in bringing up these dates is not to construct a genealogy of influences but to indicate that many of these ideas were in wide circulation by the 1920s. Lenin's *Development of Capitalism* was published in 1899, and some of Trotsky's work shortly thereafter, while Naoroji's drain theory is from a much earlier text, *Poverty and Un-British Rule in India* (1867).

22. See Guha's programmatic manifesto "On Some Aspects of Historiography in Colonial India" that claims, "the historiography of Indian nationalism has for a long time been dominated by elitism – colonialist elitism and bourgeois-nationalist elitism . . . . What clearly is left out of this un-historical historiography is the *politics of the people*" (38, 40, original emphasis). Guha's exposé of the nationalist elite's "collaborationist aspect" owes much to the neglected interventions of vernacular intellectuals, which I discuss in Chapters 3 and 4 of this book.

23. The prominent example is Chibber, *Postcolonial Theory*. Responses to Chibber are collected in Warren, *The Debate*. For earlier discussions on

Marxist and Foucauldian frameworks: Chaturvedi, *Mapping Subaltern Studies*, especially Sumit Sarkar's essay "The Decline of the Subaltern." For Orientalism and the conservative implications of difference, see Kaiwar, *The Postcolonial Orient*. Craig Brandist's current research illuminates an alternative intellectual history of "Soviet Indology," where Indian visiting scholars at Leningrad University such as Dharmanand Kosambi (1876–1947) and Rahul Sankrityayan (1893–1963) were significant contributors. The elder Kosambi (father of D.D. Kosambi) worked with ancient Pali and Sanskrit Buddhist texts and wrote almost exclusively in Marathi. Sankrityayan was a polyglot scholar and activist with pioneering work on Buddhism and Marxism, whose writings were widely translated across many Indian languages.

24. Roy notes in *Fascism: Its Philosophy, Professions and Practice* (1938) that "It is one of the cardinal principles of the Indo-Aryan spiritualist view of life that one should bear cheerfully and with resignation all the sorrows and sufferings of life" (38). This gives way to passively accepting one's position in the caste, gender, and race hierarchies; Roy links Indo-Aryan spiritualism not only to German fascism but also Gandhian nationalism. He observes, "Nietzsche was a firm believer of this principle ... one could easily see that Nietzsche's anti-Socialist propaganda was a shadow of Gandhism cast ahead" (38). On the confrontations between Vichian and Nietzschean modes of thought in the interwar era, see Brennan, *Vico, Hegel, and the Colonies*.

25. A significant perspective on women's oppression and political-sexual agency emerges during Roy's prison writings in the 1930s in essays such as the "Ideal of Indian Womanhood" and "Crime and Karma: Cats and Women." Manjapra contends, "Roy drew parallels between imperial and patriarchal domination within the Hindu family by focusing on ... the figure of 'the deviant woman,' driven by sexual desire to trespass the bounds of marriage" ("The Impossible Intimacies" 170). Loomba, *Revolutionary Desires*, esp. 116–117, speculates that Roy's views on gender asymmetry and sexual mores might have been influenced by association with leading European Communist women such as Rosa Luxemburg and Alexandra Kollontai among others and certainly found resonance in the writings of major Indian nationalist and Communist women such as Bina Das, Kalpana Dutt, Renu Chakravartty, and Hajra Begum.

26. A subsequent vein of materialist analysis along the lines inaugurated by Roy can be traced through D.D. Kosambi, *Myth and Reality*; Sharad Patil, *Dasa-Sudra Slavery;* and Ashok Rudra, *Non-Eurocentric Marxism and Indian Society*. Marxist theoreticians with diverse affiliations contributed to the conversation, such as E.M.S. Namboodiripad, "Castes, Classes and Parties" and "Once Again on Castes and Classes," both in *History, Society, and Land Relations*; B.T. Ranadive, *Caste, Class, and Property Relations*; and Anuradha Ghandy, "The Caste Question in India," collected in *Scripting the Change*.

27. A comparison between Ambedkar and Roy would be relevant for conceptualizing an "Indian" materialism for the twenty-first century. Here I can only

outline some tentative starting positions. Ambedkar's unfinished study *India and Communism*, as well as the well-known lectures "Annihilation of Caste" (1936) and "Buddha or Karl Marx" (1956), among his other voluminous writings, trace the conceptual resources for a humanist and rationalist materialism (*The Essential Writings*, 263–319, 173–189; for discussions, see Teltumbde's introduction to the recent edition of *India and Communism*; Rao, *The Caste Question* and "Revisiting Interwar Thought," in Zene, *Gramsci and Ambedkar* 43–58). M.N. Roy came to echo, by the late 1930s if not earlier, Ambedkar's advocacy of Buddhist rationalism as a counterpoint to Brahminical ideology that both viewed as fascistic if not outright fascist. See Roy, *Fascism* (1938) and *Materialism: An Outline* (1940). Such a comparison does not make the two figures identical or interchangeable, obviously, but suggests the complementarity of their interventions against elite nationalism.

28. Chibber, *Postcolonial Theory*, 291–292, contends that the Subalternist case for a global Marx does not sufficiently account for intellectual history or the wide differences of emphases: there is little engagement with Trotsky or combined and uneven development, for example. In *Capital Volume I*, Marx notes the existence of a surplus population or industrial reserve, including those who had been displaced from land but not absorbed into factory production (chap. 25). Marx identifies four distinct groups within the industrial reserve; these include floating surplus, latent surplus, stagnant surplus, and paupers. I am grateful to Chirashree Dasgupta for drawing my attention to the *Capital* reference.

29. See Roy, *Revolution and Counter-Revolution in China*. The 1946 edition from which I quote is a revised version of a 1930 text and recounts his stay in China as the head of a Comintern delegation from early to mid-1927. Roy's observations should be taken with a grain of salt, however, as he relies on "official" Soviet and Chinese publications after 1928, when the Comintern stance against independent labor and peasant mobilization had been reversed in the "Third Period." For complementary accounts based on the Trotskyist Left Opposition in China, see Benton, *Prophets Unarmed*.

30. Roy, *India in Transition* introduces some of the themes explored by Guha, *A Rule of Property*, yet it reaches different conclusions than in Guha, *Dominance Without Hegemony*. The latter deploys Gramsci to argue that the colonial state in South Asia was coercive and non-hegemonic in character unlike metropolitan Europe. On the other hand, Thomas, *The Gramscian Moment*, revisiting Althusser's and Anderson's readings of Gramsci (but not Guha's), complicates that earlier distinction and demonstrates that hegemony involves both persuasive and coercive aspects of state and civil society.

31. M.N. Roy, "Mahatma and Bolshevism," *Vanguard* 5(2), October 15, 1924, in *Selected Works of M.N. Roy, Volume II*, 311–316. Gandhi responded by citing the need for centralized discipline – "Bolshevism or Discipline," *Young India*, 1925. Roy's own views on Gandhi evolved through the years. He described Gandhi in 1938 as "the political awakener of the Indian masses" but was still critical of "Gandhi's philosophy [that] would not permit development of the

spirit of revolt." In 1948, after Gandhi's assassination at the hands of a puny Hindu nationalist, Roy wrote of Gandhi's appeal as "moral, humanist, cosmopolitan ... [although] the nobler core of his message could not be reconciled with the intolerant cult of nationalism, which he also preached" ("The Message of the Martyr," Feb. 1948, and "Homage to the Martyr," April 1948 in *Independent India, Selected Works I*, 48).

32. This constituted another key point of Roy's difference from the Bolshevik position: "Lenin believed that, as the inspirer and leader of a mass movement, he [Gandhi] was a revolutionary. I maintained that, a religious and cultural revivalist, he was bound to be a reactionary socially, however revolutionary he might appear politically" (*Memoirs* 379).

33. The key figure in this regard is V.D. Savarkar, anticolonial nationalist turned British apologist, and his idea of exclusionary, supremacist Hindu nationalism. For Savarkar's re-contextualization of Indian and European especially Italian intellectual history, see Vinayak Chaturvedi, "A Revolutionary's Biography."

34. Dada Amir Haider Khan alias "Sakorov" worked in British India under another alias, Shankar. Khan was charged in the Meerut Conspiracy case of 1929. The details of Sakorov's early activism as Haywood recounts them illustrate the broad solidarities at work and are certainly worth repeating here: "One of the most interesting and brilliant [at KUTVA] was an Indian student by the name of Sakorov. (They all took Russian names because of the severe repression that they faced back home.) A former machinist in a Detroit auto plant, Sakorov had been sent to the school by the American party. Originally from Bombay, Sakorov had gone to sea on a British ship at the age of twelve and had been subjected to very oppressive conditions his whole career at sea. He eventually jumped ship in Baltimore and wound up working in an auto plant in Detroit. Of the group of students, he was the closest to us Blacks. He knew first hand the plight of the blacks in the United States, and as a dark skinned Indian, he had experienced much of the same type of racial abuse while there. After he left the school, he returned to India, where he became one of the founders of the Indian Communist Party ... it was my good fortune to meet many of these Indian students again in 1942, when I was in Bombay as a merchant seaman. Most of them [including Sakorov] were leading figures in the Indian revolutionary movement" (164–165). I owe a debt of gratitude to Satyanarayan Mohapatra, Vijay Prashad, and Kunal Chattopadhyay for helping me identify the Sakorov reference.

CHAPTER 3

The Lumpen Aesthetics of Mrinal Sen: Cinema Novo Meets Urban Fiction

A strange case of art miming reality: one evening in 1972 at the screening of *Calcutta 71*, a film depicting state violence against Naxalite activists, the director Mrinal Sen is confronted by two agitated young men. They ask him, threateningly, "Tell us the truth: *when* did you shoot the street fighting scenes?" Not sure how to respond, given the sensitive nature of the film, Sen tries to hedge his response. His hesitation is not unfounded. In the violent climate of 1970s West Bengal, it is difficult to predict the outcome of any conversation, howsoever mundane, for too loquacious filmmakers. Sen's interlocutors do not ask him *why* he chose to shoot those scenes. Their query is directed to a far more ambiguous end – when, they ask. Eventually, it turns out that one of the unnamed protestors depicted in the film was a friend of the two young men. They are surprised to see their friend on screen, especially because the person in question had been shot dead by the police some time ago. Sen explains to the two young men that he filmed the street-fighting scenes over a period of two years. He cannot answer when he shot the sequence since that was part of a longer footage. The cruel irony of his "shooting" is not lost on the filmmaker. Recounting this episode later, Sen notes, "People ... would watch the film over and over again, just to catch a glimpse of their friend" (Sen, *Over the Years* 67).

To contemporaries, *Calcutta 71* paralleled what they saw in their daily lives, a moment when the confrontation between the Maoist Naxalite movement and the Indian state (a "progressive" government headed by India's first and only female prime minister, Indira Gandhi, backed by the Soviet Union) reached a flashpoint. In less than a two-year period, thousands of activists were killed and many more imprisoned.[1] Citizens tried to avoid the outdoors after sunset; curfews were imposed regularly and without hesitation. It is no surprise that homelessness, unemployment, and random violence – from petty theft to political assassination – would come to feature prominently in the artistic productions of the decade. Many artists – writers, playwrights, and filmmakers among them – attempted to honestly portray the crisis of Calcutta at this time, a city literally coming apart at the seams.[2] In equal measure, many others held their peace, for fear of offending the authorities or the militants. Understandably, much of the cultural work of the period ended up being ephemeral, of questionable artistic merit. But no matter the quality of the work, by virtue of subject matter alone, these texts enabled a demotic comprehension of the everyday with its seemingly inscrutable paradoxes and endless flux.

One of India's greatest filmmakers, Mrinal Sen captured this contemporary moment of crisis through radically innovative cinema. Sen, like most intellectuals professing social commitment, saw the role of documentation as a primary artistic task, one that interlaced art and politics. Afterward, he noted:

> [*Calcutta 71*] was made at a terrible time. People were getting killed every day . . . . The Naxalites had rejected all forms of parliamentary politics . . . this was the time to talk about poverty, the most vital reality of our country, and the basic factor in the indignity of our people. I wanted to interpret the restlessness, the turbulence of the period that is 1971. (qtd. in Hood 30)

In films such as *Interview* (1971), *Calcutta 71* (1972), *Padatik* (The Guerrilla Fighter, 1973) and *Chorus* (1974), Sen aimed to be, to use his own description, "an agent-provocateur" – "My job is to provide information from a point of view which is clearly not neutral. The filmmaker has to be an agent-provocateur – one who disturbs the spectator and moves him to action" (qtd. in Gupta 19). The thematic concerns, the arguments, and above all the form of his films are distinctly related to the ferment of early 1970s Calcutta. As our opening anecdote reveals, filmgoers could and in fact did watch his films as holding a mirror to society. And it is perhaps for this same reason, because they are so unabashedly and intimately tied to a specific milieu, that Mrinal Sen's films have not received due consideration. His "didactic films" (Bishnupriya Ghosh 66) appear dated today, animated by concerns whose time has seemingly passed.[3]

The following discussion, focusing on *Calcutta 71*, seeks to re-center the cinema of Mrinal Sen along the lines of what I term a global "lumpen aesthetics." Karl Marx had, famously, disparaged the urban "lumpenproletariat" as social "refuse," including such colorful members as "rag pickers, knife grinders, tinkers, beggars" and numerous such groups lacking revolutionary consciousness (*The Eighteenth Brumaire* 75). The interwar generation of peripheral Marxists, however, had drastically revised the scope of the concept as discussed in the preceding chapter. The notion of the lumpen and its contradictory inflections for national liberation came to occupy center stage as the Bandung consensus of third-world nationalism fractured in the 1960s and 1970s, in West Bengal as elsewhere.

Our present discussion traces the creative adaptation of Latin American Third Cinema in the South Asian context, especially the work of Glauber Rocha, Octavio Getino, and Fernando Solanas. Sen incorporates their formulations on cinematic form to represent underclass resistance in the context of Calcutta. Rather than seeing this process in the passive terms of "influence," I show how the aesthetic of Latin American Third Cinema is expanded and reconfigured in South Asia, serving as an important if overlooked instance of peripheral ideational exchange. Formally, this complex process involved the overlap of distinct genres such as documentary, still footage, photography, and narrative cinema. Conceptually, literature and especially fiction play a key part in the reconfiguration of cinema.

Such a mixed aesthetic draws its impetus from – and in turn illuminates – an extra-cinematic conjuncture. The disparate and fragmentary elements of lumpen aesthetics articulate the many-layered marginalization and resistance of urban underclass groups: indigent and immiserated children, women, and youth. Classified by the state as rootless and deviant, morally suspect and criminal, even as they are exploited in economic terms, such individuals constitute the "lumpen" and "antisocials" of the city. On the other hand, the Naxalite program – inspired by Mao and the Cultural Revolution in China – of youthful "Red Guards" in the city and revolutionary peasantry in the rural countryside, fundamentally recast the questions of decolonization and the nature of the postcolonial state in India. Mrinal Sen's cinema shows the long history of the urban underclass and the equally sustained tradition of resistance. At the same time, such cinema does not valorize every act of resistance but, resisting the lure of closure, traces the limits thereof. Lumpen aesthetics articulates a dynamic social condition, serving as its shifting objective form.

Sen eschews binary distinctions between artistic form and social content. The conceptual categories that best describe Mrinal Sen's cinema of urban crisis, I would suggest, are allegory and the negative dialectic. These two terms operate to frame the local as "allegories of underdevelopment," to borrow Ismail Xavier's memorable phrase for Brazilian *Cinema Novo* of the 1960s and 1970s (Xavier 3). Here, allegory works in the precise sense of a bridge between the local, the nonlocal or foreign and the universal. Allegory reveals not the existence of an ideal reality transcending individuals and circumstances, but how these latter are surfeit with overarching yet invisible universals. The local *is* allegorical: not because the latter term abstracts from the former that *which is not itself but something else*. On the contrary, the properly allegorical mode approaches the local to tease out immanent universal tendencies. Allegory reworks, without quite giving up, the Manichean split between the ephemeral and the timeless. Instead, it unearths multiple meanings attached to everyday things, which sometimes are at odds with their stable identities. Emphasizing the transitory nature of things, allegorical cinema destabilizes the visual forms of seeing and knowing. Rather than simply showcasing a historical archive, allegorical cinema inserts the ongoing transformations of the present within the *continuum* of history. It illuminates the city's transformation through capitalist modernization and reification. This is the aspect that Mrinal Sen's cinema presents to us today.

As the Uruguayan critic Ángel Rama demonstrated for the city in the Spanish Americas, such a transformative process is brought about by an "order of signs," textual in scope and administered likewise (Rama, *The Lettered City*). In the Spanish Americas and in South Asia in equal measure, cities rise in prominence or recede to the background based on a system that is contained within them and, at the same time, constituted externally by a global set of capitalist relations. As Rama stresses, such an order of signs is both local to the peripheral city and not: what appears as the local is in fact a particular instantiation of capitalism as a world-system.

The dialectic of the local is open ended: in the South Asian context, like M.N. Roy before him, and distinguishing both of them from the dogma of diamat (dialectical materialism), Sen repeatedly refuses the "synthesis" of closed systems. At the level of cinematic form and content, Sen explores the interaction between the local and the universal, not as antithetical or irreducible but as dynamically related. It could hardly be otherwise, given the continually shifting object of Sen's work – the city. His cinema, which is resolutely committed to the local and to the universal of the city form, grasps both instances.

Sen's city films, I advance in this chapter, illuminate a historical sequence that we continue to inhabit. Material "backwardness," the point of entry for Sen and so many other intellectuals of the periphery, is articulated not only in the temporal terms of lack but also in the spatial terms of combined unevenness. The paradoxical combination of an advanced cosmopolitan (Westernized) culture and a backward material poverty emerges in Mrinal Sen's representation of Calcutta and stands in for the city itself. It is the dialectic that binds the peripheral city to the first-world metropolis (the latter the fantastic products of Hollywood's spurious dream factories). Equally, the peripheral city is made aware of its own backyard, the rural countryside. Framed between two extremes of non-identity, the city becomes a locus of enquiry. The question that Sen's audience asks of him, "when did you shoot this?" a question about time, is more properly thought of as *where* did you shoot this – a query, in other words, about urban space.

This is of course a familiar phenomenon in the periphery. Unlike Paris, London, or New York, the peripheral city is the space where history is continuously fragmented by combined and uneven development. The city becomes the dislocated, spatialized form of peripheral lived experience. The problem, a direct result of the colonial period, is exacerbated in postcolonial times as modernization forces the further migration of rural populations, stretching the allocation of already scarce resources. All of which, one would like to say, puts extraordinary pressure on aesthetic representation. Sen captures this precisely: "We have seen that in our context, historical evaluation is never representative" (Sen, *Ami Ebong Chalacchitra* 25). The reified and alienated aspect of the city, which has so captivated artists in bourgeois Europe since the eighteenth century, becomes in the periphery a much more local concern – a sensuous correlate to its objective unevenness, its links with universal modernity much more difficult to discern. As the Brazilian intellectual Roberto Schwarz would say, *re*-cognition, more than fascination, is the predominant response; it is also particularly apropos, since so much of this has to do with hunger, crime, poverty, and misery.[4]

The peripheral artist, who does double duty as a cultural representative to the world, feels compelled to own responsibility for the sorry state of affairs. Limited by the provincial obscurity of their object of representation, the artist as well as the work of art appeals to an equally beleaguered audience to participate in the meaning making of the artistic object. If she, the artist, repeatedly raises the issue of (local) audience involvement, this is because art's appeal to its audience is as much to their aesthetic sensibility as it is to their acute sense of deprivation. Indeed, it is hard to separate the two. On the other hand, the committed artist has to guard against appropriation. This is more the case for filmmakers unlike, say, poets, since the former's productivity is tied to large monetary amounts, which are in turn dependent on metropolitan recognition such as "film festivals."

To summarize the necessity of allegory then: as I explore in the following sections, Mrinal Sen's depiction of Calcutta is allegorical in that the city's characteristic aspects begin to lose their old meanings and begin to take on new ones. Sen's radically new *style* alternates between the documentary and the narrative; its purpose is not only to *capture* the city but also to *express* its increasingly unpredictable oscillations. The films do so, I contend, by valiantly restoring the struggle of marginalized social forces. Rather than documenting the disappearance of the local and the ephemeral from the city space, a task that would relegate cinema to the role of passive chronicler, cinema as allegory represents the city as constantly being shaped and reshaped by human activity. The city is no mere canvas; rather, the city comes to inform and is in turn shaped by the "labor" of the masses. By revealing as well as highlighting the mutability of meaning, cinema underscores that everyday things, objects, and events are capable of change. The dead can come alive, on screen, just as the past and the present provide glimpses of the future. In other words, emphasizing the dynamics of motion, allegorical cinema presents the city in familiar and new terms. To do so, it draws from foreign and local sources alike.

Third Cinema from Latin America to South Asia

Among India's luminous exports to Third Cinema are the Calcutta-based filmmakers Satyajit Ray, Ritwik Ghatak, and Mrinal Sen. The tendency in scholarship has been to situate Third Cinema – that is, avant-garde, self-consciously political and formally innovative cinema – along the lines of national traditions (Guneratne and Dissanayake, Ekotto and Koh, Pines and Willeman). Third Cinema critics, including such pioneering scholars as Teshome Gabriel, insisted that Third Cinema films, in terms of both form and content, were distinctly marked by a continuing emphasis on anti-imperialism, socialistic nation building, collective people's struggles, and the search for indigenous cultural traditions of decolonization (Gabriel 5). The problem with such delineation, fairly unexceptionable at first glance, would only be revealed several decades later.

First, in aiming to capture the distinct specificity of Third Cinema, scholars following Gabriel failed to adequately recognize that Third Cinema was the product of a global anti-capitalist ferment: in other words, the historical phenomenon of third-world nationalism was a necessary but not sufficient component for comprehending the resistance wrought by capitalist modernization and valorization. A second related aspect is that, with few notable exceptions, much of the scholarship ended up reifying indigeneity and cultural identity, neglecting almost every other aspect of Third Cinema. This had to do with, as Mike Wayne notes, "an undialectical approach to difference and particularity" (Wayne 117). The downside to these oversights is that the *philosophical* question of a truly autonomous cinema, in the aesthetic-critical sense of resisting capitalist reification, gets reframed in the terms of cultural difference from the "West." Such a contraption not only flattens the heterogeneous body of work that separates Third Cinema from third-world cinema but also insists, rather doggedly, on a politics of difference as the key criterion of criticism. By contrast, many of the notable Third Cinema filmmakers were keenly aware of the interdependent nature of the three worlds and the mediations produced therein, as we see later.

In Latin America, the trend of Third Cinema is inaugurated by "The Aesthetics of Hunger," the seminal manifesto for *Cinema Novo* published by the Brazilian filmmaker Glauber Rocha. Appearing in 1965 (shortly after the 1964 military coup), the focus of Rocha's manifesto is the elevation of material lack, hunger, and poverty to the realm of aesthetic knowledge. Rocha is keenly aware that doing so risks, in fact nearly guarantees, exoticizing the object of representation. "The Aesthetics of Hunger" sets for itself an impossibly ambitious task: to develop a language explaining the structure of neocolonial underdevelopment that cuts through Western exoticism and speaks directly to its own, missing audience. Such an effort has another equally pressing task: to account for the lack in "theory," since material backwardness is also conceptual lack. Aesthetics takes on the responsibility of formulating what theory or philosophy had generally failed to do: namely, come up with an adequate understanding of the non-metropolitan world in the terms of totality. To quote a few relevant portions:

> Thus, while Latin America laments its general misery, the foreign observer cultivates a taste for that misery, not as a tragic symptom, but merely as a formal element ... the process of artistic creation in the underdeveloped world is of interest only in so far as it satisfies his [the viewer's] nostalgia for primitivism .... What distinguishes yesterday's colonialism from today's is merely the more refined forms employed by the contemporary colonizer ... . It is for this reason that hunger in Latin America is not simply an alarming symptom; it is the essence of our society. Herein lies the tragic originality of Cinema Novo in relation to world cinema .... Cinema Novo reveals that violence is normal behavior for the starving .... Cinema Novo is an ongoing process of exploration .... Cinema Novo cannot develop effectively while it remains marginal to the economic and cultural processes of the Latin American continent. Because the New Cinema is a phenomenon belonging to new peoples everywhere and not a privileged entity of Brazil. (94)

It should be noted that the manifesto does not rest with the mere assertion of difference between Latin America and the rest of the world. Rather, it reorients, and thereby fundamentally reframes, the investigation of the human condition. The stated goal of "The Aesthetics of Hunger" is the decentering of Europe and the privileging of specifically Latin American concerns. Yet, let us also take note of the audacious sweep: the manifesto moves from Brazil to Latin America to everywhere. Unlike the colonial humanism of Europe, as Fanon described it, Rocha's gesture is keenly aware of its limitations and more importantly its asymmetrical existence but nevertheless unafraid of its own possibilities. It is non-identitarian (while respecting the quest for identity) and universal (while being firmly grounded in the local). It does not exclude the West, despite the severest criticism, but rather sees the possibility of the periphery renewing the metropolis for a shared postcolonial future: "Wherever there is a film-maker, of any age or background, ready to place his cinema and his profession at the service of the great causes of his time, there will be the living spirit of Cinema Novo" (96). Perhaps there can be no better statement of a peripheral humanism oriented to the future. Such formulations dispense with binaries between the local and the global, and the Western and non-Western, even as Rocha's gendered conception of history – "his time" and so on – retains another binary.

Rocha's intervention has been regrettably misremembered. Like him, a whole range of filmmakers, male and female, from Heiny Srour in Lebanon and Salma Baccar in Tunisia to Ousmane Sembène in Senegal, Kidlat Tahimik in the Philippines, and Mrinal Sen in India, speak without hesitation of the need to combine decolonizing knowledge with the spirit of a universal humanism. This capacious and demotic understanding of emancipation is one of the main achievements of Third Cinema. In addition to Rocha's influential manifesto, "The Aesthetics of Hunger," other notable documents from Latin America in this regard are by Fernando Solanas and Octavio Getino in Argentina, Julio García Espinosa in Cuba, and Jorge Sanjinés in Bolivia, respectively titled "Toward a Third Cinema" (1969), "For an Imperfect Cinema" (also 1969), and "Problems of Form and Content in Revolutionary Cinema" (1979) (for these and other Latin American manifestos, see Martin, vol. 1, 33–86). Taken together, they provide some of the finest illustrations of dialectical aesthetic thought in the periphery, making Latin America a model for filmmakers globally. To explore the unrealized "living spirit" of Third Cinema for our own globalizing times then, as the Brazilian critic Ivana Bentes has noted, is to trace how the independently developed new cinemas whether in Latin America, Africa or Asia, have been used and misused in relation to one another.[5]

Rocha's "The Aesthetics of Hunger" can be read alongside the influential manifesto coauthored by the Argentinian Solanas and the Spaniard Getino, "Toward a Third Cinema" (1969). It is to Solanas and Getino that we owe the provocative term, "guerrilla filmmaking," one that Mrinal Sen would embrace. Solanas and Getino derive their framework from the guerrilla struggle, or *focoismo*, advocated by Che Guevara and the French intellectual Régis Debray, in addition to the work of (whom they do not mention) the Brazilian Marxist Carlos Marighella. Part political theory, part film criticism, Solanas and Getino's text provides a descriptive account of filmmaking collectives and youth groups in Latin America in the 1960s. They theorize a cinematic praxis based on the reception experience of documentaries such as *I Like Students* (Mario Handler, 1968) and their own *The Hour of the Furnaces* (also 1968).

The filmmakers note, with a flourish typical of the macho militancy of the era, "The camera is the inexhaustible *expropriator of image-weapons; the projector, a gun that can shoot 24 frames per second*" (50, original emphasis). Despite the combative, and to some, problematic, phrasing, the main ideas of Solanas and Getino's guerrilla filmmaking are fairly common to the other theorists of Third Cinema. Solanas and Getino reject the notion of the passive spectator and instead posit an active, non-alienating mode of "participation" where the screening of a film, accompanied by stage events, public discussion, presentation of "poems, sculpture and paintings, posters," and so on, becomes the occasion for developing a sense of political community (54ff.). The two filmmakers emphasize that one cannot know reality without acting on it; consequently, the task of documentary cinema is not only the faithful (passive) recording of events and things but also an active intervention to transform reality itself. According to Solanas and Getino, the task of cinema is to contribute to insurgent knowledges, and not replicate the State's and industrial cinema's stranglehold over positivist "realism." Third, they argue that cinema, and culture in general, is itself a legitimate site of revolutionary struggle. Even in the midst of a political situation, the "revolutionary artist" does not have to distinguish between her artistic and political work, or prioritize one over the other. Finally, like Julio Espinosa in Cuba, they remonstrate against the goal of technical perfection in film, advocating a more spontaneous approach based on contingency.

In a separate if comparable context, Mrinal Sen incorporates Latin American Third Cinema techniques, methods, and knowledges.[6] While it is hard to determine if Sen was familiar with the manifestos mentioned earlier, his city films resonate with the thoughts of Rocha, Solanas, Sanjinés, and others. Sen writes about the achievements of Latin American cinema at several places; in a piece on Solanas and Getino's *The Hour of the Furnaces*, he commends the duo's depiction of "Argentinian history" and "fractured Latin American history" as a "cinematic model" for "third-world countries" (*Cinema Adhunikata* 41).[7] Furthermore, Sen's Latin America–inflected work informs a later generation of progressive filmmakers. As one critic remarks, "The connections between Latin America and India, so manifestly present in both the films and their makers' writings about them, has long passed unacknowledged, because even scholars of World Cinema have been loath to bring to light lateral exchanges of forms, practices and personnel that took place in the global South unmediated by Western metropolises" (Hanlon 18). Hanlon contends that in stark contrast to contemporaneous Latin American cinema, political films made by the likes of Sen and Anand Patwardhan were marginalized in the West.

Locally, that is, in the context of Calcutta, Mrinal Sen's incorporation of Third Cinema cannot be described without referencing the towering figure of Satyajit Ray. Both Sen (b. 1923) and Ray (b. 1921) came of age in the late-colonial period and made their first films in post-partition West Bengal. The first of Ray's famed *Apu Trilogy*, *Pather Panchali*, was released in the same year (1955) that Sen made his directorial debut. Their subsequent development illustrates similarities as well as divergences in style, technique, and content, not to mention reception.

Ray's *Apu Trilogy* and subsequent films, such as *Paras Pathar* (Philosopher's Stone, 1958), and *Mahanagar* (The Great City, 1963), turn directly to an exploration of the city. Refusing the seamless unity of studio cinema, and similar to Vittorio De Sica's neorealist cinema in postwar Italy, Ray foregrounds the tensions, ruptures, and dissonances of urban life. His films move beyond the drawing-room dramas of commercial film. This latter cinema is invested in the city too but with the opposite politics, presenting the metropolis as an unchanging backdrop or as a series of fleeting landscapes. Like Golden Age Hollywood, this reified form functions as filmed proscenium theater: the explicit function is to efface all signs of societal conflict. By contrast, Ray brings his films out of the studio into the open. His achievement lies precisely in juxtaposing incongruent, incommensurate aspects of the city to one another. Almost singlehandedly in the context he operated in, Ray makes cinema bear the full weight of imaginative expression and philosophical speculation. His vision encompasses the catastrophic unfolding of late capitalist modernization, while refusing the mundane nostalgia that is commonplace to so much of anticolonial and postcolonial thinking.

Yet, in the ferment of the late 1960s, Ray's work was frequently found wanting by his peers to the Left such as Sen.[8] In the series of 1970s films known as his "City Trilogy" – *Pratidwandi* (1970), *Seemabaddha* (1971), and *Jana Aranaya* (1976), Ray's individualistic urban protagonists respond to the pressing events of the era, the Naxalite movement, the Cultural Revolution in China, the anti-imperialist resistance in Vietnam, and others, in ways that appear to be uncertain, equivocal, and unduly nihilistic. The protagonists of his films, no matter how humble of station, display a genteelness that is out of sync with the proletarian "anger" that Marxist intellectuals ascribed to the downtrodden. It is perhaps fair to say, with some justification, that the quickening tempo of global and local events found a somewhat diminished response in Ray. The objectively political content of his films – of theme, of character – did not quite hold up to scrutiny in the midst of emerging social forces of dissent and rebellion. It is only with his much later film *Hirak Rajar Deshe* (Kingdom of Diamonds) (1980), polemically sparkling and almost entirely in verse dialogues, that Ray would take a strong political position.

Still it would be unwise, *pace* his strident critics, to posit too clean a break between Ray and the other practitioners of Third Cinema. Here, I wish to underscore Ray's self-consciousness as a filmmaker of the periphery, even if he is unable – and unwilling – to acknowledge the possibility of radical social transformations. The contrast between aesthetic appeal and the harshness of material life is one of the chief themes of Ray's cinema, one that he pursues relentlessly. Like Rocha in Brazil, Ray is acutely and notably aware of the paradox of cinema: the most technologically mediated and advanced of cultural forms of its time and its operation in contexts of extreme backwardness where even the basic necessities are unavailable to many. This is evidenced most sharply in his sense of cinematic form and particularly, two non-filmic conceptions: namely, music and literature. These also prove particularly generative for Mrinal Sen as they do, differently, for the likes of Ritwik Ghatak and Zahir Raihan.

Beginning with the *Apu Trilogy* and till the very end of his career, Ray cultivates a distinctive, almost signature soundscape that combined European chamber music, Indian classical *ragas*, and modernist atonal systems. The cultural theorist Keya Ganguly writes that Ray's use of sound, in a mode analogous to Hanns Eisler's notion of music's "gestural element," gestures to the combined unevenness characteristic of peripheral modernity. Music, or more properly, *music-as-cinema* signposts the patchworked cultural formation that is unevenly "matched ... through its very mismatched quality": poised between European and Indian cultural forms, such a "cinema is thus the archive of its own technological precursors" (Ganguly 142, 149). Music-as-cinema carries the weight of history, Ganguly suggests for Ray, resisting the culture of forgetting and rupture advanced by the moving image on a wheel.

The other repository for Ray's cinema is fiction. The deployment of literature for a progressive cinema, a strategy at play since his very first film, arguably turns Ray into one of the outstanding innovators of Third Cinema. Ray advances the pioneering insight that in the context of peripheral modernity, fiction captures the historical depth that cinema lacks. That a filmmaker draws so regularly from literature is significant but has gone largely unremarked.[9]

To put this in another way: one of the colloquial Bengali terms for cinema is *boi*, which literally means "printed book." This confusion of parlance, blurring the boundaries between the two media, alerts one to the particular valence of culture where the visual fact of cinema is comprehended by referencing the older medium of print. Both print and cinema, acutely foreign in origin, represent embedded aspects of the modern self but in different ways. Print capitalism mediates the interaction between the form of fiction and vernacular Bengali prose, which itself has been programmatically refashioned over the course of the nineteenth and twentieth centuries. For Ray, we might speculate, narrative fiction (*galper boi*) draws upon these symptomatic prior moments of misplaced and mismatched culture, of combined unevenness. The visual texts rely on literary texts as crutches, in a manner of speaking. At the same time, literary fiction, more so than music, offsets the novelty of cinematic practice. By presenting familiar content in a new medium, literature helps to locate cinema in a continuum of culture where it is a belated entrant.

In terms of technique, Ray's breakthrough creates a new language for South Asian Third Cinema, comparable to yet distinct from that in Latin America. This is true even if Ray stops short of fully engaging with the political implications of his own discovery. Rather, as we see in the next section, it is his contemporary Mrinal Sen who builds on this formal method in *Calcutta 71*, concentrating it stylistically, and supplying it with a new allegorical and political purpose.

Mrinal Sen's Lumpen Aesthetics

Made in the span of a few years, Mrinal Sen's films *Interview* (1971), *Calcutta 71* (1972), *Padatik* (The Guerrilla Fighter, 1973) and *Chorus*

(1974), offer arguably the most significant cinematic treatment of the Naxalite movement in the city of Calcutta. They secure Sen's reputation as one of the foremost practitioners of the Indian "New Wave," followed by luminaries such as Mani Kaul, Adoor Gopalakrishnan, and Girish Kasaravalli to name only a few. In addition to Latin American Third Cinema, and Ray, Sen's work of this period is heavily indebted to the people's theater or *gananatya* (which I discuss in the next chapter). Stalwarts of people's theater, such as Bijan Bhattacharya and Utpal Dutt, regularly acted in Ghatak's and Sen's films: Dutt would also feature in several Ray films. The internationalist tendencies of people's theater find their fullest cinematic expression in the hands of Sen.[10]

Sen's initial films made in the late 1950s and early 1960s, such as *Neel Akasher Neeche* (Under the Blue Sky) (1959) and *Baishe Shrabon* (Wedding Day) (1960), display a faithful if somewhat unoriginal adoption of the social-realist conventions of Indian cinema of the time. It is with *Bhuvan Shome* (Mr. Shome) (1969), a Hindi-language film produced during the very end of the 1960s, that Sen announced himself as a filmmaker of some significance. *Bhuvan Shome* tells the story of an aging bureaucrat of the same name (portrayed with great finesse by Utpal Dutt), whose monochromatic world view – girded by discipline, rationality, and efficiency – is destabilized by his interaction with simple and genuine-hearted rural folk, particularly a young woman, Gauri, living in Saurashtra, a remote region in western India. It is an understated political film, embarking on a subtle parody of the great monolith of Indian bureaucracy and its rigid notions of modernization and progress. Like the Ray films discussed earlier, *Bhuvan Shome* is partly based on a Bengali short story by the writer Banaphool (pseudonym for Balai Chand Mukhopadhyay). But any overt similarity with Ray ends there.

Bhuvan Shome marks the beginning of Sen's collaboration with the cinematographer K.K. Mahajan. Many of the characteristic formal strategies and techniques that came to be associated with the Sen-Mahajan New Wave style of filmmaking, such as extended montage sequences, nonlinearity of plot, documentary style commentary, multiple jump cuts and freeze frames, make their first appearance in *Bhuvan Shome*. Sen's and Mahajan's depiction of the rural countryside markedly departs from previous Indian cinema including Ray's lyricism and Ghatak's folk motifs. Juxtaposing looming, empty spaces of the countryside and exaggerated close-ups of objects and human beings, the new aesthetic introduces elements of the uncanny and provides cognitive dissonance with the representations on-screen. The film also provides a rare instance of animation in contemporary Indian cinema: a memorable scene where Bhuvan

Shome pores through seemingly endless piles of government documents and grows increasingly frustrated. In keeping with the film's parody of bureaucratic mores, this device aptly captures the unreality of Shome's world view that reduces everything to government files.

If *Bhuvan Shome* portrayed the rationalist bureaucrat's sense of helplessness when confronted with the differing world view of the rural world and its inhabitants, Sen's next film, *Interview*, shifts attention to the metropolis (*mahanagar*) and the hapless youth therein. *Interview*, as the title of the film suggests, focuses on the efforts of a young man in Calcutta to find employment. He is repeatedly thwarted in this regard by his inability to find a proper suit to wear for the interview. After multiple episodes of trying to obtain a suit, where something goes wrong every time, the young man gives up and appears to his potential employers dressed in indigenous costume, considered unsuitable for professional purposes. Like Nikolai Gogol's masterly allegory of peripheral modernity in the story "The Overcoat" (1842), *Interview* utilizes a series of absurd situations around an item of clothing, namely, the interview suit. The Western metropolitan standards of professional appearance, suits and so on, acquire a persistent reality in the peripheral metropolis of Calcutta: this reality of appearance howsoever superstructural – the film suggests – is linked to and indistinguishable from the infrastructural reality of joblessness on the subjective consciousness. Significantly, "The Overcoat" had been adapted in a previous, Hindi-language film: *Garam Coat* (1955) starring the Indian People's Theater Association (IPTA) stalwart Balraj Sahni. This earlier film ends on an optimistic note, departing from Gogol's story. It is perhaps a sign of the disenchantment that such optimism is nowhere to be found by the time Sen makes his similarly themed film in 1971.

Interview's protagonist suffers from what Jed Esty, in another context, has termed "unseasonable youth": young adults whose lack of growth becomes representative of the experience of modernity. The film teems with numerous youth whose inability to assimilate into society as proper citizens, unlike the classic *bildungsroman* of bourgeois Europe, illuminates the distorted trajectory of national mal-development in the postcolony. The film introduces a number of social types that Sen repeatedly features in subsequent films: unemployed and barely employed youth, post-adolescent men and women who slide into criminality and immorality, sons who fail to take up the patriarchal responsibilities after their fathers, and daughters who seek outside work out of hardship and suffer new forms of exploitation as compared to their stay-at-home mothers. Repeatedly, the protagonist and other characters in *Interview* break the fourth wall to talk to the audience about contemporary affairs, narrating their life stories and asking for opinions and participation. The affinity of Sen's cinema to contemporary people's theater (*gananatya*) and the latter's twin emphases on moving beyond the proscenium and encouraging audience participation are made evident in *Interview*.

Released one year after *Interview*, *Calcutta 71* takes up many of the aspects of the previous film, but in a much more concentrated and simultaneously broadened framework. Like *Interview*, the narrator-protagonist of *Calcutta 71* is a young man marginalized in society. Yet he is no ordinary person. The narrator is a Naxalite activist, a suspected urban guerrilla who is killed by the police. His narration is posthumous: a technique recalling, among others, one of the great works of Brazilian literature, Machado de Assis's 1881 novel *The Posthumous Memoirs of Brás Cubas* (see Cypess). Unlike the comic protagonist of Assis's *Brás Cubas* or even Sen's own *Interview*, the Naxalite narrator of *Calcutta 71* is an intense and tragic figure. However, the film de-emphasizes his personal tragedy by situating it within the overtly fantastic device of posthumous storytelling. Although the protagonist is only twenty years old at the moment of death, the stories he narrates are decades older.

The four stories that make up the film are given precise dates – the years 1933, 1943, 1953, and the present moment, 1971. The stories describe, variously, an indigent family in the slums seeking shelter from a catastrophic thunderstorm; another family including a widowed mother, an elder sister, and two younger brothers who take to prostitution and crime; third, a teenager and his gang of friends who illegally transport food grains from the city to the villages and are apprehended by the police. Finally, the fourth story is that of the Naxalite narrator himself who, he informs the audience in a direct address, sees himself as carrying on the legacy of these marginalized subjects. Along with these stories, *Calcutta 71* juxtaposes commentary on various contemporary events, both local and global, using a series of photographs, radio voice-overs, newspaper headlines, documentary footage, and an extraordinary musical score.

The opening sequence of *Calcutta 71* offers an excellent conceptual overview; I discuss this at some length to provide a sense of the film's highly concentrated, epic-allegorical impulse as a whole. The first shot shows an intertitle, with the narrator providing a voice-over:

> Amar boyosh kuri
> Kuri bochhor boyosh niye
> Ami ajo hete cholechhi

Hajar bochhor dhore
Daridro, malinyo, ar mrityur bhir thele
Ami paye paye cholechhi hajar bochhor dhore
Dekhchhi itihash, daridrer itihash, bonchonar itihash, shoshoner itihash.
(My age is twenty/With the age of twenty I am walking for a thousand years, even today/Pushing through the mesh of poverty, degeneracy, and death/I have been moving step by step for a thousand years/Seeing history, poverty's history, deprivation's history, exploitation's history; my translation.)

The emphasis is on the witnessing of a millennium's history from a youth's point of view. Following this intertitle, the next shot is of the famous Howrah Bridge, followed by shots of the Writers' Building and the Great Eastern Hotel in quick succession, both iconic downtown buildings of the nineteenth century. Each of these spaces, usually scenes of intense activity, is empty, devoid of human presence. The title of the film, "Calcutta 71," appears thrice, once in each of the three shots, suggesting that these depictions belong to the immediate moment of 1971. A montage, introducing urban scenes of heightened bustle both public and private, follows: we get to see commuters hanging on to overcrowded buses and trams; pilgrims jostling their way to a festival; a dancing, frenzied crowd carrying a figurine of a deity; an equally crowded nightclub packed with teenagers dancing to funk and jazz music. These scenes of activity are followed by depictions of mass media technology: printing presses rolling out realms of newsprint, typewriters hammering out documents, gigantic sound equipment playing music.

Then the sequence moves to a second montage depicting contemporary political demonstrations. Fragments of the rebellious city are visualized through photographs and handheld camera shots: activists hurling rocks, police dispersing crowds with batons and teargas, protestors scattering and running away, streets littered with the accumulated debris of demonstrations – stones, shards, barricades, broken armor, protective gear, misplaced footwear – resembling an urban battleground. These visuals are then further juxtaposed with still photographs from another era: the 1940s. In the history of the city, this is another period of social upheaval and crisis, still fresh in people's memories. Invoking the work of renowned photojournalists of the time, such as Sunil Janah and Margaret Bourke-White, the sequence shows naked, skeletal children and entire families starving to death on the pavements of the city. They are victims of the British-engineered Bengal Famine of 1943 and the partition-era religious sectarian violence of 1946–1947, driven from the villages and seeking shelter in the city. Finally, we see a young woman who is slowly collapsing; as she looks up to the camera, a radio voice-over announces in a neutral voice: "The police report that last night, in the very heart of the city in the Maidan, the body of an unidentified young man in his twenties has been found." The intertitle "I am twenty years old" is repeated as the sequence fades out. We realize that the narrator and the unknown murdered youth may be the same person.

The opening sequence described here is less than three minutes of film time. It is nonetheless of surprising density, weaving together a plethora of allusions immediately identifiable to the local audience (and unavailable to the film's international viewership, such as those at the Venice Film Festival screening in 1972).[11] The opening references contemporary events in Calcutta, such as the murder of Leftist activists and ongoing strikes and demonstrations. Some of the other, less obvious references are literary. While the narrator's announcement of walking for a thousand years suggests a sense of "deep time," Bengali audiences would recognize the direct allusion to Jibanananda Das's poem "Banalata Sen." Published in 1935, "Banalata Sen" is arguably the most prominent example of modernism (*adhunikatabad*) in poetry. A deceptively simple poem, it describes a weary poet's search for his ideal lover. The former is redolent of the itinerant figure of the *bhikkhu* (mendicant monk), such as the eleventh-century Atish Dipankar, a key figure of Indo-Tibetan Mahayana Buddhism.

As the most prominent index of Bengali modernist poetry in the 1930s, "Banalata Sen" epitomized the rejection of the promised goals of colonial-capitalist modernity and the search for a utopian messianic alternative in poetic form. Here, Das deploys the meretricious idiom characteristic of older traditions of vernacular poetry, albeit in a highly self-conscious and subversive manner. The traditional motifs are rendered devoid of meaning, and toward the second half a new poetic language emerges marked by agnosticism and a minimalist diction stripped of metaphysics. The famously haunting last line of the poem, "All that remains is darkness, and seated in front of me, Banalata Sen" (Das 5, my translation) combines tragic closure and the tantalizing possibility of a future redemption. Elsewhere, Das repeatedly invoked the anomie of urban life, simultaneously emphasizing, unlike his more conservative peers, the impossibility of returning to an organic existence.[12]

It is worth noting that *Calcutta 71* borrows the opening line of "Banalata Sen" that declares, "Hajar bochhor dhore ami path hatitechhi prithibir pathey" (For a thousand years I have been walking the paths of this earth). Thus, the very first frame that we get to see in the film, the intertitle, with its refrain of "Hajar bochhor dhore" (For a thousand years) and shift from the present perfect continuous, "ami path hatitechhi" in the poem to present continuous tense, "ami ajo hete cholechhi," implies continuity between Jibanananda's world and that of the film. Such seepage from literature to film, specifically from poetic to cinematic time, is neither accidental nor simply a matter of the filmmaker's preference. The film retroactively inserts an insurrectionary vocabulary into an *earlier* work of literature. On the one hand, Das's mythic-poetic sense of time is linked to the peripheral narrative of poverty, exploitation, and deprivation. Likewise, on the other hand, the *bhikkhu* traversing premodern South Asia is allied with the modern-day Naxalite militant. We address the first aspect next, and will return to discuss the second linkage later.

Conceptually speaking, *Calcutta 71*'s figuration of time is as much an attempt to locate "a thousand years" of Indic history within a Marxian – and Maoist – lens, as it is to extend the framework of Marxism beyond Europe and state-ized Communism. In this sense the film, and Sen's work in general, departs from Soviet diamat and Indian bourgeois nationalist notions of linear progress, even as it challenges religio-conservative notions of Indic essence. Elsewhere, Sen remarks of the bourgeois nationalist outlook that "the *theme of continuing synthesis* in Indian history ... that is unadulterated idealism, genuine exaggeration. I would say that it is the opposite of synthesis; ours is a history of continuing poverty and exploitation running through the ages" (Sen, *Ami Ebong Chalacchitra* 34, italics indicate English words in the Bengali original). Indeed, *Calcutta 71* articulates "our history" as an open-ended and interlocking series of contestations. For Sen, the native bourgeoisie's appropriation of the working masses – like Europe after 1848, tracing the dialectic of *regress* rather than progress – constituted the key event of modern Indian history. When he notes that, "our history is the history of continuing political betrayal" (Sen, *Ami Ebong Chalacchitra* 34) Sen, thus, correctly identifies the precise politico-philosophical coordinates for a contrarian history, one that emphasizes negative possibilities. We need to add that such observations, part of a conversation between intellectuals in West Bengal and beyond, emerged from a set of highly charged theoretical debates about the conjuncture in India and globally in the 1970s.

The opening sequence also references, if somewhat less directly, even older representations of Calcutta in literature. The Great Eastern Hotel, the last of the three images that follow the intertitle is vividly described in Rudyard Kipling's humorous, unabashedly Anglo-supremacist tract *The City of Dreadful Night* (1888). Kipling lampoons the supposed grandeur of the Great Eastern Hotel as well as its residents, the colonial *sahibs* who are the "best" representatives of Empire abroad. Kipling's politics notwithstanding, *Calcutta 71*, it could be said, repurposes his satire. The once-iconic hotel is now the playground of the postcolonial native elite and their equally perverse fantasies of power. The same holds true for the Writers' Building, the second image after the intertitle: once the administrative heart of the British Empire in South Asia, now reduced to the seat of the shrunken provincial government of West Bengal. The Writers' Building and the Great Eastern Hotel are surviving monuments of the "white town," a racialized term denoting the areas of Calcutta formerly reserved for the *sahibs*. In the conjuncture of the 1970s, the vestiges of the white town come to signify the postcolonial replication of older hierarchies of power and space. These spaces and hierarchies are threatened by the insurgent masses. The emptiness around these two buildings stems from the "strikes" imposed by the forcible articulation of popular will.

At the same time, the ghostly presence of the British colonizers is replaced by another, equally disembodied form of neocolonial culture: American popular music. This music makes the new *sahibs* jittery, entering their bodies like an unseen spirit – shaking and rolling, they pack nightclubs like a tin of sardines. The US-style meccas of consumerist pleasure and freedom appear to eliminate the more rigid forms of colonial exclusion. However, there is a demotic counterpart to this frenzy of consumption. The underclass of the city, unlike their peers in the private, rights-of-admission-reserved clubs, celebrate processions in the streets, enacting the carnivalesque takeover of urban space and their own freedom in popular form.

The soundtrack of the film subtly highlights the mutually opposed nature of these coexisting urban life forms. This aspect is redolent of Satyajit Ray's use of music, but the commentary is sharper. Scored by noted composer Ananda Shankar, the soundtrack brings together a remarkable range of disparate musical genres. The wailing guitar in the nightclub merges with the strains of the sitar in concert, and the jazz drums alternate with the very different emphases of the *dhak* (indigenous drum associated with the śākta religious tradition) players in the streets. On the one hand, this creates the characteristic East-meets-West style of "fusion" sound then in vogue in many parts of the world, a trend that Shankar pioneered. On the other hand, the aural and visual contrast gestures to the impossibility of fusion. Existing hierarchically and unequally, the dissonance between old and new genres as well as popular and classical music is heightened by other forms of sound, such as street noise, the sound of bombs going off, and screaming protestors running amok.

In addition, mention must be made of the sequence's use of still photography, one that incorporates the work of many photojournalists. *Calcutta 71* uses photographs at various points in the film to complement the existing narrative. The montage of still images actively defies the cultural tendency of fragmentation, forgetting, and erasure; instead, it actively reconstructs the many genealogies of the global present from the vantage point of the marginalized. The opening sequence, for instance, ties the contemporary moment to the haunting specter of the 1940s and especially the Bengal famine of 1943. The graphic visuals of naked skeletal children who lay dying on the streets of Calcutta recall the last phase of colonial rule. We witness a montage of these photographs, juxtaposed with images of urban protests in Calcutta, and in Vietnam, the United States, France, Mozambique and Angola, and elsewhere. By relating the earlier moments of local Bengali and South Asian history to the global contemporary, *Calcutta 71* inserts the former into a longer continuum. This sequence best answers the practical problem that we noted in the beginning of our discussion: the articulation of a local history that is simultaneously an allegory of the universal, a "historical evaluation [that] *is* . . . representative" (Sen, *Ami Ebong Chalacchitra* 25, emphasis added).

This task is accomplished by the integration of *literature*. Fiction writers, poets, and satirists and their representations of Calcutta are adapted; nonliterary traditions of photography and music are also retrofitted for this purpose. The film opens up the contemporary city to the figurations of previous eras. From the point of view of cinema, the most belated of aesthetic forms, such grasping and borrowing from all that comes before are unavoidable, so to speak. Such a – for lack of a better word – mongrel attitude resists the critique, so influentially articulated by Lukács elsewhere, that a modernism that furtively rummages the past is anti-realist and seeks to disavow any sense of continuity with the past ("Realism in the Balance"). Indeed, it is difficult to follow through on Lukács's remarkable insight on realism and modernism without addressing at the same time regional and historical variations, for example, in the case of South Asia or Latin America.[13] Like a palimpsest, the represented spaces of the city come to embody the accumulated weight of history.

Calcutta 71's attitude to literature – which I will term "constellation" following Walter Benjamin – is singular and distinctive in this regard. It departs from the more standard practice of committing a single literary work to film. This latter approach is evidenced in Ray's literary adaptations or Mrinal Sen's own earlier films such as *Bhuvan Shome*. With *Calcutta 71*, Sen reworks the convention. Assembling a number of literary works within its frame, the film inaugurates a narrative form that we may call "literary constellation-as-cinema." This recovery does more than bring out unremarked aspects of the original text. Nor does it merely suggest that the knowledge expressed in past works continues to be valid in the present moment.

Constellation or configuration, to invoke Benjamin, presents a mode of connecting phenomena to ideas that is altogether different in its method of operation. In the famous analogy in the Epistemo-Critical Prologue of *The Origin of German Tragic Drama*, Benjamin notes:

> Ideas are to objects as constellations are to stars ... [ideas] remain obscure so long as phenomena do not ... gather around them. It is the function of concepts to group phenomena together ... bring[ing] about two things at a single stroke: the salvation of phenomena and the representation of ideas. (34–35)

Benjamin suggests that the empirical object constituted by phenomena is only illuminated "at its extremities" by the work of concepts, moving them beyond the ephemerality of the present. Benjamin further clarifies, in his later work *The Arcades Project*, that unrelated empirical phenomena are conceptualized by the synchronic interlocking of the past and the present and allegorized through what he calls the "dialectical image": "that wherein what has been comes together in a flash with the now to form a constellation" (*Arcades* 462). Constellation, for Benjamin, thus reworks the Hegelian idea of the always-already. The fragmentary objects of the past and the present are both reconfigured; they form something altogether new and thereby "redeem" both. Past objects or phenomena gain new representation, and the present loses its commonsensical causality. In abstracting from phenomena the "obscured" ideas present therein, constellation, then, provides an illumination (knowledge) of critical history.

I suggest that the form of *Calcutta 71* registers this concept making of Benjamin's constellation, where the film is more than the sum of its parts. The film constellates an unlikely tradition: nineteenth-century satirical writers such as the Bengali Kali Prasanna Singha and the English Rudyard Kipling and early to mid-twentieth-century Bengali modernists and social-realists such as Jibanananda Das, Manik Bandopadhyay, Probodh Kumar Sanyal, and Samaresh Basu. Consciously or otherwise, despite differences in style, content, and so on, these texts were responding to the idea of universal history. It is this "general idea" that *Calcutta 71* draws out as the "dialectical image" of Third Cinema.

This is a good juncture to discuss the film's specific use of constellation. The three episodes of "1933," "1943," and "1953" are adapted from Bengali short stories and novellas published in those years: "Atmahatyar Adhikar" (Right to Suicide), "Angar" (Ember), and "Esmalgar" (The Smuggler) by Manik Bandopadhyay, Probodh Kumar Sanyal, and Samaresh Basu, respectively. Of these, Bandopadhyay and Basu, self-identified Marxist writers coming out of the socialist-realist tradition, belong to the front ranks of Bengali prose writing. Relatively lesser known, Sanyal was a member of the important modernist literary group *Kallol*. Mrinal Sen's choice of the three stories stems from their writers' sustained engagement with the themes of poverty (Manik Bandopadhyay; Sanyal; Basu; for Sen's understanding of these texts see Hood 34).

Calcutta 71 creates in Mrinal Sen's words a unified history — and filmic geography — of urban immiseration and resistance. This is similar in scope to Solanas and Getino's focus on the *villas miserias*, Buenos Aires' urban shantytowns, which the authors propose as one of the "vantage points" of revolutionary knowledge (Solanas and Getino 36). "1933" depicts the desperate struggles of a family of five, living in a slum tenement, to protect themselves from a thunderstorm. Unable to withstand the onslaught of inclement weather, they decide to seek shelter in an affluent neighbor's house. There they come across other, equally hapless members of the community. The segment ends by showing the family sharing shelter space with the mangy stray dog that they had earlier driven away from their home.

In a similar vein, "1943" focuses on Shobhona, a divorced young woman of petite bourgeois background who takes up prostitution to support her mother, two younger male siblings, and her infant son. Shobhona's mother furtively encourages her to this end, while keeping up appearances of genteel respectability. The two adolescent brothers, Hari and Guntu, work as helpers in a neighborhood factory to supplement the household income. Shobhona informs a visiting cousin, who is scandalized at this state of affairs, that at least one if not both of the brothers have taken to a life of petty thieving.

The third segment, titled "1953," directly depicts adolescent "criminal" gangs. Twelve-year-old Gora, the sole earning member and head of his household, proudly describes himself as a "smuggler." He and his group illegally carry small bags of rice grain from the city to far-off villages for a tiny profit. Riding in commuter trains, always "without ticket" (an English phrase commonly used in spoken Bengali), Gora is defiant about his activities; he passes time making fun of the ticketed passengers and generally creating chaos.

Coming after the film's opening montage sequences, these three episodes, "1933," "1943," and "1953," constitute the bulk of *Calcutta 71*. There is a fourth and final episode, titled "1971," which I discuss shortly. Formally, the film employs a range of modes including melodrama and noir, which brings *Calcutta 71* close to commercial Bengali cinema. This is a quietly remarkable point, made evident in the three segments by the almost-exclusive emphasis on interfamilial relationships between mother, son, daughter, and others. Mrinal Sen, quite unlike Ray in this regard, shares aesthetic coordinates with commercial Bengali cinema. He complicates the rigid separation between First, Second, and Third Cinema.[14]

Conventional melodrama abounds in scandals, revelations, and sudden turns in fortune. More philosophically, melodrama posits the family as a synecdoche for the "total world" (*samsara* in Sanskrit or *songsar* in Bengali, see Chapter 1's discussion of Tagore). This is both the basis of its conservative politics of mystification and the source of its hegemonic popularity among audiences. Nonetheless, as another contemporary filmmaker Ritwik Ghatak repeatedly reminded his readers, melodrama occupies a distinct niche of epic realism in the periphery. Realistic in theme and setting and unrealistic in the compressed narrativization of events and causes, for Ghatak, melodrama served as the formal correlate of peripheral unevenness.[15] *Calcutta 71* deploys this objective aesthetic form to full effect, extending the melodramatic logic so affectively and cognitively familiar to audiences to its extreme, where it ceases to be familiar and takes on unexpected valences instead. The fissures and tensions of the family as a social unit are not resolved in any one of the three episodes. Jolting expectations, rather, they are shown to be unresolvable and left incomplete. This way, both *hriday* and *buddhi*, to use Tagore's terms for the co-constituted imagination of *samsara*, grasp the "tragic originality" of Third Cinema.

It is necessary to examine the individual episodes in greater detail. The "1943" episode of the "fallen woman," Shobhona, bears a running similarity to an earlier Bengali film, *Thana Theke Aschhi* (dir. Hiren Nag, 1965), itself a faithful adaptation of the British socialist playwright J.B. Priestley's *An Inspector Calls* (1946). *Thana* is one of the prominent examples of Bengali noir, important for its use of a range of devices such as an outsider detective, a murder mystery plot, locational night-for-night shooting, and low-key chiaroscuro lighting. As readers of Priestley's play will recall, the plot centers on the suicide of a working-class woman (Eva in the original play, Reba in the Bengali film version), and the subsequent revelation of the role of an upper-class, respectable bourgeois family in her death. It is a gesture to intertextuality that the female protagonist in both films *Thana* and *Calcutta 71*, Reba and Shobhona, is played by the same person, the noted actor Madhabi Mukhopadhyay, exemplifying the rather frequent crossover between mainstream and Third Cinema. In *Calcutta 71*'s "1943" episode, however, the two themes of a working-class woman's exploitation and the hypocrisy of bourgeois moral attitudes are combined in a single family, suggesting that these are internally related rather than externally induced, inseparable as a social whole.

In another point of departure, the "1943" segment uses familiar noir tropes, but neither the "detective" nor the "victim" lives up to their expected roles. The relative from out of town, an older male cousin and substitute patriarch figure, is horrified at the family's moral decay. It is not in his power to resolve. He decides to leave, mumbling some excuse of getting back to work and offering platitudes about sending monetary help soon. Likewise, far from being an innocent victim, Shobhona herself is blind to the suffering of others. The soundtrack makes this point brilliantly. Off-screen, the voice of a woman, a beggar passing by, pleads for some food – the context is the Bengal famine of 1943 – but Shobhona is unable to hear her cry for help. The audience's witnessing of Shobhona's tribulations does not provide any cathartic release, as that possibility is undercut by other even more marginal figures that remain off-screen. The disembodied voice of the beggar woman for one, and Shobhona's two adolescent brothers Hari and Guntu on the other: neither she nor the audience actually gets to know their stories. The brothers, as per Shobhona, "stay out all day and sometimes even at night: I do not know what they are up to." These unseen and unknown characters stand in for a spectrum of outcasts and criminals who are "products" of the great famine. Shobhona's personal tragedy remains pinned to these social outliers for whom there is no resolution. Likewise, the substitute patriarch, Shobhona's visiting cousin, himself dependent on extraneous support in the form of a clerical job in distant Delhi, does not have the power to resolve things to their satisfactory end. "1943" is the negation of standard issue noir drama – unresolvable in the present.

The film's reworking of the other short stories is likewise interesting. In Manik Bandopadhyay's story "Atmahatyar Adhikar" (Right to Suicide), the basis of the first segment "1933," the story is told from the father Nilmoni's point of view. Laid off from a laborer's job on account of a leg injury, Nilmoni sees his income dry up and his family, solely dependent on his earnings, reduced to penury. The night of the thunderstorm destroys what little remains of his ramshackle homestead – it is the culmination of life's injustices visited upon him and his family. Bandopadhyay devotes the bulk of the story to a fascinating examination of Nilmoni's troubled psyche, the anomie of the male working-class hero.

Keenly cognizant of his failure as paterfamilias, Nilmoni directs his anger toward his own family, mercilessly and virulently berating their weakness and proclaiming his desire to see all of them perish – his wife Nibha, daughter Shyama, son Nimu, and another newborn infant. The ending of the story too is different from the film: after Nilmoni takes his family to the Sarkar's house, they meet one solitary refuge seeker, a distant uncle of the Sarkar's. This man suffers from a disease of the lungs, probably tuberculosis, which makes him unable to breathe properly. He forces Nibha to open the window despite the storm raging outside. Nilmoni tries to assure this unnamed old man but ends up being thoroughly rebuked. Nilmoni and the uncle, the two male adult characters of the story, are, in a sense, mirror images. Stripped of dignity, authority, and most importantly livelihood, they rage against the system but end up abusing those close to and dependent on them. The story's title, "Right to Suicide," appears to imply, nihilistically, that self-destruction is their only remaining option. Yet on the whole, Bandopadhyay's text is relatively incurious about the internal hierarchies within this male-dominated working-class formation.

On the other hand, the film emphasizes the dialectical logic of the negative, only partially pursued by Bandopadhyay's text, by dispensing altogether with the fictive unity of the family. It entirely decenters Nilmoni's individualistic and patriarchal perspective and in doing so evacuates, once again, any restorative nostalgia associated with the family, *samsara*, as worldly form. The film introduces two new elements absent in Bandopadhyay's short story. The film focuses attention on the children, especially the elder sister Shyama, and charts new narrative space through her affinity with the mongrel dog Bhulu. Further, it grounds the family drama in the context of an urban slum, absent in the story, providing specific location and connotation.

The short story's theme of dehumanization becomes, in the film, the specific and determinate outcome of this urban space. "1933" accentuates physical space through a series of carefully arranged establishing shots and low-key lighting. The family house is shown in perspective beside similar dilapidated tenements. These are arranged around a narrow, barely lit lane, made impassable from the rains. Indebted to the noir, the slum is at the same time a visual representation of Frantz Fanon's famous observation in *The Wretched of the Earth*: "The native town is a hungry town, starved of bread, of meat, of shoes, of coal, of light. The native town is a crouching village, a town on its knees, a town wallowing in the mire" (*Wretched* 39). The "1933" episode echoes Fanon in commenting on the colonial logic of the city-space of Calcutta. It is placed immediately after the depiction of the white town of the opening "1971" sequence. The film's juxtaposition of these different temporalities, 1933 and 1971, formally registers the spatial disjuncture between white town and native town. It highlights the coexistence of the "non-modern," the "primitive," and the "rural" within the city, sharing space with the cosmopolitan urbane yet incommensurable with the latter. The "crouching village," the underbelly of the ex-colonial city, speaks to the *villas miserias* of Solanas and Getino's Latin America as well.

Once inside the house, the camera lingers on and illuminates the many layers of use that the single-room tenement is put to: at once sleeping quarters, and kitchen, and sitting room, and storage, and shelter space. To be sure, this scene of domestic penury and its vivid realism risks the trap of what Glauber Rocha calls the prurient "exoticism" associated with third-world poverty. But a closer examination reveals more. The mother Nibha sits in a corner, trying to shield her newborn child from the rain pouring through the roof. The girl-child Shyama moves around the room, at times holding an umbrella over her mother and the sleeping infant, and at other times arranging and relocating vessels and utensils on the floor to capture the rainwater. Her two brothers (and not one, as in the short story) sleep on the solitary cot; the father Nilmoni idles in another corner.

The scene presents the male figures as passive but foregrounds the role of the women, the mother Nibha and particularly the girl Shyama, in their struggle against the elements. Shyama is a preternatural adult. It is through her ceaseless labors that we witness the processive interaction between the socialization of nature (trapping, storing the rainwater) and the naturalization of the social (familial hierarchies of gender, status, and caregiving). It is also she who resists her father's attempts to drive away the dog Bhulu. After the family is forced to seek shelter in another house, they find that almost the entire neighborhood has turned up there. Shyama is reunited with her precious Bhulu. Interestingly, this friendship between child and animal is the only genuine "human" relationship in the entire episode. Freed of the constraints of the patriarchal family and spatial confines of the home, the shelter promises a new if fraught beginning for Shyama, albeit one that is left unrealized in the film. Somewhat aptly, Nilmoni characterizes the gathered crowd as children of God (*bhagobaner sontan*), a description that sniggers at their rootless lack of identity and, yet, provides a perverse articulation of freedom beyond the boundaries of home, family, and patriarchy.

The plight of an entire generation of indigent urban youth, earning them stigma and worse in a conservative society deeply committed to the ideology of belonging, is further traced in the "1953" episode. Based on Samaresh Basu's short story "Esmalgar" (The Smuggler), "1953" foregrounds the violent conflict between uprooted youth and postcolonial nationalism. For this generation, rebellion is molded into shape by the conditions of material lack rather than the commodity abundance characteristic of core capitalism. Lest one be accused of economism, consider that Basu's "Esmalgar" is underpinned precisely by the question of rice, as food and saleable commodity, embodying use and exchange value, respectively. Published in 1953, "Esmalgar" registers the decade-long record of grain rationing and scarcity in Bengal going back at least to the 1943 famine. This colonial-era demarcation between country and city persists well into the postcolonial period, rendering independence (in 1947) moot.

Furthermore, fiction such as Basu's engenders an indigenous literary aesthetics of hunger in Bengal that is parallel to that in Latin America. "Esmalgar" is internationalist and not simply third worldist in outlook, with Basu modeling his children (*shishu*) and youth (*kishor*) characters on those created by Anton Chekhov and Maxim Gorky (Saroj Bandopadhyay 12). Perhaps due to Mrinal Sen's own affinity to Soviet cinema of the revolutionary period, it is no surprise that the "1953" episode closely follows Basu's Russian-inflected focus on children's maltreatment. (To mention just one example, in the epic Odessa Steps sequence of Eisenstein's *Battleship Potemkin*, a key point of pathos occurs when Cossack soldiers unhesitatingly shoot at a young boy, who is then trampled underfoot by the retreating crowd. Another harrowing image from the same sequence is that of a baby in a pram, hurtling down the steps after soldiers shoot her mother.) In Eisenstein as in Sen, such representations of children exemplify a thoroughly hollowed out social order that has no room left for its future generations.

Labeled a criminal and delinquent, Gora, the protagonist of the episode, is nothing if not a profoundly moral, ethical person. He is a devoted son and brother whose income sustains his family. It is thanks to Gora's smuggling that people in the rural areas get access to food. He is equally committed to his "gang members," children of similar background, selflessly helping them avoid the police and making sure they carry their daily loot on the train. Sen succinctly describes the relation between the police and the community thus:

> Because of our long history of colonial oppression and injustice, the Indian people have generationally inscribed the police as the enemy, outside of society and definitely not a part of the masses .... The same *tradition* has continued among the masses, a certain *attitude* has crystallized ... a *biological distaste*. (Sen, *Ami Ebong Chalacchitra*, 21 – my translation; italics refer to English words in the Bengali original)

In a perverse way, Gora is the ideal type of citizen, thwarted by the failed dialectic of postcolonial nation formation and betrayed by the democratic state.

The crucial contradiction within the value system of citizenship, between use and exchange value, is strikingly expressed through a seemingly small detail: the smugglers singing a song inside the train. It is difficult to illustrate this strain without going into a lengthy digression. This popular song of naming (*namsankirtana* or colloquially *nam-gaan*), "*bhajo gouranga*," is a praise of the god Krishna and his lover Radha, also known in Bengal as Gouranga after the sixteenth-century social reformer Chaitanya. The youth group's singing irritates the train's passengers no end. There is a deliberate misrecognition at play: the singers are actually, slyly, praising their leader Gora whose name is a diminutive of Gouranga, while the passengers are furious at the joyous ruckus.

The religious folk song comes to acquire a contradictory double movement in the film. At once, it is rendered profane by one group, the smugglers who appropriate it secretly, and deemed exclusive by the other group of passengers, including the adult male who beats up Gora for disturbing the peace. The passengers deny the worldly, oral-corporeal, and syncretic character of the naming song, just as they deny the right of *any* member of the community to sing it without restriction. Furthermore, the song underscores Gora's similarity to the anthropomorphized Krishna of the "illiterate" classes rather than the otherworldly Krishna of Dvaita scripture: the former is a truant child who steals food yet rules wisely over devoted subjects at the margins of society. Like Krishna, like the prophet (*nabi*) Muhammad, and most of all like Gouranga, the singular indigenous figure that bridges Hindu Vaishnavite, Buddhist Tantric, and Sufi Islamicate traditions in precolonial Bengal – so Gora, the smuggler, attracts the lowly and the vulgar to himself.[16]

The film and the song within it, in other words, work in opposite if complementary ways. The soundscape triggers these associations; thus, the film discovers in Gora an aesthetic-historical type well known to indigenous culture, that of the androgynous (depending on interpretation) and humanized god-king. The film's lay representation of the ordinary individual, Gora, is overlaid with the more allegorical interpretation of his significance. If the parodic song vulgarizes – in all senses – the divine, it simultaneously enables the viewer to elevate the abject human: such movement militates, orally and aurally, against the hegemonic view of Gora as a lumpen delinquent. Let us consider too the continuity and development between "1953" and the previous episodes, "1933" and "1943." In the case of "1933," the homeless children are children of God; now they are made singular as the child-god himself. Similarly, Hari and Guntu, Shobhona's delinquent brothers of the "1943" episode, make a return in the figure of Gora. By contrast, the angry, irritated commuters inside the train call Gora's group all sorts of humiliating names. One of them, a middle-aged strongman, mercilessly thrashes the twelve-year-old Gora, while reminding fellow passengers that he is doing such deeds in the "name of the nation." Bruised but undefeated, Gora gets his revenge on the strongman by tripping him just as the latter is about to disembark from the train.

The film builds on these disconnected episodes and – to repeat – constellates a narrative that progressively discards all unnecessary or external digressions. It emphasizes the *negative* role of critique. Even as the film lays bare the dehumanization of individuals and groups over several generations, it does not valorize or reify them. Rather, Shobhona, Hari, Guntu, Nilmoni, Shyama, or Gora – all of these characters, despite small victories, in the end continue to exist in the underbelly of the city. There are no spectacular victories for these characters, only small and ultimately failed acts of resistance and resilience. Indeed, the film highlights the stark limits of their actions. Tragedy in this case resists easy identification and empathy, which are so easily rendered available for hegemonic rehabilitation. By foregrounding the bounded present scope of its subjects, the film gestures, conversely, to the greater possibilities of those others who are yet to come.

The film's fourth and final episode, aptly titled "1971" – denoting the present – discloses the narrator's story to the audience. The unnamed narrator, portrayed by Debraj Bhattacharya, directly addresses the audience. He narrates how he had burst into an elite gathering including noted political and social figures. His intervention creates panic. He is shot and murdered by the police after a lengthy chase. The narrator explains to the audience the rationale behind his actions and appeals to them to join him and others in the struggle. The appeal marks the end of the film. This final episode underscores one of the key notions of Third Cinema: namely, the role of film in consciousness raising and fostering participation against the grain of passivity, apathy, and individualized anomie. Appearing at the very last, the narrator remains a liminal figure in the film as a whole, a severely diminished presence that needs unpacking.

While the film shies away from explicit mention, possibly to avoid censorship, the narrator's violent end clearly references the Naxalites in contemporary Calcutta. (In fact, the iconic Naxalite activist, poet, and essayist Saroj Dutta would be similarly murdered by the police in 1971.) At its peak, Naxalism was driven primarily by the imperative of *rural movements* composed of agricultural workers and sharecroppers, which I discuss in the next chapter. Party leaders such as Charu Mazumdar and Saroj

Dutta repeatedly articulated this rural focus, even as they were unable to reconcile urban activism with the ongoing struggles of the peasantry.

Still, the Naxalites transposed with some degree of success the Chinese Cultural Revolution rhetoric of rebellious youth participating in novel forms of cultural-political practice in the urban areas. The Naxalite tendency to see insurgent youth in Calcutta and other urban areas as Indian versions of the Maoist Red Guards created epic problems of translation. Surfeit with grand polemics of social change, the ideas of Mao Zedong, Che Guevara, and others were copied and transferred, intermittently and haphazardly, with frequent revisions depending on the existing party line, to the local context.

Sumanta Banerjee, the historian of the Naxalite movement, mentions a slogan painted on the walls of Presidency College in Calcutta, which went something along the lines of "Mao [Zedong] in the city, Che [Guevara] in the village" (*In The Wake*, 212). The combination of these quite distinct personas, Mao and Che (and the nations, China and Cuba, and beyond) is remarkable. Attesting to the impact of these figures, such a slogan – a semantic intervention at the level of language – nonetheless highlights the peculiar and mismatched aspect of their adoption in the conjuncture of 1971.[17] As scholars have noted, the Naxalite conception of violent urban struggle was chaotic at best, caught between independent underclass and youth activism on the one hand and the shifting policies of the leadership on the other (see Sumanta Banerjee, *In the Wake*; Sanjay Seth, "Interpreting Revolutionary Excess"). Such confusions, however, have less to do with the political actors themselves and more with the historical context in which these ideas took shape.

The urban Naxalite movement, even as it drew inspiration from the Chinese and Cuban Revolutions, did not have anything approximating their strategic depth. This "difference," a matter of our speculation rather than fact, is formally reflected in cinema. As a result perhaps of its relative weakness in the political realm, the Naxalite is decidedly muted on-screen. The protagonist in *Calcutta 71* and more so in Sen's subsequent film *The Guerrilla Fighter* (1973) are more ambiguous, even effete, than the idealized figure of the heroic revolutionary. Equally, Sen's overall tone is much more pessimistic, tragic, and melodramatic when compared to Latin American Third Cinema.

What *Calcutta 71* illuminates most powerfully, I would argue, are those underclass subjectivities branded by the state as "Naxalite criminals." Such illumination does not undercut radical politics but rather humanizes the actors, in both the cinematic and political senses of the term. I submit that such a cinema enables an equally if not more effective mode of participation, knowledge creation, and social transformation as the revolutionary cinema of Latin America. At the same time, it alerts us to the fact that ideas are not transposed or copied wholesale between diverse spaces such as China, Latin America, and South Asia but calibrated on the basis of historical particularity.

The film precisely captures, and at the same time lays bare, the term "lumpen" as it came to designate the vast majority of insurgents: inhabitants of the slum, with no family or social ties, and inherently prone to criminal usurpation and senseless violence. The lumpen is supposedly condemned by the forward march of history: what Sen calls the idealist and dogmatic view of "continuing synthesis." For example, Ashok Mitra, the noted Marxist economist and later finance minister of West Bengal, described the group as the "filthiest social scum" and "victims of history's retribution." Holding the entire underclass as "a community of high-caste goons," Mitra writes:

> Slummy conditions of living have increasingly engendered a slumminess (*sic*) of the mind. The absence of gainful means of livelihood has gradually led to the steady loss of values . . . one can sum up this entire episode as part of the inevitable historical process: the feudal remnants [of the underclass] are the victims of history's retribution; they are getting what they richly deserve. (22–23)

The reputed liberal journal *Economic and Political Weekly* fared little better. In Malthusian terms, it bemoaned the "population explosion" and the "influx of refugees" to Calcutta since the 1940s and explained that "congestion and pauperization" had led to the rise of "anti-social [criminal] activity" ("Urban Guerrillas" 1379). Note that these comments, roughly contemporaneous to *Calcutta 71*, reflect the dominant responses to urban crises. The resistant poor are dehumanized and treated as aberrations to progress by the "Marxist" and "liberal" intellectual alike.

By sharp contrast, *Calcutta 71* offers an alternative explanation and relentlessly exposes the elite's betrayal of the masses. It is the postcolonial native bourgeoisie (the film suggests) that is the parasitic lumpen, feeding off the misery of the marginalized and the exploited. Masquerading as leaders and intellectuals, the former pass off a spurious version of nationalist development and capitalist progress as the true and only possible option for the present and the future, even as the social contradiction between them and the rest of society reaches a flashpoint. Described in terms of its total achievement, *Calcutta 71* elucidates lumpen-ness as an objective social form, a constitutive condition of class society in the postcolonial (and nominally sovereign) periphery. This *re*-conception of the lumpen is quite unavailable to contemporaneous culture except as a pejorative designation for groups beyond the pale of the submissive poor. In this sense, Sen's film breaks new ground and inverts hegemonic understanding of the lumpen.

Undoubtedly, previous writers and filmmakers had commented on the underclass in light of their own understanding of the city and its life forms. Marxists among them, such as Manik Bandopadhyay, had even attempted to contextualize them through the prism of class analysis. But such analytics had not been free from the suspicion of the lumpen voiced by Marx and handed down by Communist as well as nationalist discourse. Working within and yet going beyond this corpus, *Calcutta 71* traces a genealogy of urban social form belonging properly to the local without giving up the universal. It does so by embracing prior works of art that had intuitively grasped the historical reality of the city and, irrespective of the stated intentions of their authors, furthered the process of social analysis through that act of intuition. By constellating older literary texts, the film parses the "idea," which, as Benjamin reminds us in the Epistemo-Critical Prologue is *timeless,* from the context-bound and specific ephemeral phenomena. It is a direct result of this conceptual imperative at work that we glimpse these texts in the film only in the form of "fragments," in revised or truncated "versions," sometimes even as marginal "allusions" and "gestures." Concept, here, directly determines style. Fidelity to the concept is the measure of its true significance. To put this another way, *Calcutta 71* complements a Lukácsian realist impulse with a Benjaminian constellation. This way, it complicates linear historical causality by pointing to alternative possibilities and lineages.

The unique formal dimension of *Calcutta 71* is a product of tensions that are at once social and conceptual. That is to say, the juxtaposition of diverse techniques, subplots, media, and temporal frames – ranging from modernist fiction and poetry to oral traditions, from noir and melodrama to socialist realism – is less an outcome of the filmmaker's intentionality and more a formally concentrated expression of what Roberto Schwarz has termed the misplacement of ideas. *Calcutta 71* re-presents the phenomenon that is urban Naxalism, gathering together, nay, reinventing a series of episodes fragmentary in scope and giving them cinematic form. The film registers the political ideology of Naxalism and the youth including, but not limited to, the underclass that the Naxalites mobilized at a particular conjunctural moment. In other words, it is in the realm of cinema rather than political ideology that the elaboration of an insurrectionary theory of the city becomes possible.

Thus, it is through constellation-as-cinema that the *lumpen character* of a peripheral society, and especially its dominant bourgeoisie, emerges most profoundly, distinct in form and content. The film turns to folk and myth, as we have seen, by joining the film's narrator, the Naxalite guerrilla, with the premodern figure of the itinerant *bhikkhu*, and the enfant terrible Gora with Gouranga. These are not identifications, in the restricted sense, but ideational constellations. Rather than being a source of unchanging values in the scriptural sense, the religious and especially the popular oral/aural traditions provide ideas that are timeless in the Benjaminian mode. The demotic hopes and desires of destitute populations that exist outside of elite domains are sedimented in these figures as myths. The conceptual emphasis laid on the figurations of *bhikkhu* and Gouranga brings out, and connects to, the contemporary present, older histories of collective aspiration, and redemption. These are, in short, elements and aspects of a little recognized indigenous humanist tradition. That in their respective historical eras the hegemonic systems of Buddhism, Hinduism, or Islam, as organized state religions, also represented specific relationships of power between elite and subaltern populations is not germane in this context. It is the idea of redemption that deserves recuperation: moreover, as we see and understand from the unhappy fate of the narrator, Gora, and the other characters in the film, such an idea fails to find the ground of realization in the conjuncture of 1971. Yet, as Benjamin observed, ideas, no matter how obscured, continue to persist for the future.

Notes

1. According to police records, 1,783 activists belonging to the Communist Party of India (Marxist-Leninist), popularly known as Naxalites, were killed between March 1970 and August 1971 in Calcutta and its suburbs (Ashoke Mukhopadhyay 3231). This number does not include activists belonging to other organizations, or those with no active involvement in politics. Amnesty International noted in its 1974 report that between fifteen thousand and twenty thousand persons were detained in West Bengal prisons on alleged charges of Left-wing extremism ("Detention Conditions" 1612). For a recent account of Calcutta between the years 1965 and 1972, see Bhattacharyya, *The Spring Thunder and Kolkata*; for the role of women activists in this period, see Sinha Roy, *Gender and Radical Politics in India*.
2. In 1971, more than 25 percent of West Bengal's 44 million people lived in areas classified as urban, with more than 5 million in Calcutta and surrounding areas (*Census*). The population density of West Bengal was 504 per sq. km, almost three times the national average of 177 (Jasodhara Bagchi 22). People poured into the city in search of livelihood, causing a phenomenal growth of 166.7 percent in the homeless populations from 1961 to 1971 (Biswanath Roy 15). According to informal estimates, between a quarter to a half of the youth did not have full employment (Sumanta Banerjee 122), while a more sober estimate put the official unemployment rate in urban areas between 2.6 percent to 3.8 percent in 1971 (Bose 110).

3. Stalwart critics such as Teshome Gabriel place Sen at the front ranks of Third Cinema practitioners. Meanwhile, South Asian scholars have mostly passed over Sen's explicitly antiestablishment films. The exceptions to this trend are Hood 19–39, Ananda Mitra 37–65, and Deepankar Mukhopadhyay 81–110. But even this latter group of critics does not connect Sen to global, especially Latin American, currents.
4. See Roberto Schwarz's brilliant discussion of Paul Lins' 1997 novel, *City of God*, about the crime-ridden neo-favelas of Rio de Janeiro. Schwarz writes, "Crime may form a world apart, with a spell that lends itself to aestheticization; but it does not dwell outside the city that we share. It is this that prevents aesthetic distancing, that forces us to a committed reading – if only out of fear. This is a literary situation with peculiar properties of its own" (Schwarz, "City of God" 108).
5. Ivana Bentes correctly identifies a move from Rocha's "Aesthetics of Hunger" to a glamorized "Cosmetics of Hunger" in post-1990s Brazilian cinema, which includes films such as *Central Station* (1998) and the cinematic version of *City of God* (2003). Increasingly, poverty-focused films and TV shows from countries like Brazil and India are produced by Netflix, Fox, and other multinational companies. The target audiences are not only Western but also middle-class consumers in the Global South.
6. This point is first made by Shamik Bandyopadhyay, who points out during a conversation with Sen, "The conscious critique of social reality as a document [in your films] . . . . That was also the kind of philosophy or attitude at work in a lot of Latin American cinema" (Sen, *Over the Years* 68; see 43–73 for the full discussion).
7. See also "Cinema par Excellence: Films from Latin America" in Sen, *Montage*, and "The Latin American Scene," in Sen, *Views on Cinema*.
8. Ray and Sen engaged in a fairly sharp exchange in 1965 in a series of letters to the English daily *The Statesman*, stemming from the former's remarks on Sen's film *Akash Kusum* (Up in the Clouds), which Ray described as naive. Sen in turn bitterly accused Ray of selling out to commercial interests in *Nayak* (The Hero). For the two episodes, see Deepankar Mukhopadhyay 258–260, and Robinson 177, respectively.
9. Ray adapts a wide range of authors, starting from Rabindranath Tagore, Upendra Kishore Ray Chowdhury, and Rajshekhar Basu; mid-twentieth-century figures such as Bibhutibhushan Bandopadhyay and Tarashankar Bandopadhyay; to contemporary writers such as Narendranath Mitra, Sunil Gangopadhyay, and Mani Shankar Mukherjee (see Robinson, *Satyajit Ray* "Appendix B" for the full list).
10. In addition to his films, Sen's voluminous writings are a good source to trace his internationalist politics. Chakravarty, *The Enemy Within* 191 ff. has a well-curated bibliography.
11. Interestingly, *Calcutta 71* received "excellent exposure in some of major festivals abroad [including the Venice Film Festival] . . . Sen was thrilled by this certificate" (Deepankar Mukhopadhyay 103).

12. Seely points out that Jibanananda Das breaks with nationalism in his critical interrogation of nostalgia, community, as well as progress. In "Banalata Sen," nevertheless, the female muse providing an escape for the male poet is a variation of an old nationalist cliché.
13. In the "Realism" essay, Lukács writes, "the attitude of the modernists to cultural heritage ... [is that] it is a heap of lifeless objects in which one can rummage around at will, picking out whatever one happens to need at the moment. It is something to be taken apart and stuck together again in accordance with the exigencies of the moment" (54). For modernism in the periphery, often taking belatedness as a starting point, such statements hold true but often have effects working at cross-purposes.
14. Such convergences are increasingly recognized by scholars: see for instance the comment, "[Third Cinema's] relation to First and Second Cinema is dialectical: i.e. it seeks to *transform* rather than simply reject these cinemas; it seeks to bring out their stilted potentialities, those aspects of the social world they repress or only obliquely acknowledge" (Wayne 10, original emphasis).
15. See Ghatak, *Rows and Rows* and Sarkar, *Mourning the Nation*, chap. 5. Bishnupriya Ghosh, "Melodrama and the Bourgeois Family," rightly draws attention to the nuanced use of melodrama in Mrinal Sen's later work of the 1980s. However, Ghosh contrasts this to the films of the early 1970s, which is not a tenable view since melodrama is clearly at work in both cases. Around the same time, Zahir Raihan's overlooked classic *Jiban Theke Neya* (1970), an allegory of national liberation in Bangladesh, uses the melodramatic form to perfection in the figure of the domineering mother.
16. On the various transformations of the Chaitanya movement and its social bases, see Bhatia, *Unforgetting Chaitanya*. Anuradha Roy's *Cultural Marxism* provides an interesting discussion of the Communist adaptation of *kirtans* as part of the cultural-front activities.
17. On a related note, Lecercle, in *A Marxist Philosophy of Language*, provides an interesting exploration of Lenin's pamphlet on slogans, and commentaries on the same by Althusser and Deleuze and Guattari, that highlights the importance of language to the events of 1917.

CHAPTER 4

Black Blood: Fictions of the Tribal in Mahasweta Devi and Arundhati Roy

Mahasweta Devi, who painstakingly detailed the Naxalite movement among tribal or *adivasi*[1] agricultural laborers, forest dwellers, and landless peasantry in the 1970s, wrote almost exclusively in Bengali. Of her works translated into English that depict Naxalism, mention must be made of the urban novel *The Mother of 1084*, the short story "Draupadi," and the novella *Operation Bashai Tudu*. Of these, "Draupadi" (1978, 1981), on the eponymous Santhal *adivasi* leader, translated and annotated by Gayatri Chakravorty Spivak, had an outsized impact in the Anglo-American academy, casting shade on its multiple other receptions in West Bengal, India, and beyond. Perhaps it would not be an exaggeration to see this text as one of *the* representative examples, in the 1980s, of non-English South Asian literature abroad. John Hutnyk, writing of "Draupadi" in 2006, argued as follows:

> This 'teaching text' [is] one of several emissaries of the politics of Naxalbari circulating through a range of global sites, reaching feminist study groups, anti-racists and anti-imperialists, First and Fourth Worlders, as well as continuist communist activists ranged across the planet and still reading the history of people's struggles as an illustrative guide for political activity today. ("Euro-Maoists" 148)

Among other examples, the critic mentions "Naxalites," a 1997 track released by the UK-based electronica group Asian Dub Foundation in the album *Rafi's Revenge*. Far displaced from the setting of rural West Bengal, such adaptations signaled entirely new cultural contexts for Naxalbari by diasporic working-class artistes in London's East End, among others. And yet, the transformation of female *adivasi* militants such as Dopdi into globally circulated "cultural matter" has not been a smooth one.

One of the pitfalls of the latter has been the tendency, as Hutnyk avers, to "celebrate 'difference' in a way that does not differentiate between poverty and romance, adversity and exotica" (146). To turn this argument around slightly: I suggest that Devi's fiction emerged and traveled in the little understood context of peripheral internationalism. To this end, I trace a series of unlikely yet remarkable "encounters." The present chapter explores the persistent and braided relation between subaltern social movements and internationalist writing by constellating Mahasweta Devi's short story "Draupadi" with the later essay by Arundhati Roy, *Walking with the Comrades* (2010). Simply put, I chart an expanded intellectual history of two well-worn terms, "subaltern" and "international," by adducing a host of minor intermediaries and cultural currents, and exploring counterpoints and counterparts to Devi and Roy. Among others, Spivak herself appears to affirm the relevance of such a move:

> Just as socialism at its best would persistently and repeatedly wrench capital away from capitalism, so must the new Comparative Literature persistently and repeatedly undermine and undo the definitive tendency of the dominant to appropriate the emergent. (*Death of a Discipline* 100)[2]

A number of scholars, among them Priyamvada Gopal, Jennifer Wenzel, Neil Lazarus, and Nirmala Menon, have interrogated the vexed relation between writers such as Devi and Roy, and their reception through dominant forms of Anglophone postcolonial theory – the latter emphasizing irreducible difference, hybridity, and apathy toward liberatory realism and consciousness.[3] Building on and departing from previous scholarship, I emphasize the unremarked connections – or gaps – between the development of literary-cultural form and horizontal solidarities between writers and communities. It is *form* that illuminates anew, I suggest, the possibilities of peripheral literature and resists the latter's erasure by counter-insurgencies of the contemporary conjuncture, material as well as ideational.

There are four main aspects to excogitate in the discussion around Devi and Roy. First, I locate a body of women's writing in West Bengal and India that consistently challenged mainstream notions of women's participation in the political sphere. Vital to the critique was the imbrication of gender with other categories such as religion, caste, class, and location. Second, I explore the interaction between people's theater, vernacular fiction, and nonfiction primarily in Bengali but also other languages. One of the key aspects of this interaction that occured at the margins of but was nonetheless influential in articulating the content of counter-hegemonic political movements was the categorical reconfiguration of *literature*. Third, I demonstrate that the internationalist trends from the 1960s to the present, pulsating through the metropoles and the peripheries alike, profoundly altered literary-cultural practices in India. A whole range of writers looked outward to emancipatory currents animating other regions of the world. And last but not the least, braiding these three aspects through extended readings of "Draupadi" and *Walking with the Comrades*, I advance the significance of literary form: as concrete embodiments of historical conjunctures and simultaneously as examples of resistance to the reification of historical teleology.

The chapter advances that a consideration of form as much as content nuances scholarship and broadens our understanding of these trailblazing authors, Devi and Roy. The dialogic nature of poetic (literary) language, to adduce Vico and Bakhtin, deserves close attention in this context, engendering what I term, borrowing Auerbach's familiar concept, a *mixed form or style*.[4] This peripheral form – and its multiple iterations in fiction, drama, and nonfiction – enabled pragmatic interrogation into and imaginative excursions beyond the bourgeois horizons of the nation-state.

Perhaps, in our context, many more women achieved prominence in fiction as compared to poetry and drama. During the second third of the twentieth century, women's short fiction often appeared in Leftist periodicals alongside a range of other, male-authored texts – poetry, serialized plays, and commentary and analysis of global events. The short story, in particular, proved to be a much-favored genre; its formal brevity encouraged and enabled innovative and pithy explorations of muted subjects, topics, and themes. Vernacular magazines, such as the previously discussed *Parichay*, provided crucial albeit limited space for the transactions between women's writing and internationalist cultures of solidarity. To this end, "translation between Indian languages and from the other literatures of Asia, the Americas, Africa and Europe," writes Supriya Chaudhuri, "was an unremitting presence in the literary culture of the 1930s to the 1960s" ("Translation and World Literature" 596).[5]

Furthermore, vernacular fiction's engagement with oral and folk culture – specifically, adapting to print what did not, and could not, exist in print – was a development of considerable import, working within and against the impact of print, electronic, and now digital media that increasingly banished orality to the margins of the bourgeois public sphere. For progressive writers and intellectuals, the affirmation of the margins was, strictly speaking, a doubly anti-modernist move, neither valorizing, to paraphrase Lukács, a rupture with the past nor determining the artwork's validity by the criterion of newness alone. The attempt to narrativize the disenfranchised sections of society, such as women, lower castes, religious and ethnic minorities, and the landless peasants, necessitated more than a sidelong glance at classical, religious, and even "primitive" traditions. At the same time, such an imperative did not imply a "reflection" view of literature or an endorsement of realism as verisimilitude. We see with Devi, as with so many of her contemporaries, that fiction frequently departed from the conventions of realist literature and engaged with experimental forms of non- or anti-realist narrative: both a deepening of fractured narrative techniques and a more acute reckoning with the neocolonial order after formal decolonization.

Mahasweta Devi – like so many others – emphasized the vital importance of engaging with subaltern self-conceptions on her own terrain: that is, not so much as nostalgia or exotica, but as negotiating demotic contestations over the world. Before proceeding to "Draupadi," I situate Devi's work within the multifarious corpus of vernacular Bengali writing, particularly women's fiction and people's theater. This is not to suggest that Devi – or any other author, for that matter – should be read solely in the terms of predecessors and inheritors, that is, through a narrow lens of influences. Rather, my purpose is to illuminate the concrete specificities of the *language* that she wrote in (Bengali) and the determinate mediations of forms and themes therein, foreign as well as indigenous. Prior to, through, and following Mahasweta Devi, the cultural traditions and the literary language of Bengali evolved in ways that are seldom captured in Anglophone translation and discussion.

Such an exegesis is doubly warranted for a writer whose reputation in Anglo-American circles gains chiefly from the English translations of selected texts. The latter corpus represents not only a fraction of Devi's nearly hundred volumes of fiction; it also elides her translation into other Indian languages, with or without the mediating influence of English, such as "Hindi, Assamese, Telugu, Malayalam, Marathi, Oriya, Punjabi, Gujarati and Ho, a tribal language" (Ghatak "Introduction," in Devi, *Dust on the Road* ix). My aim is not to pose authentic vernacular tradition(s) against the postcolonial canon of the Anglo-American academy but rather to point out that the relationship between the former and latter is objectively unequal and determinate. A subtler appreciation of Devi's, and in a later period Arundhati Roy's, literary politics is obtained by resisting their dominant reception as *sui generis* cultural producers independent of historico-linguistic context and specificity. Our gesture of juxtaposing Devi and Roy makes sense, I submit, only when they are also constellated within equally unlikely but no less vital exchanges across the metropole and the periphery. A detour through literary-cultural history becomes necessary, illuminating the multilayered relationship between form, language, subalternity, and internationalism, as well as the mutations wrought on each of these terms.

Re-Situating Mahasweta Devi

Any account of Bengali feminist fiction and mixed form preceding Mahasweta Devi might start with Rokeya Sakhawat Hossain. Her English-language story "Sultana's Dream" (1905) and the more developed Bengali-language novella *Padmarag* (1924, published in English as *Ruby*) are stellar examples of utopian fiction. These imaginatively transcribe worlds founded and governed entirely by women, and free of the militaristic presence of men. Thematically similar to and, in the case of "Sultana's Dream," preceding the American writer Charlotte Perkins Gilman's better-known novel *Herland* (1915), Hossain's work intertwines politics, fiction, and social commentary. Combining traditional and free-flowing narrative, *Padmarag*, for instance, weaves together notions of interreligious unity and the need for women's formal education. Here and in many of her other texts: "Rokeya [Hossain] sees knowledge and education in positive terms, even when originating in or mediated by the colonizing countries of the West: she thinks that to reject knowledge on the grounds that it is *'Western'* is to play into the agenda of colonialism" (Bagchi, "Ladylands and Sacrificial Holes" 174–175, my emphasis). We might add, with the due qualifications in terms of emphases, that anticolonial authors such as Hossain chart a somewhat distinct trajectory to 1980s postcolonial theory's Foucault-inflected equation of Western knowledge as inherently colonial.

Later mid-century examples include Jyotirmoyee Devi, Ashapurna Devi, Sabitri Roy, and Sulekha Sanyal.[6] Jyotirmoyee Devi's hundred-odd short stories and several novels are marked by a versatile mastery over wide-ranging themes: anti-patriarchy, Hindu-Muslim conflict, the struggle of lower-caste groups, and the partition of Bengal and India. Mahasweta Devi herself writes in an introduction to Jyotirmoyee Devi's English-translated stories, "she [Jyotirmoyee] was deeply aware of the moral calculus of patriarchy . . . at first through reading, and later, through writing, she sought liberation of her mind" ("Preface," Jyotirmoyee Devi *The Impermanence of Lies* x). Perhaps closer in spirit to Mahasweta Devi is the little-known Sabitri Roy, whose novels include the socialist-realist trilogy *Paka Dhaner Gaan* (1955–1958, published in abridged English translation as *Harvest Song*), describing the peasant Hajong uprising during the Tebhaga sharecroppers' movement of the 1940s and the more experimental novel, *Ba Dwip* (The Delta, 1972, untranslated), that uses nested narratives and multiple points of view to illuminate the lives of post-partition refugees. In the same vein as Roy, mention must also be made of Sulekha Sanyal, who wrote a number of short stories, as well as a remarkable novel *Nabankur* (1956, published in English as *The Seedling's Tale*), which is an early example of an anti-*bildungsroman* connecting the themes of youth, gender hierarchy, and anticolonial struggle.

Even a cursory survey of this fiction, a significant portion of which is now available in English translation, reveals the range of interests and styles percolating through the twentieth century that defies easy categorization of modernism and realism, anticolonial and postcolonial fiction.[7] Rather than a limited focus on the private or the familial-communal, women's fiction forayed into investigating social relations, displaying a keenly attuned awareness of the quotidian fissures of peripheral society. These writers delved widely into all aspects of civic life, into the realms of peasants and the bourgeoisie, minorities, refugees, and outcasts. They strove to portray the mythical and the historical; the material and the corporeal; the struggle over land, home, and identity; and perhaps most of all, the insurgent contours of a contrarian *consciousness*. Contrary to any notion of their exclusive scope, many if not all women writers engaged with the full spectrum of social experience, casting aside the generic expectations of female-authored fiction. By connecting gender to global systems of oppression and exploitation, many of them intervened in and shaped critical cultural analysis in their own right.[8]

Mahasweta Devi's writing of the 1950s and 1960s, before the English translations of her work gained wider recognition, belonged firmly to this tendency. Devi's distinct contribution to vernacular women's writing was the combination of fiction and nonfiction, introducing novel frameworks and techniques to better conceptualize subaltern self-cognition and articulation. Her first published work, *Jhansir Rani* (1956, translated into English as *The Queen of Jhansi*), freely constellated history, myth, and fictionalized biography to depict the nineteenth-century female sovereign Laxmibai and her leadership of a tenacious armed insurgency against the British East India Company. Significantly, *Jhansir Rani*, contemporaneous to British and French historians' efforts at history writing from below, and some two decades before subaltern studies scholars excavated insurgent peasant consciousness from the colonial archives, did comparable work in the vernacular. Devi wrote in the preface to this book: "From the outset of this project I found that learning about the 1857–58 uprising presented us with rather limited opportunities. Apart from books written by English historians, there was an acute absence of other books" (*Jhansir Rani* 3).

Jhansir Rani drew on a range of oral sources including, "popular ballads, rhymes, *rasas* (didactic poetry), and old wives' tales" (*Jhansir Rani* 5): the result of four years of fieldwork in the early 1950s (1952–1956) in the Bundelkhand region in north-central India. The book depicts a zeitgeist extending far beyond the individual sovereign, yet enveloping the latter in the folds of popular myth. One Bengali commentator points out that *Jhansir Rani* marks "the first application in the Bengali language of the subaltern viewpoint as described by Gramsci" (Ghosh, *Mahasweta Devi* 37). The significance of this claim deserves elaboration. On the one hand, in the figuration of Laxmibai who rose well above her localized class limitations, Devi presents a female guerrilla leader who anticipates the better-known Dopdi Mejhen. We shall return to this point shortly. On the other hand, we are alerted to a generally unremarked layer in the reception of Antonio Gramsci, the Italian Marxist whose work was being reviewed in Bengali periodicals around the same time in the late 1950s.

Unconventional historiographical material shaped Devi's first novel, *Notee* (The Court-Dancer, 1957) and the subsequent novels *Amrita Sanchayan* (The Nectar Grove, 1962), *Kabi Bandyoghati Gainer Jiban o Mrityu* (The Life and Death of Poet Bandyoghati, 1966), and *Andhar Manik* (The Dim Star, 1967), none of which has been translated into English. In *Amrita Sanchayan*, Devi bemoans that "we are yet to sufficiently master the notion of 'historical fiction'. Our historical responsibility [as writers] stops with treating history either as full-fledged 'romance' or filled with the clamor of myriad events" (*Rachanasamagra* Vol. I, 5, my translation). Pushing back against these idealist and empiricist trends, Devi's literary work complemented that of activist-scholars in other disciplines who were undertaking similar projects of subaltern recovery in the 1950s and 1960s: the radical historian Suprakash Ray, the polymath mathematician and Indologist Damodar Dharmanand Kosambi, the philosopher and cultural critic Debiprasad Chattopadhyaya, the anthropologist Suresh Singh, and general secretary of the undivided Communist Party Puran Chand Joshi, among many others.[9] This work, of course, was not so much interdisciplinary as anti-disciplinary.

The Bengali-language critic, Nirmal Ghosh, author of perhaps the most comprehensive monograph on Devi's oeuvre, has commented, "History is at the center of [Devi's] writing" (Ghosh 62). History, in Devi's conception, refers to the determinate interconnectedness of the modern world. In the introduction to her novel *Kabi Bandyoghati*, set in the context of the sixteenth-century humanist revival in Bengal and Orissa (the Chaitanya-inspired *bhav-andolan*, badly translated as "consciousness movement" – the term *bhav* references both sensuous and cognitive consciousness), Devi places the story of a lower-caste *Chuar* poet Kalhan as "part of a magnificent renaissance of humanist religiosity in India ... one of the foremost mother-sources [*matri-utsa*] of liberal humanist thinking of the modern world" (qtd. in Ghosh 63). Her gloss points to a double maneuver: the novel locates the consciousness movement of Chaitanya within the unfolding ambit of a coeval and singular "universal history," while centering *matrilineal* and *poetic* humanism on the figure of a lower-caste poet, displacing the hegemonic coordinates of masculinist, Eurocentric, and/or Brahminical idealism. Like Begum Rokeya earlier, Devi's recuperation of peripheral history, without distancing the latter in binary terms of difference from the West, recalls feminist authors undertaking similar work in better-recognized languages such as English, French, and Spanish – Ama Ata Aidoo, Maryse Condé, Assia Djebar, Micere Mugo, Marie Vieux-Chauvet, and Excilia Saldaña, to name only a few.

In her milieu, Devi was not the sole author professing a combined commitment to universal history as well as subaltern poetics-politics. Saurin Sen, another contemporary writer, wrote a number of books that were part political treatise and part fictional novel on the various flashpoints of the 1960s: Cuba, Bolivia, Argentina, Haiti, Vietnam, Indonesia, and the Congo. Many of these texts enjoyed wide popularity among readers, although few copies survive, including *Akher Swad Nonta* (The Salty Taste of Sugarcane – On Cuba, 1965); *Congo Theke Fera* (Returning From Congo, 1966); *Kanna Gham Rokto* (Tears, Sweat and Blood – on Bolivia, 1970); *Mekong Nodir Opare* (On the Other Side of the River Mekong); *Ferar* (The Fugitive – on Argentina); and *Nisiddha Desher Ghum Bhangchhe* (The Awakening of the Forbidden Country – on Tibet), among others. Saurin Sen heralded a new turn in vernacular fiction, reinventing the genre of the political novel. Going beyond the Gandhian emphasis on nonviolent nationalism – which especially after Indian independence had assumed hegemonic coercive form – Sen provided portrayals of ordinary people, the world of militants and their communities in Africa, Asia, and Latin America, resisting their old as well as new postcolonial masters. Written in an accessible, colloquial style and interspersed with vivid anti-imperialist polemics of the day, Sen's novels, which were often serialized in magazines, played a pioneering role in disseminating knowledge of third-world liberation struggles. To Sen belongs the credit of popularizing, to readers in West Bengal, such global figures as Fidel Castro, Patrice Lumumba, and Ho Chi Minh.[10]

A similar example obtains in the case of Chanakya Sen (no relation to Saurin Sen), the pseudonym of Bhabani Sen Gupta. Chanakya Sen wrote *Rajpath Janpath*, a novel that exposed the anti-African and anti-Black structures underlying Indian nationalist rhetoric. It fictionalized the harrowing experience of racism and sexism encountered by Kenyan and Ugandan students and activists in independent India. *Rajpath Janpath* appeared in 1960, just six years after the Bandung Conference, and four years after the Declaration of the Non-Aligned Movement. Chanakya Sen described the book as "the first attempt in Bengali, since India's Independence, to write a serious political novel" (*The Morning After*, "Introduction" 1). Sen republished a revised English version in 1973, titled *The Morning After: A Non-Novel*. Perhaps the subtitle "A Non-Novel" referred to contemporary events, just as much as it indicated the failure of the novel experiment of non-alignment, as I discuss elsewhere (Majumder, "The Poetics and Politics of Blackness").

Alongside these important instances in fiction, the internationalist turn in West Bengal was best rendered in the realm of people's theater or *gananatya*. Theater had a broader reach than fiction, extending beyond the cities, district towns, and middle-class literate members of society. *Gananatya* had an especially vital impact on Mahasweta Devi's fiction. The two figures I discuss here are Bijan Bhattacharya (Devi's onetime husband) and Utpal Dutt. Bhattacharya's 1944 production of *Nabanna* (The New Harvest) marked a milestone in Bengali drama; the play was a pioneering attempt to portray rural peasants and their collective struggle for economic and political rights. While such themes had been intermittently present in earlier theater, the actor-playwright-director Bhattacharya introduced virtuoso techniques of stagecraft and lighting as well as performance codes. The formal quality of his plays, spanning the mid-1940s to the mid-1960s, was far removed from contemporary drama.

The dialogue of Bhattacharya's plays captured the distinctive rhythms and intonations of rural and plebeian speech, very different from the polished vernacular of the literate classes, and his dramatic plots illuminated the contradiction between subaltern aspiration and the dominance of the landed gentry. Much like Mahasweta Devi in *Jhansir Rani*, Bhattacharya also raised the vexed question of religious belief as a component of subaltern resistance. In *Debi Garjan* (The Oracle of the Goddess, 1966), a play on contemporary uprisings in the Birbhum district of West Bengal preceding the Naxalbari uprising of 1967,

Bhattacharya relates the question of the Santhal insurgents' "Hindu" religious consciousness to the ongoing national liberation struggle in Vietnam, which – as we will see – directly connects to this chapter's discussion of "Draupadi." Bhattacharya fused the religious and the profane under the banner of subaltern struggles against imperialism and feudalism.

The actor-playwright Utpal Dutt, one of the premier interpreters of Shakespeare and Brecht on the Indian and Bengali stage, who we have encountered fleetingly in previous chapters, went one step further. In the 1960s, Dutt, like Bhattacharya, a former member of the Indian People's Theater Association or IPTA, broke away from the proscenium format to focus on the indigenous dramatic form of *jatra*. Adapting the spectacular mode of *jatra* (similar to Easter plays), Dutt mounted a series of nontraditional plays on contemporary Vietnam, Cuba, Indonesia, and the Congo. Combining the Brechtian *Lehrstück* and the equally didactic spirit of *jatra*, Dutt sought to articulate an internationalist sensibility in plays such as *Ajeya Vietnam* (Invincible Vietnam, 1967), *Krushbiddho Cuba* (Crucified Cuba, 1968), and *Manusher Adhikarey* (The Rights of Man, 1968, on the US Black Power movement).

These plays were contemporaneous – a connection seldom explored – to the "revolutionary model plays" of the Cultural Revolution in China that combined "the three different artistic genres of Peking opera, ballet and symphonic music" (Xiaomei Chen 138). It is possible to speculate that Dutt was drawing from and indeed familiar with the model plays: he probably came across them in *Chinese Literature*, an English-language magazine published by the Chinese state-sponsored Foreign Languages Press and readily if surreptitiously available in India. In a significant intervention, Xiaomei Chen shows that the eight revolutionary model plays, approved by state agencies during the height of the Cultural Revolution, played a key role in the global dissemination of Maoist ideology. Some of the plays frequently alluded to events in the Congo, Algeria, Vietnam, Albania, and other places and positioned China as an anticolonial force outside the sphere of influence of the Cold War rivals, the United States and the Soviet Union. Chen writes:

> In the [Chinese revolutionary] model theater ... female characters were also transformed from suffering, silent subalterns into revolutionary warriors and party leaders. No longer would Zhao's wife [a character in an older play from the 1950s, *Growing Up in the Battlefields*] patiently wait for her father and son to return home. Indeed, in some plays, women warriors took their male counterparts' place as leaders, and for traditional roles associated with

womanhood, motherhood and the intimacies of family life, they substituted a total dedication to revolutionary struggle. (Chen 137–138)

A few essential facts about Dutt's *jatra* plays illustrate their connection to contemporary Chinese theater as well as the fiction of Mahasweta Devi. The first is the representation of female activists and their leading roles in organizing communities against oppressive forces. The centrality of women's activism to radical social movements such as the 1940s Tebhaga struggle was a well-established theme in Bengali fiction. Dutt added a new dimension to this problematic. His plays emphasized the subaltern female guerrilla as an organic intellectual – an extraordinary figuration, and one that decisively captured the insurgent spirit of the era. Second, these insurgents appeared on the local stage as transnational and even transhistorical figures, active practitioners and theoreticians in rural Vietnam and urban America, as much as in contemporary West Bengal and ancient India.

Dutt's plays included such leading characters as the Vietnamese activists Aunt Kim and Trac in *Ajeya Vietnam* (Invincible Vietnam); the African American Black Panther Martha in *Manusher Adhikarey* (The Rights of Man); the Rajbangsi peasant women Debari and Gangi in *Teer* (Arrow, 1969); and the low-caste Shudra leader Indrani in *Surya Shikar* (Hunting the Sun, 1971). As organic intellectuals, such characters relentlessly "taught" both male and female members of their communities and, by extension, rural and urban members of the plays' diverse audiences. Their roles included both the positive task of ideological indoctrination and the negative task of critique: working against patriarchy and feudalism, recognizing and transforming internalized oppression at the level of consciousness. At the same time, such characters militated against the typical notion of the upper-caste, middle-class male intellectual associated with the Communist parties. The organic intellectual's wisdom and acumen derived from working (and performing onstage) among the people rather than adherence to the party line. As both leaders of oppressed communities and as women engaged in militant combat, these characters suffer twice the violence inflicted on their male comrades – torture and execution, rape and dispossession.

In a very precise sense, such onstage characters were predecessors of Dopdi Mejhen.[11] The emergence of this "typical character," to employ a term from Lukács, persistently figured in the contemporary arena, illuminates the cross-fertilization between radical theater and literary fiction of the late 1960s and early 1970s. This phase did not continue for long in the face of active state repression. But while it lasted, this moment presented perhaps the most ambitious attempt to revise the social type, and representation, of the "intellectual," fusing local and international elements of struggle and solidarity. As well, Utpal Dutt's plays elaborated another cultural process that is key to Mahasweta Devi's fiction. This is the critique of "transculturation," a term coined by the Cuban anthropologist Fernando Ortiz in the 1940s, and elaborated at length by the Uruguayan literary scholar Ángel Rama during the 1970s to describe the peripheral zones shaped by colonialism.

It is useful to recount that Ortiz, who wrote about the *failed* transculturation of Spanish ideas in the conquered New World, took a noticeably dim view of the process that he is credited with encapsulating. For Ortiz, description did not mean endorsement (see his *Cuban Counterpoint*). In the internationalist culture of the late 1960s and early 1970s, there emerged a critical attitude toward dominant transculturation whose value is well worth recounting. Rather than encouraging subaltern assimilation to transculturated ideas, Dutt's oeuvre aroused affective revulsion at and non-identification with imperial transculturaton. In *Ajeya Vietnam*, for example, the military officers Wheeler and Knight appear in Vietnam as representatives of American "law." Their very enunciation of freedom, democracy, justice, civilization, and progress renders these terms hollow from the inside. In other words, the play problematizes the very concepts on which American soft power depended during the Cold War. Other plays featured native variants of these petty tyrants: upholders of Hindu-Brahminical law as in *Surya Shikar*, or American-trained local paramilitary enforcers as in *Teer*. The unfolding of the plays' narratives revealed not so much the injustice of traditional liberal law or the distortion of individual freedom. They suggested something more drastic, namely that justice is impossible under conditions of empire – whether in My Lai in Vietnam, Detroit in the United States, or Naxalbari in India. The master codes imposed from above and without regard for consequences exact terrible prices on the lives of those who are at the receiving end: such is the logic of empire.

The resistance to these alien and alienating ideas was to be found (in Dutt) in a revivified humanism and universalism: revitalized, that is, through the unlikely assemblage of Brechtian *Lehrstück*, Maoist model theater, and indigenous *jatra*. Like other contemporaneous instances, such as the Ngũgĩ wa Thiong'o–led Kamiriithu Community Education and Culture Center in Kenya or Augusto Boal's Center for the Theater of the

Oppressed in Brazil, Dutt's group, the People's Little Theater, among many others in West Bengal served as conduits for subaltern cultural expression. Dutt's English-language essay "In Search of Form," collected in a later volume of writings on theater, captures the generous ideas and sense of hopefulness in this context:

> The proletarian myths have not yet been created; the proletarian revolution has not yet produced its Goethe and Schiller . . . . The declassed bourgeois writers who, by choice, have been trying to express the power of the proletariat, have not so far been able to explore the vast storehouse of folk memory and produce a tale of heroism and struggle that will effectively forecast the rise of the working man [sic] to power. (*Towards a Revolutionary Theatre* 155–156)

The audience of dramatic literature was encouraged to glimpse, even if they never fully got to see, the emerging contours of a *horizontal* solidarity. Undercutting his own systemic masculinist language (reflective of many on the contemporary Left), Dutt's plays posited a nuanced linkage of folk and bourgeois culture by the "working woman," where the new radical literature appropriates the old and becomes the harbinger of the future. The very range and choice of subject matter, as well as formal affiliations, should warn us against reading this enterprise in simplistic terms. Rather, through what could be seen as a kind of "reverse transculturation," *she* (the working-class intellectual) resists hegemonic culture by encouraging poetic identification with subaltern struggle: namely, those racialized, classed, and gendered subjects deemed truly alien to the national-global order. Let us now return to Mahasweta Devi: it is safe to say that the notion of collectivist poetical-political praxis finds one of its greatest interlocutors.

"Draupadi" and Horizontal Form

Mahasweta Devi's "Draupadi" embodies the trend of horizontal solidarity absorbing each of the literary-cultural currents traced earlier. The story narrates the capture and rape of the Santhal Naxalite activist Dopdi Mejhen, at the behest of the wily counterinsurgency officer Senanayak. The story, as is well known, is a damning condemnation of the "democratic" Indian state and highlights the challenges posed to hegemonic postcolonial nationalism by movements from below. Less obviously, "Draupadi" explores the contemporary contours of solidarity through its formal structure. This is the central aspect that I will focus on, namely, the relation between narrative form and the horizontal solidarities of subaltern internationalism. In this regard, "Draupadi" offers a rich tapestry of ideas whose texture remains unexplored despite – or perhaps because of – its global translations.

Some of the dialogues, such as the opening of the story, are in a mode reminiscent of drama or, more properly, people's theater. These brief and businesslike lines identify the speakers by role rather than name, "First Livery" and "Second Livery," for example, designating their function as actors in a *mise-en-scène*, commenting on events. The dialogues are interspersed with nonfictional elements, "dossiers" and intelligence reports, which feign to provide the reader information on the military operation to apprehend Dopdi Mejhen. At the same time, the narrative's naturalistic façade is broken by the fragmented nature of sentences, which convey staccato impressions of multiple narratives. The opening section offers the following:

> Name Dopdi Mejhen, age twenty-seven, husband Dulna Majhi (deceased), domicile Cherakhan, Bankrajharh, information whether dead or alive and/or assistance in arrest, one hundred rupees . . .
> An exchange between two liveried uniforms.
> FIRST LIVERY: What's this, a tribal called Dopdi? The list of names I brought has nothing like it! How can anyone have an unlisted name?
> SECOND: Draupadi Mejhen. Born the year her mother threshed rice at Surja Sahu (killed)'s at Bakuli. Surja Sahu's wife gave her the name.
> FIRST: These officers like nothing better than to write as much as they can in English. What's all this stuff about her?
> SECOND: *Most notorious* female. *Long wanted in many* . . .
> *Dossier:* Dulna and Dopdi worked at harvests, rotating between Birbhum, Burdwan, Murshidabad, and Bankura. In 1971, in the famous *Operation* Bakuli, when three villages were *cordonned* off and *machine gunned*, they too lay on the ground, faking dead. In fact, they were the main culprits. Murdering Surja Sahu and his son, occupying upper-caste wells and tubewells during the drought, not surrendering those three young men to the police. In all this they were the chief instigators. In the morning, at the time of the body count, the couple could not be found. The blood-sugar level of Captain Arjan Singh, the *architect* of Bakuli, rose at once and proved yet again that diabetes can be a result of anxiety and depression. Diabetes has twelve husbands – among them anxiety (392, italics indicate English in the original).[12]

Various factors are at play in this opening, painstakingly real and vividly unreal at the same time: a dialogic and mixed style that Spivak's English translation conveys very well.[13] The short description of the protagonist offers a wealth of detail about Dopdi's age, marital status, occupation, and location, as well as the bounty offered for her capture. The so-called dossier, framed like an intelligence or newspaper report, scrupulously details Dopdi's past "notorious" activities: yet, somewhat improbably, the dossier also admits the culpability of officers in the annihilation of three entire villages, where villagers, presumably innocent, are "cordonned off" and "machine gunned." The conversation between the two liveried uniforms that serve as narrators or *sutradhars* in the unfolding drama, likewise, highlights the frustrations of plebian soldiers. The dialogue underscores their comic inability to comprehend the English-language documents prepared by their superiors, as well as the aporia of the Santhal guerrilla's Hindu-ized name. Finally, the most incongruous part, the dossier incorporates an oral proverb, a reference to the diabetic Captain Arjan Singh's rising blood sugar levels. The transition from official report to popular speech takes place within the single continuous paragraph that does not distinguish between the two.

The opening lines provide a window into the story's main stylistic or formal feature, one that develops through the remaining pages, all the way to the famous ending. There is an admixture of a tongue-in-cheek, world-weary temperament and a subversive, nebulous colloquial sensibility. Myth and legend enter the modern-day story. The queen Draupadi of the epic narrative *Mahabharata*, married to five Pandava kings, is reborn in the present-day war between the fugitive Santhal guerrilla Dopdi and the diabetic Sikh captain Arjan (perhaps a satirical reincarnation of Arjuna, the chief warrior among the Pandava).

Such an epic-religious framing is neither incidental to "Draupadi" nor, we will see, does this device merely illuminate contemporary events in the timeless light of tradition. Rather, similar to James Joyce's novel *Ulysses* or Bertolt Brecht's play *Saint Joan of the Stockyards*, "Draupadi" establishes a narrative technique that interrogates the mythical as much as the secular. Spivak has commented on the *Mahabharata*'s "colonialist function in the interest of the so-called Aryan invaders of India" ("Draupadi" 387). There are, of course, counter-hegemonic readings of the accretive epic text that deserve our attention, and from which "Draupadi" draws its own energies. Parallel to and yet brazenly incommensurate with Draupadi's five husbands in the *Mahabharata*, Arjan's "[d]iabetes has twelve husbands." This diagnosis is meant as a joke that is partly lost in translation. The word in the Bengali text, *barobhatari* – a person supported by a dozen bread winners – conventionally referring to a harlot – conveys the sharp colloquial vulgarity of the sentiment, even as it conjures a proverb that borrows as much from ancient religious myth as from plebeian satire (*Agnigarbha* 164). By depicting the captain Arjan as cowardly and a buffoon, the short story undercuts consecrated tradition that sings the praises of Arjuna, the Pandava warrior-king who defeated Draupadi's father in battle. This is, one might add, how the *Mahabharata* would look as a *jatra* play – irreverent humor at its finest. The master-archer Arjuna's bows and arrows are replaced by Arjan's machine guns, while Dopdi's ragtag peasant army persist in using its "primitive weapons ... hatchet and scythe, bow and arrow" (394). Unlike the Draupadi-Arjuna romance in the *Mahabharata*, the increase in Arjan's blood-sugar levels precisely captures Dopdi's contemporary impact. She is like an unseen foreign substance, entering into and circulating in the bloodstream, contaminating Leviathan's body.

In this way, by inserting Dopdi's story into a longer epic-religious tradition, the narrative resists the temptation to see the female Santhal guerrilla as a pure "other," a figure of irreducible *difference* from the nationalist imagination. Seeing Dopdi Mejhen as the other reifies her subaltern position, whereas she is "already present," in the dialectical sense of negative possibility, within the structure of feeling that sustains bourgeois nationalist hegemony, namely *culture*.[14] The title of the Bengali collection in which "Draupadi" first appears, *Agnigarbha* or Womb of Fire, also provides this incentive to read culture corporeally, as something that grows inside the womb. Here it is worth underscoring that it is the wife of Surja Sahu, the upper-caste landowner, who gives Draupadi her Hindu-ized name, symbolizing the stranglehold that dominant groups (including women) have over the realms of religion and history, tradition and culture. The two liveried uniforms at the beginning of the story know who Dopdi/Draupadi is through this cultural reference even before they meet her, though of course they cannot truly know her. What Dopdi achieves is an intervention in that same order of hegemonic culture and its underlying social relations. Neither a noble savage nor standing outside, as it were, Draupadi's real agency derives from her work within and against the culture that shapes her subaltern status.

It is eminently clear in "Draupadi" that the critique of culture – textualized and consecrated high culture – is intimately tied to the social relations of production. Dopdi Mejhen is nothing if not a labor organizer, negotiating demands for a fair minimum wage for the daily laborers and tilling rights for the sharecroppers. She also appears as a character in "Operation Bashai Tudu," the opening novella in the *Agnigarbha* collection that is focused on land and wage struggles (*Agnigarbha* 1–161). In this sense, "Draupadi"'s exploration of tribal, female, rural-worker subalternity vis-à-vis the Draupadi of the *Mahabharata* is closer to Brecht's epic play *Saint Joan of the Stockyards* (1932), where the medieval Joan of Arc is transfigured into a working-class organizer in Chicago.

In other words, the problematic of subalternity harkens back to the spirited debates from an earlier period, which raised afresh the question of the proletariat and its relation to culture. *Saint Joan* asks: did the proletariat represent a complete break with classical, feudal, and bourgeois culture that came before? If so, how is such a break to be conceptualized and articulated in narrative form? Brecht provides an important response that stands in contrast to the many orthodoxies of his era, to quote from Roberto Schwarz's excellent reading of *Saint Joan*:

> Rather than make a *tabula rasa* of the past, Brecht's tactic was to assemble a strategic anthology of the [old] tradition's greatest texts, to which the language of Saint Joan's protagonists systematically alludes. He did not abandon consecrated culture altogether. Instead, he presented the vicissitudes of class conflict and the calculation of the canned-goods cartel – new material – in verses imitative of Schiller, Hölderlin, the final scenes of Goethe's *Faust II,* expressionist poetry or Greek tragedy, the latter perceived as German, *honoris causa*. The most celebrated resources of bourgeois culture shared the stage with economic crisis. To emphasize the affront, we see the latter in the satirical and bloody setting of the meatpacking industry, where slaughter, financial reasoning and hunger naturally coexist. The novelty was not in the artistic contrast between the modern world and the classical tradition [which is a commonplace in Gide, Proust, Mann, Kafka, Eliot, Joyce] .... In Brecht's work, which pertains to almost the same years, that distance between illustrious models and the tone of the present assumes its own distinctive shape. The cold yet mocking concatenation of the rawest economic interest and the loftiest philosophical and lyrical idealism of the German classical tradition, under the sign of capitalist crisis, gives birth to a Frankenstein's monster. Even today, the fierceness of that caricature sends a chill down the spine. ("Brecht's Relevance" 97–98)

"Strategic anthology" and "fierce ... caricature": these are the Brechtian strategies to expose the "consecrated culture" of the American big bourgeoisie. We may add that *St. Joan*'s critique of idealism went not only against the Euro-American bourgeois class but also the Soviet bureaucratic class's burgeoning neoclassicism of the 1930s (see Fitzpatrick, *The Cultural Front*; Clark, *Moscow, the Fourth Rome*). Brecht correctly posed the proletariat, *negatively*, against the entire international order of culture: cutting across national borders, obviously, but even across the rigid ideological separation between free market capitalism and bureaucratic socialism. In similar fashion, "Draupadi" takes aim at the nationalist veneration of ancient texts and satirizes these "illustrious models" and ideals.

Quite like Brecht, Mahasweta Devi is not restricted to a single national tradition. She articulates the question of subalternity in relation to contemporary culture *tout court*. However, the difference in historical period between Brecht and Devi, located on either side of the Second World War, assumes a specific aspect here. The expressions of indigenous myth take on new and amplified meanings, for Left and Right alike, in the context of the liberation struggles of the late 1960s and 1970s. Moreover, the contingencies of culture formation in the periphery also play a role, since the ruling classes rely, first and foremost, on imperial imports for legitimacy and only afterward on the classical national past. The situation in postcolonial countries like India, however, is not entirely dissimilar to Western nations that historically lagged behind England and France; let us recall that Greco-Roman classicism, the target of Brecht's satire in *St. Joan*, becomes a part of German or US national identity only after being re-routed through France and England, as a thoroughly derivative discourse.[15]

Alongside Brecht, another of Mahasweta Devi's interlocutors – an overlooked reference – is the colossus of Chinese letters Lu Xun. Suffice it to say that Lu Xun's multiple avatars – as fiction writer, essayist, and translator – provide Devi with a model of the internationalist writer. This is evidenced in the nonfiction long essay *Lu Xun, Samaj o Sahitya* [Lu Xun, Society, and Literature] that Devi wrote in 1981, just a few years after "Draupadi," on the hundredth birth anniversary of the Chinese writer. Here, she argues that Lu Xun articulates the "anti-imperial" and "anti-feudal" functions of literature through a range of formalist experimentation and innovation. Devi invokes Lu Xun's supposed assessment of Mao as a "grounded theorist" (*mrittikasporshi tattwik*) and claims that indeed it is Lu Xun who anticipates Mao's emphases on oral and plastic folk cultures in the Yenan Forum lectures (4–7). Another salient aspect is the admixture of literary form; Lu Xun's preference for the "modern Western" short story over "classical Chinese" prose narrative, Devi maintains, introduced a generation of readers to foreign literature. Not only that, he, that is, Lu Xun, successfully represented early twentieth-century semi-colonial China in ways that classical prose forms could not (81–89). Fictional form and especially the short story's engagement with foreign and classical elements prove to be unceasing concerns in Devi's own writing.

In a later (mid-1990s) conversation with the Bangladeshi novelist, short story writer, and cultural critic Akhtaruzzaman Elias, Devi frames the problematic of representation in terms of unevenness. She sees the periphery as the space where disparate historical eras are arbitrarily yet comparably juxtaposed:

> The events that take place today are historical; similarly ancient history *was much like modern times* . . . what we find if we pore over the *puranas* [Hindu religious literature] and history, *that must be seen as modern times* . . . . The peculiarity of this piece of land, West Bengal, Bangladesh and the rest of India, is that it simultaneously lives in the *seventh century*, in the *eleventh century*, and thinks that the *twentieth century* is ending soon. All the feudal notions and ideas, the same exploitation, the same deprivation, the same hatred, are present. When there are explosion-like outbursts against this unjust order, every now and then, we term that insurrection. (Ghosh 121–122, Appendix 2, my translation, italics indicate English phrases in the original text)

Almost directly paraphrasing her arguments about Lu Xun, Devi articulates the role of the oppositional writer as working toward the emancipation of workers and peasants, from and against "feudal notions and ideas" and "this unjust order." Committed writers, she suggests to Elias, can and indeed must tease out the world-historical significance of popular "insurrections" and "explosion-like outbursts." In the context of "West Bengal, Bangladesh and the rest of India," this implies the religious "puranas" as well as secular "history," seeing these as the simultaneous rather than separate determinations of multiple temporalities. Such diverse materials of culture constitute the ground (or space) for writerly activism. Devi's comments, however, are neither vanguardist nor reducible to communitarian nationalism in any simple sense. She finds an empathetic interlocutor in Elias, one of the outstanding Bengali-language intellectuals of the 1980s and 1990s, yet whose works went neglected in Anglophone scholarship and translation efforts.[16]

There appears in Devi's "Draupadi," supplementing the *Mahabharata* and relegating the latter to secondary import, a number of more pressing references. Politics enters into everyday language, and crucially into the realm of consciousness. Such an incursion, introducing the language of imperial power, structures the sensory and linguistic registers of the characters. The fugitive Draupadi, whose awareness of self is conveyed to the reader through stream-of-consciousness techniques, connects her fragmentary personal memories to transnational group-identities, even as she articulates a sense of localized belonging. A typical passage:

There was the *urgency* of great danger under Dopdi's ribs. Now she thought there was no shame as a Santhal in Shomai and Budhna's treachery. Dopdi's blood was the pure unadulterated black blood of Champabhumi. From Champa to Bakuli the rise and set of a million moons. Their blood could have been contaminated; Dopdi felt proud of her forefathers. They stood guard over their women's blood in black armor. Shomai and Budhna are half-breeds. The fruits of the war. Contributions to Radhabhumi by the American soldiers stationed at Shiandanga. Otherwise, crow would eat crow's flesh before Santhal would betray Santhal. (399, italics indicate English in the original)

The fleeting references to "American soldiers" and the "[second world] war" are of the utmost import in this passage. These imply that Dopdi is conscious of larger forces, if only in the manner of partial consciousness characteristic of subjective knowing. Even as Dopdi remembers the US soldiers deployed in Shiandanga during the Second World War, she obliquely invokes a contemporary parallel. This is the ubiquitous presence of the American military in the 1960s theater of the Cold War, Vietnam being the prime example. Her remembrance is counterpoised with Dopdi's fierce if equally subjective pride in her "unadulterated black blood," abhorrence of "contamination," and her forefathers' ability to "guard over their women's blood," sentiments so very jarring to liberal-minded sensibilities, and seemingly filled with essentialist, patriarchal, and racialist overtones. However, the consciousness of the international counteracts and, in fact, objectively transforms Draupadi's chauvinistic sense of belonging.

The force of this passage lies in its juxtaposition of semi-realized and incomplete perceptions of the self that act on and against each other. The result, I would claim, is a reversal of the *blut und bloten* (blood and soil) ideology of chauvinism into its polar opposite, the notion of subaltern internationalism. The text indirectly, and directly, aligns Dopdi with ongoing anticolonial resistances worldwide, whether these are in Asia, Africa, or the Black Americas. The explicit mention of American militaristic expansion suggests that such a possibility is not too far-fetched. The more significant part, nonetheless, is how the problematical formulation of "black blood" complicates – rather than reinforces – a phenotypical definition of race. If the passage invokes Dopdi's perception of an "unadulterated" Blackness, pure in terms of blood and soil, such a past exists only negatively in the present. In other words, Dopdi expresses not so much the desire of going back to the past but to the impossibility of such an enterprise; the passage articulates the absolute and irrevocable destruction of prior subaltern identities by the imperialist politics of the present. On the other hand, what her reflection foregrounds is the characteristic movement of dialectical thought: a conception of the chasm between the world as it *is* and what it could *be*. In other words, we glimpse the emergent relationship of the local conflict (Captain Arjan's "dread of black-skinned people," 393; Senanayak fear of "Draupadi's black body," 402 etc.) to contemporaneous struggles elsewhere, without – it is important to reiterate – exact analogies.[17]

Certainly, the political analogy between Asian – such as Vietnamese, Korean, and Chinese – anticolonial struggles and Black self-determination in Africa and the Americas was a commonplace for a large number of intellectuals located within the West. One only need recall, in the US context alone, the work of Black artists and activists such as Amiri Baraka, Sonia Sanchez, George Jackson, and Elaine Brown. This radical vision holds equally true in India even if these are far less known. Dopdi's "black blood" belongs to the same order of the linguistic-aesthetic imagination as Utpal Dutt's border blurring "armed Negro (*sic*) farmers" of "Naxalbari" in *The Rights of Man* (138). To be clear, such analogies paid close attention to the historical specificity of each situation on its own terms and did not attempt a blanket definition of resistance. Blackness emerges as a political category in Mahasweta Devi, just as it does for her contemporaries such as Utpal Dutt, as part of an ongoing and affinitive conversation on race and caste. In western India, the case of the Dalit Panthers illustrates yet another example of internationalist political Blackness; the passage on Dopdi's Black ancestors emerges in a fresh light when read in the terms of these and other interrelated histories.[18]

In "Draupadi," the narrative links the local to the global in other ways too. The protagonist's earthly and deeply felt sense of belonging is contrasted to the abstract, disembodied language of low-intensity warfare. We see this movement very clearly in the following passage, which ventriloquizes Dopdi's stream of consciousness and articulates (once again) a literary mixed style:

> Surja Sahu. Then a *telegraphic message* from Shiuri. *Special train. Army.* The *jeep* didn't come up to Bakuli. *March-march-march.* The *crunch-crunch-crunch* of gravel under hobnailed boots. *Cordon up. Commands* on the *mike.* Jugal Mandal; Satish Mandal, Rana *alias* Prabir *alias* Dipak, Dulna Majhi-Dopdi Mejhen *surrender surrender surrender. No surrender surrender. Mow-mow-mow down the village.* Putt-putt putt-putt – *cordite* in the air – putt-putt – *round the clock* – putt-putt. *Flame thrower.* Bakuli

is burning. *More men and women, children ... fire-fire. Close canal approach. Over-over-over by nightfall.* Dopdi and Dulna had crawled on their stomachs to safety. (399, italics indicate English in the original)

The passage begins with Surja Sahu and ends with Dopdi: in between, however, we move away from the details of local names and places to the impressionistic imagery of counterinsurgency. The former set of details is grounded in Dopdi's particular circumstance; the latter is global and inhuman, free of context and history. Dopdi herself perceives the operation as a *sensory* experience, a series of onomatopoeic sounds and fleeting images impinges on her consciousness. These are meaningful and meaningless, visceral and abstract at the same time. In formal terms, the mixed style of the passage – combining sound and image, proper names, English commands, and narrative description in one continuous thread – parallels the divided nature of her consciousness, one that is simultaneously mediated by localized and imperial forces indistinguishable from each other. In sharp contrast, Dopdi's antagonist, Senanayak, who is brought in after the end of this particular military operation, manifests the process of consciousness formation in a markedly different way.

The narrative portrayal of Senanayak precisely illuminates, I wish to suggest, the type of subjectivity formed by transculturation from above. The "chief of soldiers," Senanayak is a master of counterinsurgency, as well as a properly Brechtian study in the "fierce caricature" of tradition. In an attempt to generate confidence among the troops, Senanayak delivers a racist speech on the Sikhs' "martial genius" and assures Arjan, a Sikh, that "power also explodes from the *male organ* of a gun" (393, italics indicate English original). Here the story's retelling of the *Mahabharata* comes to a dead stop: Senanayak becomes the grotesque parody of Lord Krishna, Arjuna's spiritual guide and military advisor in the *Bhagavad-Gita* (part of the *Mahabharata*). Unlike the epic, where the benevolent Krishna – or Dharma, depending on the version – saves Draupadi's "honor" through an act of divine magic, preventing her disrobing at the hands of the villainous Kaurava kings, it is Senanayak who orders Dopdi's torture, rape, and mutilation in the story. "Make her," he calmly counsels his soldiers (401). But "Draupadi" does not merely illuminate the present-day degeneration of idols and ideas of benevolence. In a contiguous vein, the story interrogates the notion of divinely ordained authority too, one that had animated a variety of the *Bhagavad-Gita*'s classical and premodern interpreters from Sankaracharya to Madhava, and modern readers from Tagore and Gandhi to Kosambi and Matilal.[19]

There exists a neat narrative symmetry between the figures of Senanayak and Dopdi, representing, one might add, two sides of a tensely poised yet evolving dialectic. Senanayak is the lawgiver, Dharma, in the rational, bureaucratized world of counterinsurgency operations. If the hallmark of divine authority is its all-encompassing knowledge of the inhabited world (omniscient ecumenism), Senanayak is its perfect contemporary parody, one that "knows the activities and capacities of the opposition better than they themselves do" (393). He is a scholar who is scrupulously up-to date with contemporary "literature" on war and participant-trauma (400). Furthermore, Senanayak plans to "write on all this in the future" and has "published an article about information storage in brain cells" (394, 400). Senanayak is repeatedly shown reading. His materials are wide ranging: from the *Army Handbook* (which advises that guerrillas should be "annihilated" at first sight), through Rolf Hochhuth's play *The Deputy*, to David Morrell's novel *First Blood*.

Senanayak's reading choices – inseparable, one might say, from his investment in textuality, in "literature" and "writing" – have not garnered enough attention from scholars. The texts by Hochhuth and Morrell are imported from contemporary history. As somewhat lowbrow popular texts, they represent the ideological divide between the Soviet and US blocs during the Cold War. Hochhuth's *The Deputy*, whose first production was directed by Brecht's one-time collaborator Erwin Piscator, in West Berlin in 1963, controversially presents Pope Pius XII's complicity in the Holocaust. This was a topic well suited to Soviet hegemonic narrative, and the play was generally popular among Left-wing activists sympathetic to the Soviet Union. On the other hand, Morrell's *First Blood* is a novel published in 1972 about a Vietnam veteran, Rambo, and his inability to cope with posttraumatic stress disorder on his return home to the United States. In a move typical of most American representations, Morrell is almost entirely silent on the Vietnamese victims, choosing to focus on the cost visited on American soldiers such as Rambo. These texts provide significant context in "Draupadi," even as – and especially as – the reader comes across them as passing mentions. Such references invoke a history: equally, they shape the character of Senanayak, who appears (unlike Draupadi) well informed about fascism, communism, the Cold War, and a host of other issues. Such knowledge affirms his sense of superiority over his tribal, illiterate opponents.

Senanayak's knowledge is abstract and two-dimensional: it is the world viewed from above, comparable to the American bombardment of Vietnam. He sympathizes "in theory" with "harvest workers" and "Anti-

Fascist" politics. He is eager to "become one" with the enemy, both out of strategic pragmatism and genuine sentiment. However, his personal feelings are not an issue when it comes to "apprehending and eliminating" those same figures. Sagely, he avers, "today he is getting rid of the young . . . [yet] he, like Shakespeare, believes in delivering the world's legacy into youth's hands" (394). Despite or perhaps precisely because of his excessive book learning, Senanayak cannot make head or tail of the slogans used by the dying Dulna Majhi, Dopdi's husband. He has to rely on external "tribal-specialists" for deciphering language when it is three-dimensional and earthy, *as speech* (394–395). Senanayak is both "elated" at Dopdi's capture since it is a testament to his specialized skills and yet filled with "regret" since Dopdi fails to match his heightened expectation of survival skills among people of the harvest worker class (400). Senanayak fails to comprehend the language, the materiality, and the praxis of subaltern internationalism.

In embodying so many startling contradictions between theory and praxis, Senanayak's character – to be clear – does not provide comic relief. Rather, the caricature is deadly serious: he is a literal embodiment of Kant's famous maxim about arguing as much as you will, and about what you will, but obey! To put this in slightly different terms, Senanayak represents a *static* character, trapped within his own narcissism and megalomania, a docile if alienated citizen. His knowledge of himself and the world around him remains unchanged by his global reading or his interactions with other characters. Senanayak remains till the very end a deracinated individual with no social ties, identity, or even a proper name – identified only by his mercenary "private" role (in the Kantian sense) as "chief of soldiers." The story seems to suggest that like him, those with superficial knowledge of but no situated investment in subaltern history end up serving at the altar of empire.

Draupadi, on the other hand, evolves during the course of the story. It is key to any politics of liberation that consciousness undergoes subjective and objective transformation: in other words, that the subject breaks with the inherited hegemonic ideas of dominant groups and achieves her own concrete-processive ideas. At a crucial juncture, Dopdi's internalized patriarchy and chauvinism – pride in her forefathers and so on – is overcome by the radical consciousness of feminist and internationalist solidarity. This is related to, and yet distinct from, Dopdi's literal awakening to consciousness after her disrobing and rape at the hands of Senanayak's soldiers. Spivak's commentary focalizes the latter moment powerfully: "It is only when she [Dopdi] crosses the sexual differential into the field of *what could only happen to a woman* that she emerges as the most powerful 'subject'" (389, original emphasis). However, tying Dopdi's "powerful subject[ivity]" solely to her gender identity ("only ... a woman") risks erasing her identity as a political organizer, as Nivedita Majumdar has observed ("Silencing the Subaltern"). These identities, of gender, location, politics, and in the last instance embodied consciousness, are all intimately braided in the unfolding of the narrative.

If "Draupadi" conjoins the State's relentless violation of *adivasi* populations and the seizure of their material resources, such processes have only accelerated in recent decades. The essential expansion of the State in recent periods of globalization constitutes the same ground as its apparent disappearance; we see this in more detail in the following section and in the subsequent chapter. Meanwhile, artists and their communities reclaim Mahasweta Devi's short story some three or more decades after its first publication. This is to say, in other words, that the lesson of "Draupadi" continues to be recounted and relived in the midst of diverse struggles for democratic rights and more.

Two examples from community-oriented theater stand out particularly in this regard. The first is the stage adaptation and performance of "Draupadi" in the year 2000 by the noted thespian Sabitri Heisnam and her group Kalakshetra Manipur in the northeastern province of Manipur. The production preceded if not directly galvanized the memorable protest a few years later, in 2004 in the state capital of Imphal, by women activists against sexual violence, murder, and legal impunity of the Indian paramilitary forces (a detailed overview of the episode is provided by Misri, "Performing Naked Protest"). A second and even more recent example is Devi's own recasting as "Amma," or mother, in the work of Dakxin Bajrange and his group Budhan Theater, that resists the ongoing criminalization of the Chhara community in the western province of Gujarat (see Bajrange, "'Amma' and Budhan Theatre"). That both of these instances of Devi's reception are from the realm of community theater is significant yet unsurprising: the interaction between people's theater and fiction turns full circle as well as migrating to other regional contexts. In the next section, we explore – through the work of Arundhati Roy – these flowing forms of solidarity in another genre, nonfiction reportage or essay.

Roy, Nonfiction, and the Literary Narrator

Is nonfiction comparable to internationalist fiction? My answer is a qualified yes. Arundhati Roy's *Walking With the Comrades* is a formally ambitious essay, combining nonfiction, creative fiction, and photography. Originally written for and first published in 2010 in the Indian magazine *Outlook*, Roy's essay evidences signs of its journalistic intent. Roy reiterates, in an introductory form, the main lines of the issue: India's twenty-first-century push for modernization and global integration, the State-led appropriation of commonly held lands for mining and resource extraction, the resistance of *adivasi* communities, the armed conflict and "encounters" between community groups and government forces, and so on. The essay provides extensive information on the Naxalite movement and the previous history of the Gond tribals, both presumably aimed at a readership that is not familiar with either. This aspect is mostly unremarkable: well researched without being exceptional, a human interest-style narrative on subaltern resistance to capitalist globalization, another example of what is already a minor genre in India.

Viewed from another angle, the significance of the essay was not so much the content – despite its controversial reception in India – but what it stood for. *Walking* presented the first account of the Naxalite movement written by a globally recognized Anglophone writer and published in a nationally circulated magazine. Even then, the significance of *Walking* lay not in its publication venue or in the fame of its author. Roy is arguably the country's best-known oppositional intellectual, unlike, say, the no less vital but overlooked figures of Sabitri Heisnam, Anuradha Ghandy, or Meena Kandaswamy. Equally, Roy's English-language essay incorporated aspects of a genre so marginalized as to be almost invisible to contemporary readers: vernacular nonfiction writing.

Vernacular nonfiction texts such as *Jangalnama* or *Jaitrayatra,* written in Punjabi and Telugu respectively, locate a twenty-first-century constellation of internationalist writing that is largely unknown to most Anglophone and metropolitan readers. Yet the very fact of its (negative) presence complicates the free-floating dissemination of a text such as *Walking,* and illuminates Roy's intervention as part of an ongoing, if obscured, conversation among like-minded writers in India and elsewhere. Furthermore, these texts attest to the persistence of an older tradition of anticolonial and internationalist "reportage." Over the course of the twentieth century, reportage conveyed the struggles of popular movements to millions of readers worldwide. Examples would include the work of activist-intellectuals such as John Reid, Agnes Smedley, Basil Davidson, Stephanie Urdang, and Ryszard Kapuściński (see Zubel, "Literary Reportage," for an excellent survey). In the Indian context, figures such as Saurin Sen and Nirmal Verma, who wrote in Bengali and Hindi, respectively, provide similar examples. In the profusion of contemporary web journalism and platforms of print, visual, and digital media, we should treat the persistence of such a marginal, contrarian corpus with greater attention – not less, for reasons I highlight next.

I wish to suggest that *Walking*, in ways that have been little discussed so far, belongs to as well as draws from the tradition of reportage. I do not use the term "reportage" in the pejorative sense of passivity, as Lukács once did in applying it to Brecht among others ("Reportage or Portrayal?"). Rather, I contend that Roy's renown as a literary figure has, quite paradoxically, obscured the fact that *Walking* shares remarkable parallels and differences with a host of other texts. A corollary to this argument is that such counterpoints, far from flattening or reducing the individual text to its generic identity or historical context, in fact, highlights the text's particular and contemporary intervention. In other words, I am arguing that any discussion of the specificity of a text, fiction *and* nonfiction alike, needs to be complemented by considering its formal affiliations. Not only do the latter enable contextualization, where form is the concrete manifestation of history, it also sheds light on how that history is constructed in its material content. Finally, by re-constellating *Walking*, my reading seeks to problematize the academic abandonment of Roy as an essayist. Nagesh Rao has previously drawn attention to this aporia in a 2008 essay, remarking, "Roy the novelist was easily welcomed into the liberal multicultural classroom but Roy the essayist has been asked to wait outside" ("The Politics of Genre" 161). More than a decade later, the situation has not changed.[20]

To that end, I turn to *Jangalnama*, a first-person nonfictional account of Gond *adivasi* activist camps located in Chhattisgarh province's Bastar district in central India. Written by Satnam, pseudonym of the writer Gurmeet Singh, *Jangalnama* was published in Punjabi in 2004 and soon thereafter translated into Hindi and then to English. The reportage text, which describes in painstaking detail the extermination of *adivasi* communities and resistance movements under the security state's rhetoric of "counterinsurgency operations," serves as an early model for several accounts. This includes the example of Roy's *Walking*, published six years later, as well as a host of subsequent texts written in English and other Indian languages. Of course, it needs to be underscored that a Punjabi-language text on Gond *adivasi* resistance (or the theatrical reclamation in Meitei of a Bengali text, as with Sabitri Heisnam and "Draupadi") participates in a kind of subnational, regional-linguistic internationalism that is nearly impossible to conceptualize. I discuss the regional-linguistic in greater detail in the next chapter.[21]

Jangalnama serves as an immediate precedent for *Walking*, in terms of both thematic content and narrative form. A comparison of form is especially helpful to illuminate this point. *Jangalnama* and *Walking* similarly deploy the structure of the "travelogue," nestled within this form one finds generic elements of the "diary" and the "essay." Both texts claim adherence to nonfiction reportage, with *Jangalnama* terming the literary as "fantasy." At the same time, despite their affinity to nonfiction, Satnam and Roy as we will see engage with specifically literary-formal categories to construct their narratives. Such formal and generic aspects, to repeat, are not marginal to the more serious thematic concerns of *adivasi* resistance and the articulations thereof. Rather, form and content shape each other. The mixed form of the travelogue-diary-essay-reportage enables these texts to negotiate the content of present-day internationalism.

Jangalnama's "Preface" declaims, "*Jangalnama* is not a book of research on jungles, nor is it an imaginary, literary piece, part truth and part fantasy [...] . The characters in this book, who are always prepared to sacrifice themselves for their ideals, are living human beings" (vii). The preface sets the tone for the rest of the text. The author trenchantly claims verisimilitude and truth, while, interestingly, eschewing the twin realms of "research" and "imaginary, literary ... fantasy." There is a suggestion here that the paradigms of research and "literary piece(s)," with their respective emphasis on impartial and subjective assessment, are equally complicit in furthering the status quo. These statements might be taken as classic examples of what Priyamvada Gopal terms "oppositional writing," a point we will return to shortly.

By contrast, in describing *Jangalnama* as "a diary or a travelogue," the narrator claims a more intimate yet objective space of engagement that is neither exclusively empiricist documentary nor subjective experiential. A representative passage will illustrate this best:

> There was also talk of organizing an anti-war movement. On the whole, the kitchen was an active platform for political debates and discussions.
>
> 'How will the tribals participate in an anti-war movement?' I asked out of sheer curiosity.
>
> They told me that they had been preparing people for the last two months, first against the threat of war and then against the war itself. They had organized a number of activities: several protest rallies had been carried out, effigies of Bush and Vajpayee burnt, and conferences held where hundreds and thousands had participated.

> I don't think news of these activities was published anywhere in the press. There was no mention of them at all. 'Civil society' controls the newspapers and the 'civilized world' has no interest in reading about the political activities of the people living in the jungles [...].
> Later, as I journeyed further into the jungle, I found out that most inhabitants of the jungle had only recently heard, for the first time, the names of Bush, Vajpayee, Musharraf and Afghanistan. The war had introduced these names to them as well as put them in the 'league of traitors'. Of course, these people do not know the meaning of treason. The only thing they know is that the contractors, helped by the police, loot the forests, and the government supports them. For them, America is an entity that backs this government and so, this entity too, is their enemy, just like the government. (22–23)

The narrative works laterally, incorporating the oral testimony of the participants and assimilating multiple points of view. In prioritizing the oral over the written, the text claims a horizontal affiliation to the very community it represents. *Jangalnama* refuses, as it were, the impulse to establish an independent authorial perspective. The passage illuminates too the processes, as well as the obstacles, of forging a localized vocabulary of resistance in the twenty-first century. Discussion, education, and organization are central to the former articulation, starting from the activists' communal kitchen and extending outward into the nonactivist sections of Gond society. Matters of local political economy, such as the exploitative role of private contractors and their nexus with the police, are connected to the role of the government. Distant names, places, and events are understood in terms of their relation to the same entity – the government. Ongoing global events such as the American intervention in Afghanistan or the role of India's neighboring nation Pakistan in the so-called War on Terror, signified by "[George W.] Bush," "[Atal Behari] Vajpayee," "[Pervez] Musharraf" and "Afghanistan," enter into and become part of the daily idiom.[22]

The Gond *adivasi* adaptation of the term "the government" deserves emphasis: in the remote activist camps, the postcolonial nation-state – signified by the term "government" – continues to be *the* arbiter, antagonist, and concrete horizon of activist orientation and democratic aspirations. The nation-state so considered is distinct from the notion of a postnational globalized order. In the latter, the existing structures of the nation-state are (said to be) reduced in importance if not rendered altogether irrelevant. What the activists articulate is a much more nuanced understanding of the globalized nation-state: that the latter is reconfigured and altered, for sure, but far from obsolete. Rather, the telos of anticolonial nationalism has converged, in the distinct figure of the state, with that of capitalist globalization. In the same passage, an unnamed activist captures the transformation as follows: "'Today, in India, nationalism means accepting American imperialism,' one of them said, triggering laughter all around. 'This is the new globalization,' he continued, 'where the national interests of countries like India and imperialist interests have been *merged* into one'" (22–23, emphasis added). Conceptualizing "the government" as a merger of national and imperial interests allows the activists to see continuities, in other words, between local resistance and the global order, as something that is mediated through and by the nation-state.

Jangalnama articulates the notion of "civil society" in similarly intertwined terms. The radio aids information retrieval for the activists, enabling news of global affairs to circulate in the remote camps. At the same time, as we see in the earlier passage, newspapers ensure that "the political activities of the people living in the jungles" are never disseminated outside. The civilized world of India's metropolitan cities, where public opinion is shaped by corporatized print and visual media, is separated from the forest dwellers of Bastar by much more than geography. Once more, we see the conflict between the textual of the newspapers and the aural/oral of radio. Interestingly, the jungle, despite its exclusion from the civilized world, represents continuities with the latter. In both instances, the same vectors of dominant social relations determine the flow of information.

The narrator dramatizes a key question: "How will the tribals participate in an anti-war movement?" (22). This provocation directly gestures to the interrelations between subaltern movements and internationalist writing. *Jangalnama* highlights what many recent works of theory simply ignore: namely, that internationalism cannot be measured simply by the positive ability to cross state borders. For subaltern groups in the peripheries, on the one hand, challenging imperialism means *in effect* resisting the altered conditions of their own mediated existence, often within the bounded parameters of the nation-state and civil society. This is not simply a matter of pragmatic expediency, strategic failure, or the limited scope of the imagination. On the other hand, the narrator's ironic query foregrounds the distance between the perception and recognition of solidarity and the vexed possibility of their *articulation*; the former remains no less internationalist in essence even when – and especially when – coercively rendered local, regional, or subnational in appearance.

In contextualizing antiwar agency in Bastar, *Jangalnama* raises once again those issues so very familiar to intellectuals of earlier decades: the intransigent state, civil society, and bourgeois hegemony over language and representation. At the heart of *Jangalnama*'s narrative are the material struggles of communities and the related question of their alienation from others. The same pattern of exploitation and resistance is seen worldwide, yet the ways in which affected populations can exchange ideas *among* themselves are severely limited. This is as true for forcibly dispersed and/or localized Gond activists in India as for indigenous movements elsewhere: in the Amazon basin in Brazil and Bolivia, in the northern United States and Canada, or in Australia and New Zealand.

It follows that the crucial issue of self-representation (in the dual sense of politics and aesthetics) is necessarily related to, and draws its intellectual energy from, another key concern: locating a particular text within a broader poetic-literary history of representation. *Jangalnama*'s interrogative "how will the tribals participate?" is then simultaneously a question of "how will such participation be recorded for posterity?" The text itself suggests that articulation is overdetermined within the structure of global signification. Overdetermination ensures that these resistant communities – and the texts that articulate them – are either ignored or appropriated within a narrative of "development." Still, rather than *accepting* this scenario as yet another instance of subalterns' inability to speak, *Jangalnama* traces an alternative archive of counter-hegemonic representation, through oral testimony, among other things. In other words, we are back to the impossible yet familiar territory of Mahasweta Devi's nonfiction text *Jhansir Rani,* on the 1857 rebels, its sources comprising "popular ballads ... and old wives' tales." Still, the writerly engagement with subaltern self-conception on the latter's own grounds has been rendered far more intractable in recent decades.

Arundhati Roy's *Walking* charts a similar path to *Jangalnama*, drawing from and elaborating on many of the themes of Satnam's comradely text. It is interesting to note – as an aside – that *Walking* is not the first instance of Roy's engagement with the Naxalites. That credit goes to the novel *The God of Small Things*, published in 1997, which features the character of Velutha, a Paravan (untouchable caste) factory worker and Naxalite activist in late 1960s Kerala. Velutha's trajectory illuminates the patriarchal and caste fault lines of Malayali society. His twin acts of resistance and defiance, namely political organizing against the upper-caste factory owners and romantic relationship with an upper-caste woman, condemn Velutha to violent police torture and death in a prison cell. He is an outlier – as are most major characters in *The God of Small Things*. At the same time, the novel relegates Naxalism as a movement to the background. By contrast, *Walking*, written more than a decade later, focalizes the Gond Naxalites of Chhattisgarh both as discrete powerful individuals and as a powerful community of resistance. Perhaps such a change can be attributed to Roy's amplified political commitments in the intervening period; more plausibly, it is a function of nonfiction's greater flexibility regarding content.[23]

Unlike Satnam's explicitly solidaristic text, however, Roy's essay is situated in the bland genre of embedded journalism. *Walking* marks an ambitious – and to my mind, successful – attempt to redefine the scope of the latter. It accommodates and reverses the widespread trend in contemporary fiction and nonfiction alike that incorporates elements of social and political history. By contrast, Roy's text inserts an exaggeratedly subjective and naïve component into a work of nonfiction, highlighting its ability to articulate resistance. What distinguishes *Walking* is this literary sensibility, manifested most prominently in its narrative "voice." Going beyond the emphases of objective naturalism, the essay attempts to create a new domain of critical thought that militates against the status quo. Such a move toward a mixed form but from the other end is not limited to social justice movements though, arguably, the latter inspire it. To frame this differently, Roy pushes against the permissible and the possible limits of the real through the realm of the imagination. By deploying language, orality, and media in creative – and as we see later, entirely unanticipated – ways, it problematizes existing knowledge and simultaneously gestures to the unseen and unknown. In so doing, *Walking* formally aligns itself with the dialogic literary practice of "Draupadi" and other internationalist writing.

Walking deploys the figure of the observer, a standard feature in reportage such as *Jangalnama*, to unsettling effect. For the narrator venturing into the forests of Dandakaranya, the tribal people are very much an unknown entity. She, too, is equally a surprise to the militants, who expect to see "a man rather than a woman" (*Walking* 38). This leads to the possibility of misunderstanding; the narrator fears that she and the guide she is supposed to meet may not recognize each other. There is parity, at the very outset of the text, on each side's unpreparedness for the other. The same is also true of the reader perhaps. The title of the essay sets up deliberately misleading expectations. "Walking with the comrades" implies a sense of affinity, where "walking" implies traveling together, and "comrades" references its dual meaning, both the Gond activists' communist political identity as well as their implied camaraderie with the narrator and the reader. This sense of fellowship between subject and object is severely and abruptly destroyed – "for them [the militants], roads are not meant for walking on. They're meant only to be crossed or, as is increasingly becoming the case, ambushed" (68) – creating a conflict between the title's implied purpose and what the essay actually does.

The essay is both a *testimonio* and an *anti-testimonio* (see Chapter 2's discussion). The narrator's first impressions of Dantewada, the town from which she begins her journey to the forests, is striking in its invocation of opposites and inverted sense of reality: "There are many ways to describe Dantewada. It's an oxymoron. It's a border town smack in the heart of India" (38). The town is an unreal space, like an enchanted land in a fable yet dystopian in its harshness, where, "the police wear plain clothes and the rebels wear uniforms .... Women who have been raped are in police custody. The rapists give speeches in the bazaar." As the narrator placidly suggests, Dantewada is "an upside-down, inside-out town" (38). The emotionless, objective tone of this statement further serves to accentuate the horrifying implications of state violence, such as the use of rape as an instrument of counterinsurgency.[24] The guerrilla-controlled territories beyond the town of Dantewada are described later in the same passage as "the place the police call 'Pakistan,'" implying that its inhabitants are enemies of the Indian nation on whom violence can be legally justified. It is the classic binary logic of both nationalist and imperialist "othering."

The placid tone soon begins to disappear. Later on, the narrator comes to revise her previous description of the "enemy aliens" as she comes to know them intimately. In a description that almost invites the reader's skepticism, the narrator is overjoyed to find: "My private suite in a thousand-star hotel. I'm surrounded by these strange, beautiful children with their curious arsenal" (57). She also notes with surprise, "Dandakaranya was full of people who had many names and fluid identities" (89). The narrator is similarly amazed by the unexpected at many points. This is far from uncritical sentimentalism or hyperbolic style, charges leveled by Roy's critics.[25]

Amazement and surprise, I wish to underscore, serve as *organizational motifs* in the essay. The seemingly arbitrary juxtapositions of incommensurable objects and ideas have more than a formal implication: these defamiliarize and re-constellate the old and the new alike. Thus at one point in the essay, the narrator compares – through a remarkable jump – the Gond Naxals to the putative father of the nation, in terms of their respective environment-friendly practices: "I cannot believe this army. As far as consumption goes, it's more Gandhian than any Gandhian, and has a lighter carbon footprint than any climate change evangelist" (94). The narrator's sense of wonder is borne out of two factors: the unexpected nature of life in the forest and the series of encounters with other individuals. The testimonies of these persons, "Comrades" Kamala, Venu, Raju, Madhav, Rinki – some named, many more unnamed – constitute concrete objects. As oral testimonies, these manage to complicate the narrator's vision and anxiety about this "army." The text delicately weaves in an intertextual reference to the protagonist of Roy's own novel *The God of Small Things*, as well: the narrator wonders, "Who should I be tonight? Kaamraid [Comrade] Rahel, under the stars?" (60). In this vein, the essay moves away from verisimilitude to take on greater and extended speculative dimensions. Documentary description, so essential to establishing objective authority – such as that of the "climate change evangelist" perhaps – is revealed to be an artifice, since it is impossible to sustain objectivity in the face of contradictory appearances and multiple points of view. Meanwhile, it may be said that the essay remains true to Roy's earlier novel, and the former's insistent stylistic-political commitment to consider the "footprint" of armies and God alike from the perspective of "small things."

By drawing our attention, repeatedly, to the narrator's amazement as a recurrent motif, *Walking* reworks the generic conventions of the neutral observer and objective reportage. There is the attendant problem of incomprehension, too, in the litany of languages spoken by the comrades – "Gondi, Halbi, Telugu, Punjabi, and Malayalam," and only one person speaks any "English" (62). The text subtly highlights the fraught position of the narrator. This is done through a growing distinction between Roy the author and the narrator as a separate entity. At least one reader of *Walking* has remarked that the latter's persona seems marked by a litany of "usual liberal prejudices" (Gopal, "Concerning Maoism" 122).[26] With increasing visibility, the separation between author and unreliable narrator – characteristic of fiction rather than nonfiction – is deployed in the nonfiction text. Let us consider the following passage:

> I'm not sure whether I'm looking forward to the Bhumkal celebrations. I fear I'll see traditional tribal dances stiffened by Maoist propaganda, rousing, rhetorical speeches and an obedient audience with glazed eyes. We arrive at the grounds quite late in the evening. A temporary monument of bamboo scaffolding wrapped in red cloth has been erected. On top, above the hammer and sickle of the Maoist party, is the bow and arrow of the Janatana Sarkar [local people's government], wrapped in

silver foil. Appropriate, the hierarchy. The stage is huge, also temporary, on sturdy scaffolding covered by a thick layer of mud plaster. Already there are small fires scattered around the ground, people have begun to arrive and are cooking their evening meal. They're only silhouettes in the dark. (97–98)

The off-guard, seemingly innocent remarks at the beginning, as well as the all-important last sentence, provide the interpretive key to the rest of the passage. Guised as negative non-anticipation, "I'm not sure whether I'm looking forward," the narrator confesses her personal feelings to the reader. In any case, her initial sense of unease is belied by the mundane events that follow: as a matter of fact, these are wholly incommensurate with the former. The opening sets up false anxieties, belied by the rest of the passage. But the significance, the genuine thrust of the description lies elsewhere. The narrator's remarks color the passage with a particular world view, revealing itself for what it is, a *class perspective*. This is the voice of the bourgeois intellectual "I," animated by a well-intentioned concern that feckless tribals might, once more, succumb to "Maoist propaganda," associated with the "totalitarian" tyrannies of a bygone century. It encapsulates the tortuous benevolence with subaltern practices and beliefs (mimicking Devi's Senanayak) and presents a rhetorical form of "I understand ... but."

On the other hand, it is the narrator's own vision that is shown as static and two-dimensional, "glazed" and "stiffened." In the "hierarchy" of things described, she can – literally – see the banners and the stage but not the people sitting below. In what surely counts as an example of narrative aporia, the "people" are unfinished spectral sketches. They appear as "only silhouettes in the dark"; the lack of "evening" light, a naturalistic detail, becomes a metaphor for the narrator's own benighted perspective. By highlighting the narrator's overdetermined perspective, *Walking* connects representation to determinate social relations. The hegemony of a dominant history is expressed as a formal aspect of the text, I suggest, in the figure of the sympathetic narrator. Such a formal attribute is both shaped by and in turn illuminates material social relations between metropolitan middle-class intellectuals and Gond tribals in the periphery. Many such examples can be cited from the text. Far from showing naïveté, the narrator's anxiety is a function of the real yet unstable power that she wields over the others by virtue of class status, location, and stranglehold over culture. In other words, and without stretching the comparison too much – the naïve narrator belongs to the same (bourgeois-cosmopolitan) order of things as the counterinsurgency chief, Senanayak.

Yet, nestled within the heart of the passage, undercutting the narrator's dominant position, is a radically contrarian presence, another social force. The "Bhumkal celebrations," mentioned in passing by the narrator, commemorate a popular indigenous resistance to land seizure, dating back to the 1910 uprising of the same name. The 1910 Bhumkal that engulfed major areas of Chhattisgarh (then part of the blandly named Central Provinces), in turn, was the culmination of smaller insurrections going back to the early and mid-nineteenth century. Could it be that the "rousing speeches" and "tribal dance" assemble a "temporary monument" to subaltern counter-history, one that variously incorporates religious, anticolonial nationalist, and Maoist, in short, conjunctural idioms to articulate itself? Such articulation is necessarily transient and still registers the twists and turns of sustained historical *movement*. In a jungle reality constituted by contradictory appearances, the Bhumkal celebrations of the present moment trace the remarkable persistence of the oral and the plastic of collective memory; these are etched in "bow and arrow," "hammer and sickle," "bamboo," "mud plaster," "red cloth," and "silver foil." Resisting the narrator's expectations of "traditional tribal dance" (the perfect empty signifier of bourgeois description), the constellation of material objects in and around the "stage" of performance gestures to a dynamic and evolving tradition of the people, one that, significantly, the narrator does not get to witness – and which the passage postpones to the future. The text hints at the possibility of subaltern expression, too, unrealized yet manifested in the "small fires scattered around," and the patient waiting of the "people [who] have *begun to arrive.*" The reader, like the narrator, does not get to see or know this gathered collective in action.

Thus it is the narrator, initially presented to the reader as an individual with complex feelings, who proves impervious to nuance in the end. By contrast, quotidian objects and barely visible subjects, nondescript when seen through the narrator's eyes, take on greater layers of illumination at second reading. The artistic achievement of the passage (not to be confused with the perspective of the narrator and even less with the author) lies in this unexpected inversion. Such a reversal signals what is really at stake in the narrative. The text forces us to question neutral descriptions and the presentation of subjective facts. By presenting the narrator as partial, despite herself, and simultaneously gesturing to a submerged discourse that resists the narrator's views, *Walking* dramatizes – or stages – social *agon* within its own narrative structure.

I would extend this proposition further: *Walking* formulates in narrative *form* what for its fraternal texts, *Jangalnama* – and earlier "Draupadi" – is still a matter of narrative *content*. The key issue is subaltern self-representation, one that *Jangalnama* framed as a terse question – "How will the tribals participate in an anti-war movement?" If Gond consciousness and activism are absent in the proliferation of contemporary media, which *Jangalnama* describes at length, then *Walking* reprises and reenacts the same alienation-displacement as a formal component of its narrative. The text promotes a speculative and partial narrative voice to achieve this task, just as it encourages a false sense of communication between the narrator and the reader that is actually revealed to be insulation from the tribal "other."

Such layering, moreover, does not contradict *Jangalnama*'s injunction against "literary fantasy." Rather, as diverse oppositional texts, *Jangalnama* and *Walking* complement each other in unexpected ways. If anything, what is interrogated in the literary is the exclusive focus on alienated textuality that undervalues the oral, corporeal, and material components of civic life. Both texts call into question scientific objectivity and complicate the empiricist notion of research; each in its own way demonstrates how the proliferation of contemporary knowledge as an assortment of facts and feelings – in 24/7 news and social media, in the public sphere of civil society – mediates the gradual erasure of agonistic interrelations between subject and object. Like Mahasweta Devi and others earlier, Satnam and Arundhati Roy strive for a more capacious understanding of the dynamic between the objective and the literary.

Another aspect to consider is *Walking*'s innovative use of photographs. The essay is interwoven with a series of photographs taken by the author, and her commentary on them offers unexpected contrasts, reversals, and inversions. These photos juxtapose the visual register to the nonfiction narrative and further unsettle the expectations of the reader/viewer. One photograph titled "The Long March" depicts a line of men and women carrying supplies, bags, and guns walking through the forest grass: the caption underneath says, "We are moving in a single file now. Myself, and one hundred 'senselessly violent,' bloodthirsty insurgents" (n.p.). The statement satirizes the notion of the liberal intellectual gone rogue, perhaps like a modern-day Indian metropolitan version of Colonel Kurtz among the "non-Indian" or "anti-Indian" natives.

Another striking example is a photograph of an empty forest with a close-up of blades of leaves. It is titled "Iron Ore Dust on Mango Leaves," and the commentary below reads, "There's an MoU [Memorandum of Understanding] on every mountain, river and forest glade. We are talking about social and environmental engineering on an unimaginable scale" (n.p.). Such a statement, once again, achieves narrative impact through the multimedia form of the essay, juxtaposing corporeal belonging against the abstract violence of national-global corporate capitalism. "Engineering" and "Memorandum of Understanding," science and commerce, combine in unanticipated ways: these terms trace the invisible and indeed "unimaginable" forces that shape the forest's tryst with so-called globalization. Within the space of the photograph, the commodification of nature is made palpable by the "dust" on "mango leaves." The barely visible mineral dust counters any notion of pristine nature and the latter's exact correlate, the traditional tribal; it also makes legible what is absent in the image itself – the unimaginable figure of the social. The photograph that is seemingly devoid of human presence negatively reveals the dialectical – interlinked and oppositional – presence of social mediation. Nature and corporate personhood mediate each other. To phrase this as a paradox: the image represents a leaf that is, at the same time, *not* a leaf. Perhaps the Gandhian ethic of (non-) consumption, riddled with myriad contradictions, acquires fresh urgencies of renewal at this moment.

The photographs in *Walking* explore the human-natural encounter at the very moment of capitalist climate catastrophe by juxtaposing unlikely objects and persons. Contrasted to the text's emphasis on the narrator, the images focus on the activists themselves: sometimes on individual figures, at other times on groups. The majority of the photographs profile women militants. Defying the expectations of the narrator, perhaps, they are dressed not in traditional Gond costume but the fatigues of a people's army. (Recall here Spivak's pointed remark: "Given the nature of the struggle, there is nothing bizarre in 'Comrade Dopdi,'" 390.) Rather than reifying these comrades as bloodthirsty insurgents (or equally stereotypical noble *adivasis*), the women are shown participating in the mundane activities of the camps alongside the men. Each photograph synchronically presents a slice of everyday life, depicting human beings in dynamic interaction with the world. Yet, by the very exceptional status of the insurgency itself, the everyday and diachronic submissions to social hierarchy that such interaction entails – in gendered labor, for instance – are refuted, temporarily if at all. The volubility of these subjects-in-image provides a sharp contrast to their deeper silence *within history*. Supposedly nonlocal, foreign idioms and objects, such as people's army and fatigues, form part of the activists' conjunctural identity. Such becoming, I have argued in this chapter, is best grasped as "encounters," emphasizing the unrealized, the unknown, and the impossible within each moment.

Finally, we conclude by highlighting a seemingly minor detail in *Walking* that strikes me as symptomatic and curious at a number of levels. This is the description of one activist that the text identifies as "Comrade Maase (which means Black Girl in Gondi) who has a price on her head . . . . Only Maase speaks English . . . from the way she hugs me I can tell she's a reader" (62). The text does not offer further details on Maase. Yet the terms deployed, "Black Girl," "English," and "reader," nevertheless suggest an unsolved paradox. The reference to Maase's reading might be taken to mean that there are alternative networks of readership, even within the reified domain of English, than the customary class of upwardly mobile citizens. Maase is not only an object of representation and expropriation (there is "a price on her head") but also someone who interprets and contests such processes on her own terms. But what does "Black Girl" mean?

Does the essay conjure an intertextual image from another realm, Sembène Ousmane's iconic short story and film *La Noire de* (Black Girl)? This could be a deliberate move, and the fact that the text emphatically marks the moment of translation by parenthesis and capitalization "(which means Black Girl in Gondi)" would then imply that "Maase" embodies the spirit of Sembène's "Diouana." If this is a plausible interpretation, then the detail is indeed about the essay's attempt to reclaim an older, now shrunken internationalist terrain. In other words, *Walking* encounters and situates Maase within a longer history of solidarity, as much to the blackness of Diouana as to Dopdi Mejhen. But how far does this relate to Maase herself – can she conduct a dialogue with her counterpart Diouana, in either English or French, or Gondi and Wolof? Can and should non-subaltern writers such as Roy intervene in such conversations? Obviously, *Walking* does not offer any answers but the question, I think, persists just under the surface of the essay.

A consideration of aesthetic style and narrative form is crucial to answering this question. Critique, we have seen, emerges through mixed form and provides a rejoinder to the false separation of autonomous art from social activism: form is indeed inseparable from the text's critique. This is a good juncture to coordinate our reading of the two primary texts, by Devi and Roy, respectively. As discussed earlier, Devi's "Draupadi" strategically combines various techniques such as stream-of-consciousness, interior monologue, caricature, and satire. Likewise, the story deploys a series of local and foreign intertextual references, ranging from classical and popular epic, people's theater, and transnational literature. This mixed style in "Draupadi" activates the horizontal and worldly solidarities of internationalism through explicit (thematic) and implicit (formal) means, while avoiding overt didacticism. Thus, Vietnam, the US empire, the Cold War, and pan-Africanist Black struggle, all can be said to impinge on the narrative without hindering for once the situated history of the Santhal resistance in Shiandanga and Radhabhumi.

Formally, too, as I have tried to show, "Draupadi" highlights the dialectical movement of consciousness as situated matter. On the one hand, Dopdi's grounded and cognitive-corporeal awareness evolves from chauvinism to internationalism. Senanayak's unanchored cosmopolitanism, on the other hand, remains stagnant and tied to his parochial and statist class function. Right at the end of the story, in her only direct address to Senanayak, "counter me" (colloquial for the English "encounter," an euphemism for state murder), Dopdi challenges the chief of soldiers (402). Perhaps, the short story's greatest achievement is the illumination of insurgent consciousness and its processive-transformative encounter with the State and the world.

Like "Draupadi," *Walking* illuminates a conceptual relationship between and across disparate conjunctures. Our reading of these encounters illuminates histories that are quite identical and non-identical, suspended between disparate forms of text and dispersed modes of consciousness (Dopdi and Saint Joan, Maase and Diouana, Gandhian Naxals and climate change, etc.). The common running thread is a *speculative* and *critical* concept of subaltern internationalism. Speculative, in the sense that each of these moments in the text reveals historically situated perceptions of the self and the world, and critical, because these – in constellation – negotiate a singular movement of history that remains unfinished. Speculation and unfinished form are always two sides of the same movement, as Theodor Adorno observed:

> Discontinuity is essential to the essay; its subject matter is always a conflict brought to a standstill. While the essay coordinates concepts with one another . . . it shrinks from any overarching concept to which they could all be subordinated. *What such concepts give the illusion of achieving,* their method knows to be impossible and yet tries to accomplish. ("The Essay as Form" 16, emphases added)

In an earlier passage, Adorno describes this in slightly different terms: "The way the essay appropriates concepts can best be compared to the behavior of someone in a foreign country who is forced to speak its language instead of piecing it together out of its elements according to rules learned in school" (13). The conceptualization and actualization of form, in other words, rely on interaction and engagement with as much as – perhaps or more than – a priori or objective knowledge of the world. The question of literary form here is not about the stylistic preferences of individual writers but the concrete conjunctures of unrealized history. The specific role of the non-subaltern, committed writer emerges in this context.

On the one hand, the act of representation – or mimesis – resists the pressure of teleological history and on the other hand seeks to connect the fragments to unity, by dispensing with the binaries between modernism and realism, literary and oral expression, the local and the foreign. Each of these, equally, embodies "concepts" or "culturally preformed objects" that are incommensurate with one another ("The Essay as Form" 3). "Draupadi" and *Walking* grapple with, to use Adorno's terms, "discontinuity" and "concepts" of the "foreign." The twin poles of subalternity and internationalism are conceptualized in a similar fashion. The texts articulate (and accordingly reflect in their own mixed formal structures) the content of social unity constituted by perpetually evolving forces in struggle with one another. If we express this in the dialectical language of Adorno, the method of the internationalist writer "coordinate(s) concepts with one another." This is a strategy that is aware of its impossible limits but still tries to accomplish them. Considered as a whole, internationalist writing is best described as speculative attempts (*Versuch* as in the essay), or what I have called "encounters," by writers to come to terms with the myriad ways in which subaltern individuals and communities articulate totality.

The attitudes of Devi, Roy, and the vernacular corpus I discussed offer a sharp contrast to the conceptual tendency to see subalternity as shapeless and lacking definition. In the latter, fragmented identity, signaled by the repeated invocation of intimate voice, affective location, and non-generalizability are valorized – in the strict sense of expropriated surplus value – to such an extent that the very idea of illumination central to internationalist writing is lost. What is forgotten, perhaps erased, is that capital as telos localizes subaltern labor while globalizing the alienation thereof, either as commodities or ideas and often both.

Equally, a conflation of internationalism with post-national cosmopolitanism as always transcending the nation-form ignores the mediations of combined and uneven development, dependency, and imperial domination – all of which determine the question of representation *negatively*. The alternative reification and downgrading of the local and the national – unwittingly and paradoxically – complement each other. The celebration of the local cannot be countered by denigrating the same, in theory, but rather by grasping the unrealized possibilities of this relation as I argue elsewhere.[27] We may here summarize the heart of the matter, that is capital and its determinate mediations of human labor: multiplied and proliferated through different levels not only of the nation-state, civil society, dominating and dominated classes, but also – as peripheral internationalist writers such as Devi and Roy are keenly aware – language, representation, and recognition. The following chapter discusses the specific literary-cultural forms of capitalist mediation in the New Indian Anglophone novel.

Notes

1. Tribal and *adivasi* (autochthonous or original inhabitant) are disputed umbrella terms referencing widely disparate ethnic minority groups who number in the hundreds of millions in India as well as other parts of South Asia. The Indian Constitution provides various safeguards for peoples classified as "Scheduled Tribes," though these are generally observed only in violation. I use the terms tribal and *adivasi* through the chapter and use specific ethnic identifiers such as Santhal and Gond wherever possible, to retain consistency across Mahasweta Devi's, Gayatri Spivak's, and Arundhati Roy's renditions of the term in Bengali and English.
2. The categories of "dominant" and "emergent" that Spivak draws on are best explored in Williams, *Marxism and Literature*. In comparative world literature scholarship, these are often focalized and not without controversy through another socialist activist-thinker Antonio Gramsci. To take just one example: Srivastava and Bhattacharya, *The Postcolonial Gramsci*, especially the essays by Cheah, Mignolo, Young and the interview of Spivak, and the review essays by Brennan, "Joining the Party," and Green, "On the Postcolonial Image of Gramsci." Further recent explorations of Gramsci's reception are Thomas, "Reconfiguring the Subaltern" and Shapiro and Lazarus, "Translatability, Combined Unevenness and World Literature." The freshly translated classic, René Zavaleta Mercado, *Towards a History of the National Popular in Bolivia*, renders a vital Latin American perspective on Gramscian categories.
3. Taking issue with the "talismanic reiteration of privileged conceptual categories such as 'hybridity' and 'ambivalence,'" Gopal comments, "even when an unambiguously liberationist and realist author such as Mahasweta Devi is brought to metropolitan academic attention by a distinguished theorist such as Gayatri Spivak (making for a salutary consideration of non-Anglophone texts), she must first be made fit for refined theoretical company" (*Literary Radicalism* 3). Wenzel points out in her reading of Devi's stories "Draupadi," "Douloti the Bountiful," and "Dhowli" that these emphasize the repeated *contests* over forests as socio-ecological spaces rather than peaceful coexistence, thereby illuminating the limits of postmodern and nativist ecocritical approaches (see Wenzel, "The Epic Struggle over India's Forests" and "Forest Fictions and Ecological Crises"). Lazarus's exploration of Mahasweta Devi (*The Postcolonial Unconscious* 41–45, 152 ff.) adumbrates, "what, in the postcolonial discussion, has tended to be indefinitely deferred: namely, the *content* of

subaltern consciousness" (155, original emphasis). Finally, as Nirmala Menon shows in her fine study that situates Kiran Desai and Arundhati Roy to non-Anglophone writers such as Mahasweta Devi, O.V. Vijayan, Lalithambika Antherjanam, and Girish Karnad, the postcolonial lacunae can be addressed by "moving beyond Anglophone and Francophone literatures to varied literatures" (*Remapping the Indian Postcolonial* 2–4).

4. On dialogue in fiction, see Bakhtin, *The Dialogic Imagination*. For philosophical humanism and mixed form or style, see Auerbach, *Mimesis*. Auerbach discusses the importance of Vico in several essays, such as "Giambattista Vico and the Idea of Philology," "Vico and Aesthetic Historism [Historicism]," "Vico and the National Spirit" et al., collected in *Time, History, and Literature*.

5. Chaudhuri suggests that vernacular periodicals such as *Parichay* were both "local and cosmopolitan." ("Translation" 596) A task for scholarship would consist of recovering the underexplored presence of women in these publications, not as marginal associates but as intellectuals on their own terms. On the one hand, Bengali-language periodicals and magazines served as "local forums for dissenters" (Nag, "Little Magazines" 110); less happily, on the other hand, in some cases these were key sites of reactionary ideology among the intelligentsia and the reading public.

6. The last name Devi "reflects a Hindu-Bengali social convention of referring to upper-caste women as 'Devi' meaning 'goddess.' Although the practise is now outdated, women writers from the past few generations, most of whom were from the upper castes, are habitually referred to using 'Devi'" (Mookerjea-Leonard 45). Mahasweta Devi is the only recent writer who maintained this upper-caste convention, perhaps to avoid using the patronymic. In this case, the intersection between anti-caste and feminist politics is complicated, to put it mildly.

7. In the bibliography, I list the English translations for these writers except in cases when I directly cite a Bengali-language text. Additionally, a new generation of critics has reclaimed the significance of mid-twentieth-century women's writing. See Barnita Bagchi on Rokeya Hossain, Debali Mookerjea-Leonard on Jyotirmoyee Devi, Dipannita Dutta on Ashapurna Devi, and Debjani Sengupta on Sabitri Roy.

8. Ania Loomba's recent work on activist women in anticolonial and postcolonial radical movements summarizes this point succinctly: "Partly because women's emancipation in India was, as in large parts of the colonized world, intertwined complexly with the struggle for independence, feminist scholarship in India has always been sharply conscious of the historical connections between women's personal, sexual, and political freedoms and the larger structures of social power" (*Revolutionary Desires* 12). Loomba unpacks the pitfalls of two tendencies: first, the empirical erasure of women from social movements and, second, the conceptual neglect of the interconnections between feminist and other types of solidarity politics.

9. Of these figures, perhaps the most influential in West Bengal of the 1960s and 1970s was Suprakash Ray (real name Sudhir Bhattacharya). For an appraisal of

Ray's importance in South Asian historiographical debates, see Gangopadhyay, "Biography of a Name."

10. To the best of my knowledge, no scholarship exists on Saurin Sen, either in English or Bengali. Yet, even as our too-abbreviated discussion indicates, Sen is a crucial literary figure in linking the various sites of 1960s radical struggles, perhaps more so than any other contemporary author.

11. Himani Bannerji's *The Mirror of Class* (1998) remains the compelling account of people's theater, especially tracing the significance of Bijan Bhattacharya's *Nabanna*. For analyses of Utpal Dutt's plays mentioned here: Nandi Bhatia, *Acts of Authority*; Rustom Bharucha, *Rehearsals of Revolution*; Abin Chakraborty on *Ajeya Vietnam/Invincible Vietnam*; and Auritro Majumder on *Manusher Adhikarey/Rights of Man*.

12. All subsequent quotations, unless noted otherwise, are from Spivak's English translation, which italicizes the English words and phrases in Mahasweta Devi's Bengali language text (cited as Devi, "Draupadi"). When needed, I have referenced the Bengali text (cited as Devi, *Agnigarbha*).

13. A dissenting note on the translation of "Draupadi," and especially the use of italics for English words and phrases is struck by Minoli Salgado, who writes: "While Spivak, the translator, is busy advocating cultural difference and disjunction in Mahasweta's text, the author herself is keen to focus on the generalized tribal experience in her work … which undermines Spivak's claim that Mahasweta's work punctures nationalist discourse" ("Tribal Stories" 135). In my own reading, I posit the dialectical and inseparable relation between "difference" and "generalized" forms. It is harder to accept Salgado's contention that the tactical demand for "mainstream" rights, in "Draupadi," is quite the same as accepting "nationalist discourse."

14. Here, quite obviously, I draw on Williams's *Marxism and Literature*, but also from his earlier texts, *Culture and Society* and *The Long Revolution*. Over the course of his own evolution as a thinker, Williams came to emphasize culture not so much as tradition, a body of texts etc., but as that which is acquired through lived experience.

15. For specific iterations of the postwar/postcolonial Brecht: in India, Dalmia, *Poetics, Plays, and Performances*; in Kenya, Thiong'o, *Moving the Center*; and Brown, *Utopian Generations*; in East Germany and South Africa, Kruger, *Post-Imperial Brecht*.

16. Among other Bangladeshi writers, Elias's novels *Chilekothar Sepai* (The Attic Soldier), *Khowabnama* (Dream Elegy), stories, and essays, *Sangskritir Bhanga Setu* (The Broken Bridge of Culture) illuminate the persistence of internationalist writing in the 1980s and 1990s. For commentaries, see Dasgupta, *Elegy and Dream* and Ghosh, *Akhtaruzzaman Elias*.

17. To be sure, the turn to the *volk* of blood and soil was characteristic of conservative thinkers in India as much as in Europe: in Heidegger's philosophy or Yeats's poetry, such a turn triggered a revanchist reaction to modernity. Conservative nationalism as well as modernism looked back, yearningly,

at a vanished past, which was often located, like Gauguin's Polynesians, in the figure of the distant other. This strategic evocation of absence, deliberate and precise, accentuated the isolation of the present-day atomized subject. Such formal overlaps between Left and Right need not distract from their key differences: in attitudes toward race, caste, and gender hierarchies, and social challenges from below and outside.

18. The Dalit Panthers, an important group of untouchable caste writers and activists, named themselves in a conscious reference to the Black Panther Party. The journal *United Asia* claimed, in 1972, "It may be that the American negro (*sic*) is fighting not only for himself and for his brethren in America but for all the . . . blacks of the world whether they be in America or in India" (qtd. in Slate, *Colored Cosmopolitanism* 134). In their 1973 manifesto, the Dalit Panthers extended the term "Third Dalit World" to mean not only untouchable castes in India but also the "working people, the landless and poor peasants, [and] women," in "Cambodia, Vietnam, Africa, Latin America," and other sites of anti-imperialist struggle ("Dalit Panther Manifesto," Joshi, *Untouchable!* 145).

19. For the contestatory readings of the *Bhagavad-Gita* and the *Mahabharata*, I draw the reader's attention to Matilal, "Krishna: In Defence of a Devious Deity," and earlier Kosambi, "Social and Economic Aspects of the Bhagavad-Gita," and the essays in the collection, Chakrabarti and Bandyopadhyay, *Mahabharata Now*.

20. I would qualify the critic's description of Arundhati Roy's "radical cosmopolitanism," which seems to conflate the internationalism that Roy draws on. Still, the stark contrast between Roy as a public intellectual and her academic underutilization, both in India and in the United States, illuminates a genuine problem. The omission of Roy's essays – as compared to her novel *The God of Small Things* – in academic scholarship reveals a narrow and conservative attitude toward what "counts" as literature.

21. Noteworthy accounts in English are Sudeep Chakravarti, *Red Sun: Travels in Naxalite Country* (2008); Gautam Navlakha, *Days and Nights in the Heartland of Rebellion* (2012); and Shubranshu Choudhary, *Let's Call Him Vasu: With the Maoists in Chhattisgarh* (2012), Alpa Shah, *Nightmarch* (2018) and in Telugu, D. Markandeya, *Bastarlo Janatana Jaitrayatra* (2013). These texts robustly expose the state's mistreatment of *adivasi* communities as evidenced by counterinsurgency operations since late 2009. Alongside, these writers make many judicious criticisms of the State's chief antagonist, the Communist Party of India (Maoist) and its strategy of armed struggle.

22. For a related theorization of imperial democracy in the aftermath of the War on Terror, see Roy's sharply polemical essay, originally delivered as a lecture in 2003, "Instant-Mix Imperial Democracy: Buy One Get One Free" (*An Ordinary Person's Guide*).

23. Roy's depiction of contending Marxist currents in *The God of Small Things* is the subject of a significant debate. On the one hand, Aijaz Ahmad charges *The God of Small Things* with, first, a hostile depiction of the parliamentary Left in

India and second, spuriously advocating sexual desire as the only antidote to social oppression ("Reading Arundhati Roy Politically"). On the other hand, Pranav Jani convincingly answers this early critique and demonstrates that the sexual and the political are far more interlinked in the novel than Ahmad is willing to allow. In a significant move that aligns fiction with nonfiction, Jani asserts, "Roy's novel and her essays, far from moving in divergent directions, are bound together by a political paradigm that is unmistakably progressive and leftist" ("Beyond 'Anticommunism'" 48).

24. It is worth remembering Arundhati Roy's review of the Shekhar Kapur film *Bandit Queen*, on the lower-caste female outlaw turned politician, Phoolan Devi. Published in 1994, Roy's review exposes the link between upper-caste militias, organized sexual violence, and their consistent erasure in mainstream Indian cinema. Roy's memorable line "Rape is the main dish. Caste is the sauce it swims in" anticipates her later and better-known interventions such as *The God of Small Things* (see Roy, "The Great Indian Rape Trick").

25. I agree with Rao and Jani that criticisms about overblown style fail to grasp the implications of literary language. See also Bernard D'Mello, "Arundhati Roy, Anuradha Ghandy, and 'Romantic Marxism,'" who points out that the core of "romanticism" is the question of "human emancipation."

26. Priyamvada Gopal, "Concerning Maoism," constitutes a rare academic engagement with *Walking*. I am indebted to Gopal's essay, and especially its emphasis on the narrator, to think through the relation between literary and nonfictional form. Recently, Joel Nickels has compared Roy's *Walking* to Claude McKay in terms of a "non-state internationalism," a welcome braiding of early twentieth-century and current anticolonial impulses (*World Literature and the Geographies of Resistance*, chap. 2).

27. Majumder, "Toward a Materialist Critique of the Postnational." To take just one example: Bruce Robbins's neologism "cosmopolitics," perhaps seeking an antidote to the postcolonial insistence on difference, entirely dismisses "the romantic localism of a certain portion of the left which feels it must counter capitalist globalization with a strongly rooted and exclusive sort of belonging." (3) Robbins's recommendation of the alternative "affective" subject of "multiple attachments," inhabiting a "newly dynamic space of gushingly unrestrained sentiments, pieties" (9) etc. is compelling, no doubt, but only if one overlooks the inconvenience that such dynamic spaces and unrestrained sentiments are seldom equally accessed.

CHAPTER 5

The Disappearing Rural in New India: Aravind Adiga and the Indian Anglophone Novel

> How strange it is though, that the contemporary tsars of the Indian establishment – the State that crushed the Naxalites so mercilessly – should now be saying what [Naxalite leader] Charu Mazumdar said so long ago: China's Path is Our Path.
> (Arundhati Roy, *Walking with the Comrades* 121)

The Anglophone Novel as Parody

Aravind Adiga's Man Booker-winning debut novel *The White Tiger* (2008) is contemporaneous to *Walking with the Comrades* (2010). The politics of the novel, however, is quite different from Roy's essay – in ways that I hope to illustrate in this chapter. The protagonist and narrator of *The White Tiger*, Balram Halwai, is a self-made entrepreneur running a start-up company in the metropolis of Bangalore, India's information technology hub. The story of his life is captured through a series of letters that he writes, at night, to visiting Chinese Premier Wen Jiabao. Styled after the nocturnal tales of *The Arabian Nights*, Halwai's audacious notes, however, reveal his ambitious personality as well as the quirkiness of the social types that he encounters. Halwai traces his odyssey from India's rural eastern hinterland, ravaged by the violence of upper-caste landlords' militias, to prosperous New India of the cities, New Delhi and Bangalore. Interestingly – and this is the tale's twist – the protagonist achieves "success" by robbing and murdering his employer, and establishing a business venture with the loot. The novel is both humorous and unsettling and mockingly depicts the pervasive structural violence of twenty-first-century Indian polity.

Hailing from a humble peasant background, Halwai appears to represent the emerging middle class in India: affluent, savvy, and asserting both a distinctive national identity *and* a claim to globalized consumer citizenship. Yet hidden inside the brave façade and display of wit, there is another dissonant and discontinuous layer that surfaces in the novel. I focalize an aspect of *The White Tiger* that has hitherto gone unremarked: namely, the novel's relation to, and representation of, Naxalism. *The White Tiger* simultaneously parodies and disavows the Naxalite movement. Attention to form, I suggest, illuminates the centrality of Naxalism as a literary, political, and spatial "figure" in the novel. More broadly, the text's recoding, appropriation, and expulsion of peripheral internationalism reveal, at the level of form, the fundamental disjuncture within the Indian Anglophone novel. My purpose is to constellate two phenomena, which are unrelated at first glance but nonetheless share a common point of emergence.

The resurgent Naxalite movement and the Anglophone novel coincide with – and arguably are results of – the restructuring of political and cultural economies in New India.[1] To situate the national and global articulation of the likes of Halwai, I draw on the term "New India" from Kanishka Chowdhury, who observes, "an unprecedented combination of dispossession, legislation and intimidation has been set in motion to abolish these remnants of the 'old' [India]" (30). If the old country indexes an antiquated and outdated ideology, New India, by contrast, is characterized by "a trumpeting of the importance of the global . . . and the ideological logic of *the global Indian subject*" (17, emphasis added). Ostensibly, India's lurch to the political Right runs parallel to the economic liberalization since the early 1990s, but the roots of both go back further to the late 1970s. In that sense, Arundhati Roy's pithy quip on India's *Chinese* path, quoted earlier, perfectly captures the nation's trajectory.[2]

On a higher scale, the capitalist world-system undergoes significant alterations in the, for lack of a better term, "neoliberal" era. I use the term with some hesitation because all too often, as scholars have remarked, neoliberalism indicates a monolithic idea bracketed from the previous history of capitalism. Chowdhury is at his most insightful in suggesting that influential think tanks and cultural theory, alike, affirm the contrast between past and present:

> The duality of the old and the new is an important ideological trope employed by advocates of neoliberalism . . . a necessary accompaniment of the new economic order is to link the 'old' to an antiquated and outdated economic system . . . on the one hand, [to] any institution or law, such as a regulatory commission or a system of tariffs, that is seen as a barrier to the accumulation of wealth and the free flow of international capital; on the other, the specter of workers' and agricultural laborers' rights, or public investment or expenditure. (30)

Nonetheless, neoliberalism summarizes well, I think, the exacerbated misery of the past four decades arising from financial deregulation and the demise of the welfare state; the erosion of workers', women's, and minorities' rights; state-backed and corporate-led expropriation of lands, forests, and oceans; humanitarian and environmental disasters; among many other issues – all under the auspices of freedom. Global transformations – between the end of Fordism and the collapse of the Soviet bloc and the redistribution of metropole, semi-periphery, and periphery – impinge on national formations in Asia as elsewhere.[3]

The White Tiger's formalization of the new periphery and its unevenness, I advance, illuminates the ways in which fiction registers (to slightly adjust Franco Moretti's evocative phrase) the foreign, local, and *subterranean* forces within a given social formation. I quote the opening in full since it captures the novel's unconventional style and lays out some of the key themes I want to discuss, namely, capitalist valorization (in the Marxist technical sense) and its registration and formal displacement in Anglophone fiction. The novel situates:

The First Night
For the Desk of:
His Excellency Wen Jiabao
The Premier's Office Beijing Capital of the Freedom-loving Nation of China
From the Desk of:
    "The White Tiger" A Thinking Man And an Entrepreneur Living in the world's center of Technology and Outsourcing Electronics City Phase 1 (just off Hosur Main Road) Bangalore, India
    Mr. Premier, Sir.

Neither you nor I speak English, but there are some things that can be said only in English.

My ex-employer the late Mr. Ashok's ex-wife, Pinky Madam, taught me one of these things; and at 11:32 p.m. today, which was about ten minutes ago, when the lady on All India Radio announced, "Premier Jiabao is coming to Bangalore next week," I said that thing at once. In fact, each time when great men like you visit our country I say it. Not that I have anything against great men. In my way, sir, I consider myself one of your kind. But whenever I see our prime minister and his distinguished sidekicks drive to the airport in black cars and get out and do namastes before you in front of a TV camera and tell you about how moral and saintly India is, I have to say that thing in English. Now, you are visiting us this week, Your Excellency, aren't you? All India Radio is usually reliable in these matters. That was a joke, sir. Ha!

That's why I want to ask you directly if you really are coming to Bangalore. Because if you are I have something important to tell you. See, the lady on the radio said, "Mr. Jiabao is on a mission: he wants to know the truth about Bangalore."

My blood froze. If anyone knows the truth about Bangalore, it's *me*. (The White Tiger 1–2, paragraphs resized for readability, emphasis added)

As we learn in the subsequent pages, Halwai grows up in Bihar (a province in eastern India) in the 1980s, in the midst of violent clashes between Naxalites and upper-caste landlords' militias. In the letters to the Chinese premier, Halwai refers to his journey from the rural countryside to India's capital city of New Delhi as moving from "Darkness" to "Light." The heart of Darkness is his birthplace, the village of Laxmangarh. When Halwai murders his employer Ashok in New Delhi toward the end of the novel, he does so in full cognizance of the fact that Ashok's family, the landlord "Stork" and his goons, would certainly kill his (Halwai's) remaining family members in the village as retribution. Deliberately or otherwise, the Laxmangarh of the novel resonates with the real-life incident of Lakshmanpur-Bathe. In a notorious event in December 1997, the Ranveer Sena (literally, army of brave hearts) militia massacred sixty-one villagers in Lakshmanpur-Bathe on the suspicion of being Naxalite sympathizers. This was part of a wider, State-backed and *bhumihar* upper-caste-led onslaught against untouchable caste Dalit communities during the period.[4]

To be clear, the text does not invite such real-life comparisons, here or elsewhere. Its overall tone is mocking and tantalizing, with allusions that are never fully explained. The novel drops contextual information from its content; it nonetheless encapsulates a precise social history. When Halwai mentions the term "Naxals" to the Chinese premier, he adds – "Naxals – perhaps you have heard of them, Mr. Jiabao, since they are Communists, just like you, and go around shooting rich people on principle" (21). Later on, as Halwai seeks employment from his absentee landlord, the latter's cronies assure the man that Halwai's family has "no history of supporting Naxals and other terrorists" (56). "What are you? A Naxal?" the landlord asks the boy Halwai at one point. For his prospective employers, that is "a very important piece of information" (66). The infamous events of Lakshmanpur-Bathe and the massacre of Dalit agricultural laborers surface in the novel, inverted and doubly disguised – "I was born there [in Laxmangarh], but Father sent me away as a boy. There was some trouble with the Communist guerrillas then" (69); then again, "the fighting between the Naxal terrorists and the landlords was getting bloodier" (73). Despite his father's scrupulous attempts to dissociate from the "Naxal terrorists" and earn the overlords' favor, in the end, Halwai's murder of the landlord's younger son transforms him, by his own reckoning, into "a virtual mass murderer" (337). Arguably, these seemingly minor details insert the Naxalites directly into the text.

In a similar mode, the travails of Halwai, who hails from the sharecropper class of rural peasantry, and who subsequently – as an economic migrant – takes up a chauffeur's job with the same landlords' family in the city, are reinvented as entrepreneurial stories of integration. However, the sojourn to the "Light" is never complete: rather, in key moments of dissonance, the novel marks the repressed return of Naxalite discourse. When the narrator-protagonist asks his fictional reader, the Chinese premier, if he has "heard about" the Naxalites, it is because the Naxalites shape his own life and perspective. The narrator interiorizes Naxalism's historical affiliation to Maoist China: Halwai's confession of murder to "His Excellency" is a parodic reincarnation of Maoist "self-criticism," and a reprisal of the personality cult of the "Great Helmsman." Halwai's progress from the country to the city and his act of killing his employer perversely parallel the older Maoist dicta of encircling the city, and the semi-feudal and semi-colonial class enemy, with the revolutionary peasantry from the countryside. Yet such structural similarities and resonances are contradictory to the ethical imperatives of the novel, which advocate (albeit mockingly) social Darwinism as the sole available mode of liberation. In place of critique – of neocolonialism, caste, and race-based inequality, the rural-urban divide – linked in turn to the internationalist affiliations of the Naxalite movement – *The White Tiger* appears to substitute the apolitical ethos of a protagonist focused on wealth acquisition and social mobility. Halwai's success within the capitalist system necessitates the repression of realism and critique: between its unstable narrative voice and transparently didactic message, the novel balances two diametrically opposed tendencies.

The White Tiger's deployment – and recalibration – of Naxalism has gone largely unnoticed among scholars and commentators. Perhaps this is not surprising in itself, owing to the text's obscure and deliberately indirect frames of reference. At the same time, and this is the second part of my argument, the formal elements of the novel gesture toward the broader aspects of peripheral internationalism. This has also not been adequately recognized. Specifically, *The White Tiger* draws on the protest novel, epistolary fiction, and the indigenous form of *tamasha* popular theater to convey what Ulka Anjaria has termed the "new social realism" of twenty-first-century Indian Anglophone fiction ("Realist Hieroglyphics" 114–116).

How should one conceptualize the novel's intertextual references and gestural appropriations, some direct, others more fleeting and nebulous – mediations operating at various levels of the text? These undercut the dominant message of the novel. They indicate, I suggest, the presence of agonistic tendencies and aspirations, malleable and mutable at various levels of fictional *and* societal form. Capitalist valorization enables fresh articulations of middle-class subjectivity in New India, speaking for and at the same time irreconcilably opposed to subaltern groups and popular classes of the majority. The form of the novel registers, yet by no means confirms, these multilayered, dynamic, and persistent struggles. This is precisely because form is material, that is, disaggregated and discontinuous, yet immaterial, subjected to perception alone, testifying to forces that only exist negatively. Let us elaborate.

To consider some of these aspects one by one: *The White Tiger* reconfigures the interwar genre of the protest novel to depict Indian society. The novel's indebtedness to the African American protest novel, especially its similarity of plot to Richard Wright's *Native Son* (1940), is fairly obvious. Wright's iconic protagonist Bigger Thomas operates in racially segregated Chicago of the 1930s. Halwai's world, likewise, is fractured by radical dichotomies of class and caste – "India is two countries in one: an India of Light, and an India of Darkness" (12). After departing from the rural country, Halwai finds Delhi as well as its peri-urban extension, Gurgaon, to be divided between Light and Darkness. A second plot parallel is that of profession: Bigger is employed as a chauffeur by the Daltons, who are wealthy and white, and he develops a peculiar relationship of admiration and distrust toward the Daltons' daughter, Mary, and her Communist boyfriend Jan. This is echoed in Halwai's role as a driver to his upper-caste landlord's son, Ashok, and his wife, Pinky Madam, who are recently returned from the United States. Halwai, moreover, plays on the landlords' "Hindu" sentiments to get the job, tricking, blackmailing, and getting rid of the previously employed Muslim driver who was "passing." Ashok and Pinky are kind to Halwai, and after their own cultural exposure to the West, unable to fathom his complete lack of status in a quasi-feudal setting. Halwai wants to be like Ashok and lusts after Pinky. Yet, he despises them and treats their kindness toward him as a sign of weakness. While Bigger kills Mary by accident and is duly convicted by a racist legal system (recalling the infamous Scottsboro trials) for the murder, Halwai kills Ashok by conscious design and successfully gets rid of Pinky, who returns to America.[5]

The resonance between these two novels, one set in interwar Chicago and the other in early twenty-first-century New Delhi, has not gone unnoticed. As Sara Schotland observes, "a comparison [between *The White Tiger* and *Native Son*] proves very useful" ("Breaking Out of the Rooster Coop" 1). Scholtand's reading of this usefulness, however, is decidedly ahistorical and focuses on the ethical aspect: "both novels examine the extent to which poverty, frustration, hopelessness and humiliation figure into the complex of causes that result in violent crime" ("Breaking Out of the Rooster Coop" 1). Beyond this criticism, which is doubtless valid on its own terms, we ask another question – what enables, and equally, necessitates Adiga's engagement with Wright? Both novels cast into sharp relief the social-historical forces of combined unevenness. As "typical" main characters, to use Lukács' term, Bigger Thomas and Balram Halwai are paradoxically free and unfree. At one level, these characters index the persistently similar operations of race and caste regimes in the dissimilar conditions of core and peripheral capitalist "free" society. At another level, Halwai's resemblance to Bigger is made possible by the refraction of African American solidarities in Indian internationalist culture, a tradition that coalesced over various nodes (Maoist, Dalit, etc.) as we addressed in previous chapters.

The White Tiger further emphasizes historical, twentieth-century peripheral internationalism, and its critique of capitalist freedom, through the formal device of epistolary fiction. Halwai's act of writing to Wen Jiabao might be said to borrow from the series of fictional letters, or public epistles, *Chacha Sam Ke Naam* (*Letters to Uncle Sam*), penned by the notable Indo-Pakistani Urdu writer Saadat Hassan Manto. Published shortly after partition, Manto's letters castigate Uncle Sam or the United States in a mock admiring and devastating critique of neocolonialism. *Chacha Sam* begins with – "Dear Uncle, greetings ... my country is not your country which I regret" (Manto, *Chacha Sam Ke Naam* 27). Like Lu Xun in another context, Manto's epistolary style combines modernist experimentation and progressive critique.[6] Not surprisingly, Uncle Sam never responds to these epistles. Neither does Wen Jiabao. Nevertheless, the framing of these letters, unidirectional unlike the traditional epistolary novel, allows their writers to engage in faux dialogues that are, in actual terms, exteriorized monologues. Echoing Manto's sarcastic regret of not being an American citizen, Halwai's admiration for twenty-first-century China goes one step further. He gloats, "You Chinese are great lovers of freedom and liberty" (*The White Tiger* 7). Yet, this is a double parody in that the internationalist critique of American capitalist and Chinese Communist "freedom and liberty" is turned inside out.

The White Tiger does not simply invoke the antiracist and anti-imperialist texts of Richard Wright and Saadat Manto, does not only deploy the forms of the protest novel and epistolary fiction, but does so to imagine their perverse antithesis – the figure of a new, hyper-real *Asian capitalism*. Properly speaking, this is where the tropes of parody and mock appropriation reveal the full, and unified, implications of the novel's literary style. In a reactionary claiming (and erasure) of race-caste, Indo-Chinese, and Afro-Asian solidarities, Halwai remarks to Jiabao, "in twenty years' time, it will be just us yellow men and brown men at the top of the pyramid, and we'll rule the whole world. And God save everyone else" (262). In the same passage, Halwai also reveals to Jiabao his fascination with "golden-haired" white women, who he pays for sex in "five-star hotels." Halwai's tone of assumed intimacy, as well as his locker-room talk (to borrow a term from a real life leader) with the Chinese premier is markedly homoerotic and homophobic at the same time. In a passage that makes for painful reading, for both its racism and homophobia, Halwai slyly ascribes the "decline of the white man" to "buggery" and excessive "cell phone" use, noting of the latter that "the Japanese invented them to diminish the white man's brains and balls at the same time" (262). Not only brown Indian and yellow Chinese men, but the Japanese too are adduced to Halwai's projected image of a post-Western world, characterized by the total alienation and commoditization of sexual relations among other things.

In a review penned for the *London Review of Books*, soon after the novel's publication, historian Sanjay Subrahmanyam rightly criticized *The White Tiger*'s attempt at reactionary humor:

> A framing device that should be mentioned [in *The White Tiger*]: each chapter consists of a message sent by Balram to Wen Jiabao . . . . This *adds nothing to the novel* beyond permitting Balram to present himself as a Third World rather than a merely Indian racist. Consciously or not, it also imitates far funnier and more successful examples, such as John Barth's 'Petition' from *Lost in the Funhouse*, addressed to the King of Siam. ("Diary," n.p., emphasis added)

Consciously or otherwise, however, Subrahmanyam misses the import of Halwai as a "Third World" rather than an exclusive, "merely Indian racist." The formal movement beyond the nation, India, is not simply limited to the Third World as Subrahmanyam seems to assume, a point I will return to later. The novel's framing device – a matter of its form, above all else, rather than content – does add something very significant to the novel. Form parallels, and registers, the movement of history. At the level of concept knowledge, we have something here originating in and from *historical materialism*; namely, the insight that historical movement is the effect of developing contradictions (which the novel formalizes as a tasteless joke) within immanent contending forces. Thus Lenin speaks, in 1914, of the crisis of Western imperialism made manifest by the Great War, and the resultant possibilities of post-capitalist transition opened up by anticolonial struggles in the East. Nearly a century after Lenin, after Rosa Luxemburg, and so many others, the novel turns such critical solidaristic notions on their head – displaces and reconfigures them – to express the current conjuncture of post-neoliberal crisis: the decline of Western dominance, the emergence of contending power blocs in Asia, and the corresponding shifts in subjective human consciousness.

A second level of formal reference to rising Asia over and above Halwai's crass caricature of fraternal solidarity occurs in the title of the novel. It is a direct adaptation of Robert Stuart Nathan's little-known work *The White Tiger* (1987), a lowbrow spy thriller that charts the Chinese Communist regime from its egalitarian beginnings to its subsequent transformation into a bulwark of the global capitalist-bureaucratic order. As described by Nathan, the "white tiger," a folk motif popularized in the work of the ninth-century Chinese poet Li He, makes its appearance during moments of social upheaval (Nathan, *The White Tiger* 4). This motif is repeated almost verbatim in Adiga. Halwai quizzes Jiabao, "what is the rarest of animals – the creature that comes along only once in a generation," adding later, "So that's how I became the White Tiger" (30). "Tiger" in Halwai's self-fashioned vocabulary of domination is also a reference to the rapid expansion and subsequent collapse of the Asian "tiger economies" of the 1990s – South Korea, Singapore, and Taiwan – in which Halwai proves to be a late entrant.

Finally, it is possible to speculate that *The White Tiger* draws on older indigenous forms to frame its new articulation of individualized ambition. Halwai explicitly claims to be inspired by the Urdu poet and anticolonial thinker Muhammad Iqbal to pursue freedom from slavery. Second, *tamasha* refers to the popular theatrical tradition in western India deployed by Dalit communities to mount a critique of upper-caste elites: "Mahars [former untouchables] seem to have been the chief musicians and actors in *tamasha*," Paswan and Jaideva remark in their monumental *Encyclopedia of Dalits in India* (62). They note the parallels with another untouchable caste group, the Bhangi caste of northern India, and their cultural claims of self-improvement to rise above outcastes and criminals in mainstream (read upper-caste) representation. While *tamasha* is invested in articulating a critique of the Brahminical caste system specifically from the point of view of untouchable caste groups, the narrator of *The White Tiger* brackets the possibility of such critique. To clarify, there is no transparent or sustained analogy between the novel and such popular theater. Invisible at the surface level, the trace of *tamasha* can be mapped rather by the atypical presence of seemingly minor, incongruous details.

In *The White Tiger*, the formal characteristics of the *tamasha* are put to use, namely, the motif of self-improvement and satire of upper-caste mores, which furnish the protagonist with his subaltern "voice." Halwai ventriloquizes to Jiabao, "I was destined not to stay a slave" (35). He borrows the theme of lack of formal education, a common feature of the *tamasha*, to declaim, "I never finished school, to put it bluntly. Who cares! ... We were never allowed to complete our schooling" (4, 8). Halwai is racially distinct with a "blackish face" (10), lives in the village periphery alongside "families of hogs" (16), and is considered by the landlords as a "fallen human" (85), all markers of caste untouchability. These are curious details given the fact that Halwai is a member of a middling caste, as he admits, and *not* in fact an untouchable. At one point in the narrative, his employer specifically asks him, "Are you from a top caste or bottom caste, boy?" (54). Halwai elides his true caste identity and answers – "Bottom, Sir," but as noted earlier, he is at pains to disavow any personal connection to Dalits (and Naxalites). The novel tantalizingly raises, and subsequently elides, the questions of untouchability, formal education, and caste-based literary representation.[7]

The existing scholarship on *The White Tiger* is significant owing, not in the least part, to the novel's award-winning celebrity. But these are generally speaking inadequate to the subject at hand. While scholars recognize that *The White Tiger* highlights socialized inequalities, less understood are the modes in which the novel advocates for greater leeway for the free market and middle-class participation in the same. Indeed, for some critics, Adiga's novel squares inequality to social traditionalism. To provide a few examples: Kathryn Hansen insists that *The White Tiger* articulates "a new sensibility of class" that differs from "the old Marxist rhetoric" ("Who Wants to be a Cosmopolitan?" 297). Robbie Goh extrapolates, similarly, that *The White Tiger* links "India's hopes for modernization and economic progress to its transnational connections ... even as it explicitly and excruciatingly ties its many social problems to *socio-religious traditionalism*" ("Narrating 'Dark' India" 337, emphases added). Lena Khor contends that

Halwai's act of "saving himself" through his quest for prosperity is a critique of human rights discourse, as is his "ironic" appeal to the premier of Communist China, "a [known] violator of universal human rights" ("Can the Subaltern Right Wrongs?" 63). Another scholar, Ana Christina Mendes, sees *The White Tiger*'s connecting of backwardness to tradition as (yet again) an ironic move, deliberately playing into stereotypes. Mendes speculates, "Adiga seems to be quietly mocking the longing for the ideal of authenticity [and] the appeal of a Dark India in the literary marketplace" ("Exotic Tales" 287, 289).

In these, admittedly selective, instances, the commentary remains restricted to positing either liberal critiques of traditionalism or the postmodern celebration of irony as the only two options represented in (and by) the novel. Even when the social *agon* presented in the novel is read as symptomatic of the frictions of India's integration into the global economy, what is ignored is the overarching problematic of uneven development of social form. On the other hand, scholars such as Betty Joseph, Snehal Shingavi, Mrinalini Chakravorty, and Ankhi Mukherjee offer welcome correctives to this trend.[8] Either way, the tension between dynamically poised forces is resolved by accelerated incorporation into or a playful subversion of capitalist globalization. Seldom is the negative potential of this conjuncture – abolition of its own conditions of possibility – probed at length. What is equally if not more telling, I would submit, is the manner in which many of these critics' reading of the New India novel quickly disposes of backwardness and inequality – the direct effects of capital's dynamic universalization – by connecting them to the past and causally linking to culture: blaming tradition in short. This sociological-empirical move both acknowledges the difference of India as a peripheral space from the metropolitan core of the West and at the same time disavows any explanation of that difference.

Likewise, authorial intention insufficiently accounts for *The White Tiger*'s narrative structure. In comparison to the likes of Arundhati Roy, who is frankly critical of globalizing impulses, Aravind Adiga's politics appears lukewarm, to put it mildly. One comes across such self-congratulatory statements as this one from the author: "[A]t a time when India is going through great changes, and with China, is likely to inherit the world from the West, it is important that writers like me try to highlight the brutal injustices of society" (qtd. in Wagner, "Aravind Adiga" n.p.). While echoing a disinterested sense of justice, Adiga's sensibilities are firmly rooted in the bourgeois imaginary of the new middle class; he avows that "I am not – and will never be – an opponent of the great economic boom .... [T]hose who interpret my novels as opposing *liberalization are misreading them.* They are marked by ambivalence, not opposition, to the changes (qtd. in Das, "They Mocked Me" n.p., emphases added). Adiga's "ambivalence" about "liberalization," let us add, should be read in conjunction with his bracketing of materialist history. In an interview to *The Guardian*, he sagely opines, "Class is a boring topic to write about. Big divides are not what people are interested in" (qtd. in Higgins, "Out of the Darkness" n.p.). In yet another characteristic instance of new middle-class perceptions of victimhood and upward mobility, Adiga, an Australian citizen, recalls his own "underdog" experience growing up in small-town India and achieving success through individual effort as he moved to the city of Bangalore.[9]

What disappears from these perspectives, scholarly as well as authorial, is the negative presence of peripheral internationalism or, more locally, the purported Dalit Naxalites in Bihar. To fully comprehend the form of the novel is to reenter this allegation once again. Of course, that which is invisible to the author is transparent to all the rural characters in the novel: the landlords and their assorted coterie of thugs; Balram's hapless father, siblings, and grandmother; as much as Balram Halwai himself. In contrast to contemporaneous texts (such as *Walking*) that directly engage with the Naxalite movement, our protagonist seeks to disown – vociferously – any personal connection to the Naxalites. Yet, as we have already seen from his voluble and intimate admissions, both the resonance of Halwai's natal village Laxmangarh to Laxmanpur-Bathe and his own career as a peasant migrant that takes to violence and usurpation against the landlord "class enemy" haunt the novel's main narrative. To balance the tension between the Naxalite subtext and the capitalist rags-to-riches fairy-tale text, the narrative appropriates – through parody – elements of the internationalist affiliations of the former. It is this peculiar relationship we have explored, the novel's simultaneous disavowal and appropriation of Naxalism, which is (to borrow from Althusser) the most symptomatic element of the text.

But the symptom percolates much deeper in fact, more so than previously described. The novel's appropriation of subaltern positionality – Halwai and others like him – marks a rare convergence of middle-class, upper-caste, and masculine, in short, normative nationalism and heterodox internationalism. This is to say, in other words, that the novel not only negotiates but also articulates two divergent and – in the last instance – irreconcilable tendencies at once. On the one hand, it reprises the domestication of dissidence at an ideational plane. Social struggles in the periphery, over caste patrimony and surplus for instance, are confined within the limits of the nation-state and trammeled by the logic of liberal democracy. This is the "new sensibility of class" (Hansen) and "new social realism" (Anjaria) that critics discover in the text, where the classical Marxist question of struggle over surplus – and its representation in realist fiction – gives way to piecemeal rights for the oppressed as well as liberal apologetics of justice. In the related but separate context of Naxalite *adivasi* militancy in central India, the political scientist Saroj Giri has perceptively argued that a "humanitarian model" that co-opts "undemocratic" and "violent" rebels within civil society discourse complements the State repression of *adivasi* communities. These progressive approaches see recalcitrant groups as a local or intra-national problem, as the manifestation of "'social discontent,' 'democratic overload,' 'crisis of democratic governance' and the 'need' to address these 'genuine grievances'" (Giri, "The Maoist 'Problem'" 471). Giri correctly observes that the liberal-humanitarian model propagated by NGO organizations, rights-based and livelihood-based activism, and so on forecloses, "a[ny] possibility for a more radical resistance from the masses ... that is unmanaged by one or the other faction of capital or state" (Giri, "The Maoist 'Problem'" 471). Through containment and recoding, the trenchantly anti-humanist narrator of *The White Tiger* replicates the real-life humanitarian model of transnational NGOs.

On the other hand, the novel unsettles its dominant message – and its underlying, affirming ideology – in at least two ways. First, Halwai's acts of murder, usurpation, and circumvention of the law, on his way to "Light," reveal the embedded violence that is constitutive of the state and the market in New India as elsewhere. It gives the lie to foundational fictions of liberal-capitalist democracy: freedom of entrepreneurship, property ownership, and hard work. The ideological expressions of capital, namely, globalization and opportunity, with their promises of freedom to the benighted masses, arrive in bursts and spurts, in selected circles, and always to the benefit of the elect few. They map onto, overlap with, and perpetuate non-capitalist social and economic hierarchies of oppression. Second, and more importantly, the aesthetic-formal transactions of the novel illuminate lineages that are international and not simply intra-national. *The White Tiger* marks the inverted presence of peripheral internationalist solidarities and the overlapping histories of anti-caste and anti-imperialist activism in India. These latter open up alternative, expansive imaginations and genealogies of *redistributive*, rather than *retributive*, desire.[10] This is to say that generalized cooperation replaces, if only as a negative possibility, Halwai's vision of capitalist competition.

In what may count as its signal achievement, the novel activates the negative possibility within the current conjuncture. This is very far from, and indeed at odds with, the politics of the author. The novel, I propose, rather than blaming "tradition" for the various ills of the present day, does something much more interesting – it illuminates that capitalist progress not only creates but also sustains backwardness in the new periphery. To rephrase this operation in a mildly abstract idiom, *The White Tiger* underscores the determinate role of universalizing mediations that transform the essence of things into the contrary appearance of objects. That is why at one point in the novel, Halwai describes to Wen Jiabao the hunt to capture him [Halwai] as follows: he becomes "[a] photograph: blurred, blackened, and smudged by the antique printing press of some police office, and barely recognizable even when it was on the wall of the train station, but now, transferred onto the computer screen, reduced to pixels, just an abstract idea of a man's face" (34–35). "Blurred, blackened, and smudged" and "reduced to pixels" – these abstractions transform Halwai's identity from a suspected Naxalite to an insignificant everyman, and back again to a fugitive from the law. The specificities of his life and person are doubly mediated in the compressed space-time of the narrative. Not only that, within the limits of the single sentence, the novel allegorizes the extended journey from old to new media technologies, from the "antique printing press" to the "computer screen." Such intense compressions at the level of narrative unit – the sentence – index the protracted forces of capitalist generalization and expropriation unleashed in New India.

Thus, *The White Tiger* offers a remarkably precise and clear-eyed view of the "various stages of capitalist penetration" (Jameson, "Third World Literature" 68) that coexist in twenty-first-century India. Despite the narrator's repeated proclamations distinguishing the rural countryside of stagnant tradition from the urban centers of mobile opportunity, the text, once again, undermines such rupture. Instead, it highlights the contentious if sporadic interlinkages between the two spaces of country and city. The accumulated structures of kinship, patriarchy, caste, and class travel back and forth between the country and the city, surprisingly plastic and rigid at the same time. Halwai's job as a chauffeur, first in the provincial town of Dhanbad and subsequently in the capital city of New Delhi, is but a continuation of his vassalage to the landlords' family. The "Stork," head of the landlords, employs him for his younger son on the basis of their village relationship; this employment (like Bigger Thomas's) is both a capitalist wage relation and a contract of caste patrimony. In similar fashion, the Stork's family is itself representative of a larger compression and unevenness, composed of older, conservative landed gentry and their younger, Western-educated, liberal progeny. The combined and uneven impact of free and unfree servitude, class and caste patrimony, and conservatism and liberalism, each hardly distinguishable from the other, is brought to life or realized in the novel. In New India, the chauffeurs' urban living quarters parallel those of the untouchables of the traditionally class and caste segregated village, as do the shopping malls and other glitzy parts of the national capital where Halwai is the perennial outsider.

In the light of these audacious – if unauthorized – insights into combined unevenness, the novel's central, recurrent thematic trope can be reexamined anew. The novel posits the synchronicity of the nonsynchronous, to borrow from Ernst Bloch, and interrogates rather than affirms the ideology of the new. The so-called contrast between Light and Darkness, and between the city and rural country, is revealed to be a fiction that does not correspond to its own reality. It is, therefore, an unstable artifice, susceptible to dynamic interpretations and, even, entirely different conclusions.

Likewise with the novel's key event: by murdering Ashok, the Stork's son, Halwai makes a remarkable leap from the humble status of his birth to join the ranks of the privileged. An interesting narrative strategy in the text is activated only through the utter annihilation of the master. "Ashok Sharma" (Halwai usurps the first name of his employer and adds an upper-caste surname, 258), the self-made entrepreneur narrates his previous struggles in retrospect. Such a framing device allows the narrator, Sharma/Halwai, to proclaim his individual success. At the same time, the story of Halwai makes it clear that such a trajectory is impossible – in the conceptual sense – in New India. To put this differently, fictional form articulates a fantasy that content denies to the narrator. By collating these two aspects of the novel, of central trope and key event, a certain unifying principle of composition is revealed.[11] It is this: the narrator's articulation of rupture and rebirth – externalized, in what he says – does not correspond with his internal – that is, what he feels and knows – sense of causality. I argue that Halwai's seemingly forthright yet insincere *tone* exactly captures the uneven inscription of social relations in the New India Anglophone novel. In other words, the novel's formal principles of discrepancy and incongruity, focalized in the figure of the narrator, provide what one might term with due qualifications an inverted national allegory.

"Only in English": The Anglophone Novel and the National Allegory

What role does English, in the twin forms of the Anglophone novel and global language of commerce, play in suturing the strategic extension from New India to the vanished third world? The answer to this query necessitates a somewhat lengthy detour; the exchange between Fredric Jameson and Aijaz Ahmad (arguably, one of *the* debates in postcolonial literary studies) contains vital clues to our present conundrum. In the opening chapter, I advanced that Jameson's notion of national allegory is key to the figuration of a (non-Western and non-capitalist) world literature of emancipation. Meanwhile, Aijaz Ahmad's critique elaborated later in *In Theory* contains valuable and unremarked points of departure. I contend that the two theorists approach the problematic from different but not entirely antithetical ends. In short, I propose reading Jameson *and* Ahmad, together, rather than opposed to each other. At stake in *The White Tiger* are the categories "third world," "socialist culture," and "English," and their emphatic reconfigurations under neoliberalism. A brief summary of Jameson and Ahmad is helpful to enter our argument.

In the "Third World Literature" essay, Jameson asserts that the allegorization of third-world literature is a historically specific process occurring in the age of multinational capitalism and in relation to metropolitan ideologies of determinate mediation and power. Jameson advances two related observations in this regard; he affirms the democratizing of the literary curriculum to include what one might call, in shorthand, "postcolonial," "ethnic," or more recently "non-Western world literature" (his own reference is to Goethe and *weltliteratur*). However, Jameson interrogates the very forms through which such democratization-as-appropriation would take shape. Third world texts are "necessarily ... allegorical" not only because of the texts' thematic content but also the way they appear as forms (I am interpolating here), as formal commodities. Nearly two decades after Jameson's intervention, and adducing a welcome consideration of Aijaz Ahmad among others, the critic Sarah Brouillette strikingly illustrates these interlinked processes by emphasizing, in the following terms, the specific yet determinate mediation of the "global literary marketplace" – the novel as a literary commodity is distinct from a bottle of Coca-Cola, but nonetheless mediated by similar relations of production, circulation, and reception. The border-crossing postcolonial novel evidences, perhaps more so than Coca-Cola, the sweet triumph of the market. In this regard, Jameson diagnosed literary-cultural trends that would solidify later.[12]

It is useful to recall that "Third World Literature" narrows down on the novel as a literary form particularly fitted for the marketplace of ideas. Thus, Jameson writes, "[a] popular or socially realistic third-world novel tends to come before us, not immediately, but as though already read" (66). To be acknowledged by the metropolitan reader – the "us" – the novel undergoes a series of mediations in receding order of visibility, of "taste," of "canon," of "our modernisms," and finally, the "sheltered life" of the reader (66). These mediations not only inflect circulation but also modulate the *content* of the "popular or socially realistic" text. The abstract determination of value, in other words, works for the consumer and the producer of novelistic fiction alike. Which is to say that such a text, in turn, sustains and ordains a dominant tendency: the circle of the reader and the writer includes the critic as well. Having "already read" the third-world novel and the "seemingly old-fashioned" reality the novel transcribes, the critic's claim to objective judgment is legitimized.

Further, the "TWN" (third-world novel) repeats the dialectic of identity and non-identity as a *parody*, as it were: its current preoccupations are those which metropolitan novels once had, supposedly, but which have now been left behind by the latter. In framing our present as not only dissimilar to but also differently oriented from that of the third world, the TWN-as-commodity obscures the structural determination that gives rise to such differences, namely, the universal, combined, and uneven expansion of capital. Put this way, Jameson's formulation is not so much Orientalist endorsement but rather the description of a dependent relation at the level of ideas, what he terms elsewhere a "spatial dialectic." To be recognized, and admitted, to the emerging canon of world literature, a TWN is alienated and abstracted as such. The novel's formal (allegorical) relation to the third-world nation (another form of TWN) emerges by simultaneously testifying to a recognizable ground of similarity with, and distance from, the West. The collective "us" and possessive "our" in these statements, I suggest, signal a relational vantage point that need not be restricted to Jameson's specific example of the US academy but extends to metropolitan platforms more broadly.

Recall Ahmad's response, "Jameson's Rhetoric of Otherness": Jameson's characterization of "all third world texts" as overt national allegories, Ahmad noted, flattens the heterogeneity within and without the third world. For Ahmad, Jameson ostensibly repeats the cultural cliché of the third world as an "embattled situation," as if the rest of the world were free of such battles (against capitalism and imperialism). Furthermore, Ahmad distinguishes between the conceptual tension and the polemical deployment of the third world, especially when concept and polemic overlap with each other ("Jameson's Rhetoric" 4). Tracing the multiple genealogies of the third world, and their evolving, often-contestatory relationships to one another, Ahmad justifiably bemoans that "the only choice for the 'third-world' is said to be between its 'nationalisms' and a 'global American postmodernist culture'. Is there no other choice?" (8). Interrogating the binary between nationalism and postmodernism, Ahmad's analysis emphasizes diachronic relation over synchronic structure. Diachrony not only problematizes the hermeneutic construction of the postmodern West and the nationalist non-West but also demonstrates the mutually constitutive relation between them. Both Jameson and Ahmad, one may point out, employ a dialectical method of analysis.

In an extended later discussion, "Three Worlds Theory: End of a Debate," Ahmad delineates not one but three uses of the term "third world." The first sense of the term is bourgeois nationalist: institutionalized in the Bandung Conference of 1955 and the Non-Aligned movement of the 1960s, the language of third-world nationalism (according to Ahmad), articulated by the likes of Jawaharlal Nehru in India, Gamal Nasser in Egypt, and Sukarno in Indonesia combined the rhetoric of anti-Communism with a state-led public and private developmentalism. The second usage derives from the Soviet Union, which described its own area of direct influence, namely, the European periphery or the Eastern bloc, as the socialist second world. Simultaneously, the Soviet Union advocated alliances in the – by corollary definition – "non-socialist" third-world periphery with "progressive" regimes such as India, Egypt, Indonesia, and others. The third and final deployment of the term is Maoist: especially during the Cultural Revolution and after, the People's Republic of China posited both the USSR- and the US-led blocs as imperialist first worlds. From this perspective, the third world was said to be composed only of poor and agricultural nations. While the Soviet Union supported third-world nationalisms for its own policy and ideological ends, China, after the Sino-Soviet split, and since the 1970s, steadily backed by the United States, sought to distinguish the third world from the socialist bloc (Ahmad, *In Theory* 306–307). The limit horizon of the third world according to all three definitions came to be "not socialism but nationalism" (307), or more to the point, nationalism *without* self-determination and substantive autonomy. Thus, I would argue, Ahmad illustrates the historical, ideological, and importantly linguistic forces at play in the theoretical cohering of post-Cold War nationalisms.

Ahmad decenters the concept(s) of third world, so to speak, by locating and situating them within Cold War knowledge formation. The content of these individual formulations may be true or false – for instance, were the Soviet Union and China socialist or state capitalist – were Nehruvian India and Nasserite Egypt bourgeois nationalist or sub-imperialist, and so on. What matters much more is the manner of their affiliation or formal relationship to one another, which illuminates – yet again – the diachronic contestations underlying the formation of concepts. In a striking gesture, Ahmad introduces socialist *movements* by way of unsettling the empirical fixity of dominant meaning.[13] He writes: "Socialism, one would have thought, was not by any means limited to the so-called second world (the socialist countries) but a global phenomenon, *reaching into* the furthest rural communities in Asia, Africa, and Latin America, not to speak of individuals and groups *within* the United States" ("Jameson's Rhetoric" 10, emphases added).

Subsequently through the decades of the 1970s and 1980s, Ahmad reckons, the third world increasingly came to mean an absence of socialist movement not only for anti-Communist Cold War warriors but also for many on the Left. This is where the quotidian shorthand use of the term "third world" overlaps with cultural theory, and not without controversy. Ahmad avers, "Marxists who ... deploy the Three Worlds theory, identify socialism with the Second World [and] uphold Third-Worldist nationalism as the determinate ideological imperative of our epoch" (*In Theory* 308). In the unexpected, conjunctural convergence between Left and Right, Ahmad maintains, "a thing called socialist and/or communist culture ... vanished from our discourse altogether" ("Jameson's Rhetoric" 8). Ahmad's contention not only qualifies Jameson's penetrating insight on the shortcomings of postmodernism but also, the former points to a greater contradiction: namely, that metropolitan and specifically Anglo-American theory implicitly reified nationalism as the limit of peripheral desires, while increasingly deemphasizing the sovereign importance of the nation-state. "Theory," implicitly or otherwise, provided positional cover to the maneuvers of the Right, if one may put it so.[14] By recuperating socialism – as a relational operation rather than static notion – beyond the confines of the Cold War, Ahmad extolls two basic principles of peripheral internationalism as we have defined them in this study: first, the periphery as a relational concept deriving from the capitalist world system and second, the importance of national sovereignty not as an end in itself but for patiently developing, without guarantees, a generalized "socialist culture."

Unforegrounded by Jameson, *language* is a key element of composition in his account of "Third World Literature." Aijaz Ahmad, correctly, draws attention to the prominence of English and French vis-à-vis non-European and non-Indo-European languages. Generalizations about third-world literature have to be made on the basis of a restricted corpus of novels written in, or translated into, English or French. To put this differently, the defining concept and its innumerable positivist-empiricist and micro-knowledges co-constitute and reinforce each other. The metropolitan conception of the (third) world has to – and can only – be substantiated, augmented, and made autonomous through the exclusive forms available to the metropole. The continuity between world literature thus constituted and older frameworks of metropolitan knowledge is unmistakable, as Aamir Mufti among others has recently argued (*Forget English!*). Equally and perhaps more to the point, non-unidirectional and less hegemonic interactions, exchanges, and translations across other language complexes are marginalized: English and French, surely, but also Arabic, Bengali, Chinese, Hindi, Russian, Spanish, Swahili, Urdu (which in turn exert determinate pressures on one another, on "minor" languages, and so on). In short, each of these languages and literatures – as well as English and French – is denuded of its worldly textures and becomes idealized reflections. One might add that Aijaz Ahmad anticipates, more so than a comparable critic, say, Pascale Casanova or Franco Moretti, the troubling implications of English and French dominance in the literary world system.[15]

In addition to illustrating, first, the waning of non-hierarchical socialist cultures, and second, the sidelining of non-Anglophone and non-Francophone literatures, Ahmad indicates a third aspect in his work. This is the dialectic of regression and defeat, a diagnosis that emphatically aligns him with Jameson. If for Jameson, third-world literature is a concept for the new, "multicultural" metropole to project its present by disavowing the past, and vice versa, for Ahmad the term is the formal expression of neoliberal capitalism's obliteration of past and present articulations of systemic resistance. For both theorists, form is historical: the concept's crystallization marks the conjuncture when literary and cultural forms, at the level of socialized ideology, express the real subsumption of labor under globalizing capital. Seemingly, multiculturalism rather than essentialism marks the reconfigured form of the first-world West: meanwhile, the erstwhile second and third worlds, converted to the Global South in the image of the West, represent that conceptual space that might, in turn, have been or not have been, but – crucially – will *never* again be socialist. Such operations at the level of terminology, which rewrite the past and impose upon the future, continue the Cold War by other means.[16]

That is not all: Ahmad provides the truly underappreciated insight that in such a situation, social reality can and would only exist in an allegorical, that is, discontinuous and disjunctive relation to privileged form (the Anglophone novel among others). Within the mediated space-time of the novelistic text, the negative possibilities would appear to be receding, amorphous and foreign, otherworldly and not belonging to this world. These would be at a remove from and residing in

> [O]ther kinds of cultural productivities – not archival but local and tentative, generated not by colonialism per se or by the East/West binary oppositions but by *histories at once older, more local, more persistent,* more variegated and prolix, more complexly and viscerally felt . . . .I have in mind here genres which are essentially oral and performative, sites of production located at great remove from the great cities, entire linguistic complexes as yet unassimilated into grids of print and translation. (*In Theory* 81, emphases added)

By foregrounding the contestations *within* textual representation, as well as without, Ahmad's critical reading revises, supplements, and ultimately deepens Jameson's account.

This is a good juncture to return to *The White Tiger*, with a better-grounded understanding of the central processes at work in the text, namely, first, the articulation of national specificity as a parody of identity and difference from the West; second, the subtraction of socialist culture from peripheral nationalism; and third, the subsumption of "local and tentative . . . linguistic complexes" under the banner of a global English. To be clear, these dominant determinations are not merely reflected by the novel; which is to say, the former shape the latter at each and every level of signification, but neither absolutely nor without resistance. Rather, the manner in which individual texts and genres negotiate and articulate these broader forces – at the level of form and utterance, character development, and plot – alerts us to ongoing contestations in the terrain of narrative, and within a given social formation at large. As Raymond Williams explained in *Marxism and Literature*, the "dominant" engages with distinct forms of the "archaic," "residual," and "emergent." By foregrounding the incompleteness of powerful determinations, I emphasize the highly stratified but still sovereign nature of the Anglophone novel.

These determinations – and their underlying antagonisms – reverberate throughout *The White Tiger*. But it is the moment(s) of their symptomatic appearance, of which we offer further examples, which concretely focalize narrative and social agon. Sharma/Halwai's communiqués to Wen

Jiabao – which are epistolary and public, retrospective and discrepant – offer the preeminent instance of co-constituted form and content in our text. The narrator recounts earlier Indo-Chinese alliances as an antidote to the imperial, material domination of the West: not only the Naxals of the 1970s but also the Bandung-era Panchsheel Treaty of the 1950s, and the even prior anticolonial period of shared resistance against the British. All of these are invoked in passing; however, the prime example derives from Halwai's personal past, from the depths of his own childhood as it were: the "Great Socialist," a self-satisfied leader who lords over his natal region with a combination of cunning, thuggery, and mesmerizing rhetoric (astute readers might discover in the parody the real-world chief minister of 1990s Bihar, Lalu Prasad Yadav, one of the legatees of the socialist, anti-caste tradition of Ram Manohar Lohia). The former resembles – and is in fact compared to – the Buddha, not only in terms of appearance and sphere of activity but also, crucially, the promise of upliftment for the caste and class oppressed: "Any boy in any village can grow up to become the Prime Minister of India. That is his message" (30). In a sense, the Great Socialist would be a kindred spirit for the likes of Halwai, representing the myriad popular castes and classes. The novel's repeated invocations of the Buddha, the "original" great socialist, would form another instance – a premodern one at that – of localized community, demotic reason, and non-nationalist solidarity across South, Southeast, and East Asia.

But the novel invokes these possibilities only to describe their failure. Like another "Great Helmsman" (Mao Zedong), the Great Socialist manipulates subaltern aspirations and state institutions alike to ruthlessly consolidate power. These are unexceptionable criticisms of course: yet, in Sharma/Halwai's retelling, the cult around the leader stands for an entire, undifferentiated, and benighted region (Bihar), in toto, rather than a noncontiguous index of popular mobilizations against entrenched feudal power. The Great Socialist becomes, retrospectively, *the* preeminent symbol of Darkness (81), rather than the contradictory and statist mediation, say, between Dalit Naxalites and Ranvir Sena in Laxmanpur-Bathe or the novel's fictional Laxmangarh. At another signifying level, the former continues to inhabit the protagonist's and the nation's contemporary life in both positive and negative terms. Not only does Sharma/Halwai exhibit the same duplicity as the Great Socialist, so does the entire class of successful businessmen, real estate barons, and politicians in the New India of the Light. Arguably, as the plot shifts from the regional to the national capital, the Light effaces the socialist leader just as much as it obscures "the faded mural of the Lord Buddha" (25). Nonetheless, it takes the reader to recognize the narrator's move for what it is, a simple *burlesque*, to see through such mystifying effulgence (and read the story against the grain). The twice-born Halwai is aware, though he cannot articulate this properly, beyond a nostalgic yearning that pervades his epistles, of the critical content of state-ized socialisms in Bihar.[17]

At another juncture, describing to Jiabao the "Great Indian Roster Coop," the narrator inserts a pointed aside: "[Unlike China] in India we have no dictatorship. No secret police. That's because we have the coop" (149). Overlapping with the structure of the Indian family, the rooster coop imprisons, dehumanizes, and regulates the majority. The coop is at once physical and symbolic, whose operations the passage describes in unsparing detail. On the one hand, such a figuration correctly calls into question the ideology of the dominant classes; on the other hand, it obliquely ties the latter to authoritarian state practice, such as "secret police," "raid[s] . . . at night," and "jails" (149). India and China come to represent unfree societies, albeit in distinctive ways – hierarchical traditionalism and Communist dictatorship respectively – in ideology as much as in living social practice. Evacuated from this (non-) comparison, or as I would contend, appearing in an inverted fashion, is the residual trace of twentieth-century peripheral internationalism.

These instances substantiate the novel's key "principle of composition" (Roberto Schwarz's phrase): namely, the non-correspondence between the narrator's external articulation and internal causal perception, or put another way, the gap between what he speaks and what he knows but cannot say. The forceful unpacking of the Great Indian Rooster Coop – as well as the cult of the Great Socialist – draws its strength from the internationalist, and Leftist, critiques of stratified caste-class, community, and imperialized nation-state that we have traced in previous chapters: the heterogeneous thought traditions represented by the proper names Phule, Roy, Ambedkar, Lohia, among so many others. What the novel's digressions evoke, and simultaneously bracket, are discussions of Aryanism and Brahminism in India, white supremacy in the American South, and fascism in Europe – between indigenous hierarchies in the East and their imbrication with the imperial West, in other words. The substance of diverse (and even heretical) translations of Marx and Marxism in the periphery, however, is filtered through or re-translated through a post-Marxist, and Western lens. As much as prior lineages of peripheral thought, Sharma/Halwai borrows from an enduring metropolitan idiom of Oriental despotism. In other words, the novel appropriates *Left* intellectual-social histories and turns them into *Right* caricatures of hidebound Eastern societies. The logically discrepant comparison between present-day India and China, as well as the negative, "No," occurring twice in the passage previously noted, signals the text's own resistance to such ideological impositions. Nonetheless, it is precisely through these accretive asides to his fictional comrade-in-arms, Wen Jiabao, that Sharma/Halwai conjures a "Third World ... racist" (Sanjay Subrahmanyam's phrase) vision of Asian domination over an emasculated, too-liberal West.

What this entails is a process of ideational translation that is as much literary as it is historico-political. To expand on the gist of our close reading: the narrator's oscillations of tone and voice, while intimate and personal, precisely index the mediation of global, structural forces of capitalist valorization. The braiding may be expressed as follows: the vector of globalizing neoliberal capitalism cannot measure up to, and indeed increasingly works against, its core premise of inalienable liberty – in democratic India or Communist China, as elsewhere. But at the same time, the universalizing value-form of capital can only measure those articulations that are identifiable with the conscionable self-image of the metropolitan West. To resolve this tension, the Anglophone novel undertakes its own loose but nonetheless determinate version of historical revisionism. Borrowing, without citation, from old and new texts such as *The Origins of Totalitarianism* (1951) and *The Black Book of Communism* (1997), the narrator pits socialism and fascism as the twin totalitarianisms of the previous century and exculpates if sarcastically so a liberal – that is, non-imperialist and post-socialist – West.[18]

The consolidation of this metropolitan revisionist perspective might be further expressed in four discrete steps if only for analytical convenience: at one level, the (third-world) national allegory is downgraded from grasping the combined and uneven capitalist world system. At a second level, it is transfigured into a parody of its dialectical self – an essentialized binary difference between the West and the non-West. To put this differently, national allegory is sublimated in culture not as the diachronic commitment to a shared post-capitalist future but – as Jameson already observed – the synchronic assertion of identity and non-identity, similarity with and difference from the West. In this scenario, aspirational epigones – in countries such as India – can and do appropriate the discourse of national self-determination to speak for those below, as well as to those beyond the limits of the nation-state (such as its nationalist diasporas). Language, and more precisely the English language, is a decisive factor in this hierarchical transformation. We might, profitably, recall Ahmad's intervention: "Only the literary document produced in English is a *national* document, all else is regional, hence minor and forgettable" (*In Theory* 75, original emphasis). At yet another, third level, non-English or "regional ... minor and forgettable " languages – and literatures – are denied their respective claims to border crossing and intercultural dialogue, either in the past or present, but more vitally for the future. Ahmad duly observes, "major literary traditions – such as those of Bengali, Hindi, Tamil, Telugu, and half a dozen others from India alone – remain, beyond a few texts here and there, virtually unknown to the American theorist" ("Jameson's Rhetoric" 5). Correlatively, at the fourth level (and I can only make this point very schematically), "ethnic," "women's," or "minority" texts produced within the metropole – in English – are rendered similarly but differentially national, that is, as American, Canadian, or British, and so on, therefore eliding the counter-hegemonic articulations of "individuals and groups within the United States," to use Ahmad's phrase. As such, *The White Tiger* and Wright's *Native Son* could and yet cannot be conjoined as fraternal texts. (We keep aside the related case of French and the Francophone world for the present discussion.)

These are the constraints of national allegory in *The White Tiger*, then, ones that repeatedly reduce the difference of capitalist combined unevenness to symbols of "unfree," "native" culture. Indeed, a novel that is otherwise so thoroughly ironic cannot admit, overtly at least, its most unironic operation: the subtraction of non-Western and non-capitalist cultures of resistance, solidarity, and broad internationalism. These cultures can only be admitted in the language of negation, and monstrous, exaggerated parody. Literary language comes to bear the accumulated weight of deliberately erased histories, and it is only by unpacking the former, one might say, that the text can be made to speak what it cannot say otherwise. Or perhaps *The White Tiger* does say it, at the very outset, in the first dialogic sentence occurring in the novel: *Neither you nor I speak English, but there are some things that can be said only in English* (1, emphases added). As the chosen medium of Anglo-American, Indian, and Chinese, in other words, the globally privileged of the contemporary order, English is not one language among many, but the meta-language of dominant though not absolute determination.[19]

The same dynamic is reflected, at yet another level, in Sharma/Halwai's disaffection with government officials. Thus, the narrator introduces himself, to Jiabao, as someone who exposes the official lies peddled by "our Prime Minister and his distinguished sidekicks" (2). Here as elsewhere, we witness the fraught convergence between mutually opposed middle-class and subaltern political desires. By (falsely) claiming to speak truth to power, à la the oppositional intellectual, Halwai-as-Ashok Sharma articulates the new middle class's formal push to reinvent the *content* of the state, while appropriating Halwai's *discontent*. The literary critic Snehal Shingavi correctly pinpoints that Sharma/Halwai mutates a "liberationist" critique of the state into a "populist libertarian solution" to do away with the regulatory functions of the state altogether ("Capitalism" 8). Disaffection with the state, once used to describe seditious activities in the colonial era, encapsulates the beleaguered nature of the narrator's middle-class prosperity in New India. But there is also the tantalizing suggestion – which the novel displaces – that calling the prime minister's bluff entails material reconstruction, and working through immanent archives, memories, idioms, and currents that are "as yet unassimilated into grids of print and translation" (*In Theory* 81). One might go so far as to suggest that the novel's opening, quoted in full at the beginning of the chapter, provides a perspective as well as a reading method that is key to unpacking the novel as a whole.

To summarize, *The White Tiger* gestures to the persistence and indeed the renewed emergence of a constellation of intra-national forces that resists the deregulated market and nominally democratic state in India: the peasant worker, the criminalized migrant, the oppositional intellectual, and others, those individual types ruthlessly exploited and rendered superfluous by patriarchal caste, gender, and class structures in New India. Yet, and still, the novel affirms a dystopic horizon of faux liberation where the challenge to the extant nation-state (and the normative capitalist world system) is mounted by revanchist class nationalisms. Between its repeated and alternative knowing and saying, or negative gesturing and sanguine positing, there emerges a literary construction of an internationalism of the Right. Such an edifice is built on, and yet painstakingly denies, a Left conceptual foundation. The text, as we have already noted, describes a fiction that does not match its own reality.

The processes of Rightist consolidation on the other hand, as Ahmad suggests in his later work, recall the Gramscian notions of cultural hegemony and passive revolution, a shift in "common sense."[20] The reorganization of historical blocs (Gramsci's term) in New India, as Leela Fernandes explains, is manifested "through the process of enframing in which the boundaries of this group [the new middle class] are delineated through a set of public discourses, cultural narratives and economic shifts" (*India's New Middle Class* 31). These evolve out of, yet only partially displace, tendencies that are previously present in a given social formation. Fernandes writes:

> The 'newness' of consumption practices in liberalizing India includes large segments of the middle class that do not have the kind of disposable incomes associated with the upper middle class and upper classes. Despite widespread national anxieties around the spread of Western-style consumerism in India, there is economic uncertainty in the Indian middle class that has not allowed the kind of consumerism associated with advanced industrialized societies. (Fernandes 80–81)

This is a classical peripheral predicament. The internally differentiated, English-speaking middle class – making up 7 percent to 10 percent of India's population by Fernandes's estimate – is both fiercely willing and yet in the final instance unable to dispense with those below and outside the reconstituted national order. It is not a minor detail that their fictional representative, Sharma/Halwai, writes from "the world's center of Technology and Outsourcing Electronics City" in the city of Bangalore (*The White Tiger* 1). Such a "world's center" is simultaneously the world-system's margin, a digital plantation providing subsidized labor to the core regions – the advanced industrialized societies – of the world. There emerges, in the novel, the precarious image of a service-provider *economy*, dependent on outsourcing without a productive industrialized base. At the level of middle-class consciousness, this base determination generates uncertainty around commodity consumption (as Fernandes notes) but also consumptive anxieties around servility and disposability. Properly speaking, it is the service relation – corresponding to the real subsumption of peripheral labor to globalizing capital – that binds the industrious entrepreneur, the informally underemployed, and the abject unemployed. In this vein, one can speak of service as *the* structural relation of the New Indian periphery. This is a national characteristic, cutting across the antagonisms between the rural and the urban, the locally stagnant and the globally mobile, the precarious "floating populations" (M.N. Roy's term) and the privileged middle classes. Capital's subjectification of labor engenders subjection to service, and vice versa.[21]

To summarize these remarks for literary-allegorical representation: the novel space of exchange that world literature (specifically the Anglophone novel) both inaugurates and secures indicates the *limit conditions* of capital. The (neo-) liberal embrace of the margins, while salutary at some levels, nonetheless generates newer, and reinforces older, illiberal forms of underrepresentation and dispossession at other levels. The greater the democratization of the literary marketplace and the reading lists, incorporating previously marginal voices, themes, regions, and so on – the further the dialogic and contrarian complexes of languages and literatures are appropriated and mistranslated, if not erased altogether. (This is the summary essence of the Jameson-Ahmad debate in our view and its continuing relevance for the present moment.) The determinate and contradictory unity of world literature places peripheral cultural productions, in short, in a relation of continued dependence.

Not only does *The White Tiger* articulate this structural relation in form, as an allegory for the embattled nation, this is also why it fails to completely banish the rural. As I have already suggested, the text stages its narrative failure, which has its real roots in the situation of persistent national dependence, as a drama of contending forms. The rural (and the regional, the traditional et al.) – with their range of negative associations and connotations – is summoned to witness the march of urban (and national, global, modern) progress, made to reappear afresh, only so that the former can be buried anew.[22] The profound tensions underlying such a maneuver mark the repressed return of critique. The social antagonisms – at the level of form – are reinforced by the thematic presence of the Dalit Naxals of Laxmangarh in Halwai's life and in New India. Indeed, the novel is remarkable in this persistent figuration, giving the lie to the mythos of globalization as a seamless break from the antiquated past. The uneven interaction of foreign and local forms is suggested by the novel's incorporation of the African American protest novel (Wright), intertextual references to China and Maoism (Nathan), and indigenous forms of satire (Manto, Iqbal, *tamasha*). These appropriations formally illuminate the continuing material difference of peripheral social form from the metropolitan core. On the flipside, the Left internationalist desire to transcend capitalism through national sovereignty and cooperation is reversed and flows, first, into the Right's fantasies of boundary-less globalization, and then, further along, into the latter's antithesis of nativism and expunging all others from its borders. *The White Tiger* frames the dilemma brilliantly in the figure of the eponymous narrator. Progressively and at various levels, the narrator's projections, transfigurations, mutations, sublimations, desires, and fantasies – socio-historical operations at the level of subjectivity so familiar to psychoanalysis – mark the objective struggle to redefine peripheral internationalism in the neoliberal present.

On the one hand, their parodic versions enable the appropriation of the militant and the contrarian in the form of pro-market virulent nationalism, specifically the Right-wing narrative of development. The novel, accordingly, incorporates the multilayered contestations in New India within the more "palatable" framework of Sharma/Halwai's consumerism, sexism, and upper-caste racialism – that is properly speaking, fascistic in scope. On the other hand, and in another reading, the novel retains if only as a negative possibility, the subterranean lineages that refuse the border-crossing fantasies of capital and its generative uncertainties of consumptive crisis. It is not possible to fully *re*-present these figurations and affiliations in the free market of ideas: they remain as ghostly traces, as objects to be parodied, and ultimately disavowed. My discussion of the novel illustrates two critical lineages: first, it locates contemporary resistance to systemic crisis in terms of a much longer social and intellectual history. Second, by emphasizing the mutability of narrative and social forms, I illuminate the conceptual space to link localized struggles to insurgent ideas and movements elsewhere. Dialectical reading, one might say, pushes against the current conjuncture in unpredictable but clearly defined directions, either toward a renewal of socialism and internationalism or, failing that, a descent into barbarism.

Notes

1. According to one scholar, twenty-first-century Anglophone fiction in India, similar to that in countries like Malaysia, Singapore, and Kenya, is "less and less recognizable by the tropes and guises of postcolonial literature" (Varughese, *Beyond the Postcolonial* 2). The retreat from the postcolonial is the subject of significant scholarly debate; these are cited in subsequent footnotes.
2. For a comparison between these two Asian countries, see the essays in Yokokawa, Ghosh, and Rowthorn eds., *Industrializing India and China*. Important discussions of neoliberal development in the Indian context, among many others, include Elizabeth Armstrong, *Gender and Neoliberalism* and Kenneth Bo Nielsen and Patrick Oskarsson eds., *Industrializing Rural India*. These studies complement Kanishka Chowdhury, *The New India* and Leela Fernandes, *India's New Middle Class*, which I discuss in the chapter.
3. To its many critics, neoliberalism continues if in a modified form older processes of imperialism. For an updated overview of the subject, see Utsa Patnaik and Prabhat Patnaik, *A Theory of Imperialism*. For the implications of the "Asian century" on cultural theory, see Gayatri Spivak, *Other Asias*.
4. A comprehensive discussion of the Lakshmanpur-Bathe massacre and its broader context of Dalit Naxalism in Bihar is Kunnath, *Rebels From the Mud Houses*. Drawing attention to the role of the state, George Kunnath observes, "Dalits, marginal peasants and other victims of the Ranveer Sena felt that the state agencies, especially the police, colluded with the Sena. The investigative reports of the Sena massacres published by human rights organizations, and the coverage of such incidents in the newspapers, reflected common man's perceptions of the state-Sena-police nexus" (188).

5. William Maxwell's *New Negro, Old Left* deftly illustrates the many interactions between African American writers and international Communism in the interwar era, including Claude McKay's Soviet sojourn, the impact of the Scottsboro case, and the debates following Wright's *Native Son*. For the Indian side of this global story, which extends beyond the interwar era, see previous chapters of the present book and especially Chapters 2 and 4. Aravind Adiga cites the work of Ralph Ellison and James Baldwin as influences but notably excludes Richard Wright (see, e.g., Wagner "Aravind Adiga," n.p.).
6. In *The Pity of Partition*, Manto's biography by his grandniece and noted historian Ayesha Jalal, the latter discusses Manto's "reading and translating [of] French and Russian writers like Maupassant, Zola, Hugo, Chekhov, Tolstoy and many others" (26). However, Jalal appears to disavow Manto's relation to Marx, observing, "Marx ... he [Manto] had read none" (27–28). This is a surprising claim, not only given Manto's familiarity with modern European literature, which Jalal illustrates, but also because he (Manto) like many leading contemporary Urdu writers such as Sajjad Zaheer, Ismat Chughtai, and Ali Sardar Jaffri had a deep and conflicted relationship with the Communist parties of India and Pakistan.
7. Toral Gajarawala, *Untouchable Fictions*, chap. 4, provides a compelling reading of Halwai's caste identity in terms of the invisibility of caste in Anglophone fiction. The critic notes, "While several generations of novels before this one elided caste, Adiga presents a caste analysis but rhetorically persuades us of its anachronism via the worldview of a deprived and depraved character" (150). Again, English is materially significant in this episode. Going back to the colonial period, the relationship between caste status and class position is mediated through access to English-language formal education. See, for example, Modhumita Roy, "Englishing India." After independence, the pattern of upper-caste dominance was consolidated with the state privileging of higher education and neglect of primary literacy: "education became a central arena in which state-middle class relationships of patronage and dependence were consolidated" (Fernandes, *India's New Middle Class* 21).
8. See for readings of *The White Tiger*, Joseph, "Neoliberalism and Allegory"; Shingavi, "Capitalism, Caste and Con-Games"; Chakravorty, *In Stereotype*, 108–118; and Mukherjee, *What is a Classic?* chap. 5. These critics provide theoretically sophisticated discussions of neoliberal capitalist violence, urban immiseration, accumulation in India, and literary canon formation. But my larger point stands: these insufficiently explore the figuration of Dalit Naxalism in the novel.
9. Rather disingenuously, Adiga claims, "I was humiliated by the rich boys there [in Bangalore] – all of whom I had beaten [in exams] – because I had a thick accent when I spoke English and I did not know who Lionel Richie was" (qtd. in Das, "They Mocked Me"). The interview in question was conducted by *The Times of India*, the oldest English-language newspaper in India.

10. Here, I depart from Deleuze's formulation on desire and its associated notions of deterritorialization, machinic assemblages, and incorporeal transformation, etc. With mixed results, Deleuze displaces the Marxian analysis of contradiction between modes and relations of production. Among recent French critics, Isabelle Garo and Jean-Jacques Lecercle, some of whose works have been translated into English, provide excellent explorations of this shift. See Garo, "Deleuze, Marx and Revolution" and Lecercle, "Deleuze, Guattari and Marxism."
11. I adopt the phrase "principle of composition" from Roberto Schwarz's discussion of Machado de Assis's method (*A Master*). Schwarz observes that the description of society in Brazil does not match the felt perception of the same, even at the level of idea (ideology). Here as elsewhere in the book, my analysis remains indebted to Schwarz's pioneering theorization of peripheral literature.
12. Brouillette's fine study builds on underutilized critics, such as Aijaz Ahmad (*In Theory*), Arif Dirlik ("The Postcolonial Aura"), and Graham Huggan (*The Postcolonial Exotic*). She writes, "The average novel is not a commodity in the way that, say, Coke is a commodity" (*Postcolonial Writers* 49). Each book is different from the several million other books in print, and there is considerable separation between what a novel articulates and how interpretive communities or readers receive it. Most importantly, novels (or books in general) cannot cross borders easily without being translated and undergoing modification. Despite these important differences from other commodities, there are material conditions of publishing, reviewing, and popularizing, production and circulation in short, that structure the corpus of non-Western literature.
13. Here the issue is one of scale. To consider Asia alone, not only did Communist countries such as China, Vietnam, North Korea, Laos, and Cambodia comprise a significant part of the then-existing third world, these were populated by almost a quarter of the world population. In non-Communist India, there is the example of the elected Left Front (1977–2011) in the province of West Bengal, whose population (around 90 million) is larger than that of the most populous European country, Germany, and almost a third of that of the United States. The tripartite division of the first, second, and third worlds is not only inaccurate; it obfuscates the existence of the majority world.
14. This is of course not true of Western Marxist attitudes *tout court*, but a certain historical tendency inattentive to the national question. On the other hand, Soviet Marxism's early mishandling of the national question had serious implications for socialist movements in the peripheries. See Chapter 2 of this book.
15. An instructive comparison can be made between Ahmad, *In Theory*, especially chap. 2, and Casanova, *The World Republic of Letters*, chaps. 1 and 3. Surprisingly, Ahmad's intervention finds little mention in subsequent scholarship on vernacular Indian literatures, though these are the very traditions he cites. See, for example, the critique of Moretti and Casanova by Orsini, "India in the Mirror of World Fiction" and the essays in Prendergast, *Debating World Literature*.

16. Like the third world before it, the Global South becomes simply the belated image of the West. The Global South is far more than a neutral description; it is a relational concept made legible by the equally ideological notion of the multicultural West with its own set of contradictions. The Global South and the multicultural West are identical in the sense that both are untainted by socialist struggle, yet non-identical in that the former continues to offer an inexhaustible resource of "traditional culture" and scope for "development."
17. For a contemporaneous assessment of the Lohiaite legacy, see Yogendra Yadav, "What Is Living"; my point is quite simply that these are alternative entry points for reading the regional and socialist politics portrayed in *The White Tiger*.
18. Among others, Losurdo, *War and Revolution*, provides a stellar account of historical revisionism in the West, particularly the erasure of colonialism. I will provide two instances of why postcolonial scholars should take revisionism seriously: first, its imported nature – there is no comparable term for "totalitarianism" in Indian languages, though there are nearly century-old critical traditions in Bengali, Hindi, etc. on actually existing Communist regimes. Second, the post-Cold War, English-language discourse of liberals and conservatives that equates historical Communism to European colonialism and/or fascism is almost always unaware of vernacular texts and lineages that sharply distinguish between these processes.
19. To provide a few examples: as early as 1995, India was the third-largest publisher of English-language books, including textbooks, in the world (Brouillette, *The Postcolonial Exotic* 79). Still earlier figures from 1975 are even more compelling, giving credence to what Philip Altbach termed, "literary colonialism in the third world" – "In India, about half of the book titles are in English, while only two percent of the population is literate in English" (Altbach "Literary Colonialism" 230).
20. Ahmad, *Lineages of the Present*, especially chap. 5 on Gramsci and Hindutva in India, and Ahmad, *On Communalism and Globalization*. Like Arundhati Roy, Aijaz Ahmad's work on culture, capitalist globalization, and Right-wing fundamentalism constitutes a signal if academically neglected critical corpus.
21. Admittedly, the relation between service and peripheral dependency needs fuller theoretical and historical elaboration. Here, I refer in passing to the Marxist, ex-Subaltern Studies historian Sumit Sarkar's *Writing Social History*. Sarkar outlines a similar trajectory in a study of the nineteenth-century saint Ramakrishna and the elite followers that gathered around him in the then-capital city of Calcutta. The vagaries of colonial service put the native bourgeoisie in a situation of dependency that was both comparable to, and yet starkly different from, the quasi-feudal vassalage of their class subordinates or *chakors*. The bourgeois anxiety regarding colonial service (*chakri*) led to the outpouring of an affective devotion (*bhakti*) that seemingly ran counter to the liberal Enlightenment notions of reason and logic. In the colonial frame, the language of *bhakti* articulated the spiritual sublimation of dependency to

a higher power, while *chakri* – and its cognate *naukri* in Hindi and Urdu – retained the mixed aspect of wage and vassalage relations.

22. On this point, I am indebted once again to Raymond Williams's classic study of the rural in literature, *The Country and the City*. This is a text that needs urgent reclaiming for its singular insights on the popular forms of resistance, a key concern of peripheral writing.

CHAPTER 6

Conclusion

One of the main themes addressed in the preceding pages is the revaluation of the past in terms of literary activism. Here, I wish to revisit two salient aspects of the discussions that deserve underscoring: first, a consideration of the role of literature in understanding, and reconfiguring, the interconnectedness of the modern world; and second, the extents to which literary traditions help us militate against the culture of forgetting and appropriation. I offer these as examples of the kind of resistance that literary criticism and/or theory can pose in the present moment.

In the age of access, surveys, data, and information at our fingertips, certainly it is easier to gather knowledge about all manner of things. However, what remains problematic about such acquisition is its narrow emphasis on facts. By contrast, literature, as is well known, offers a fundamentally different way of comprehension and articulation. Through its emphasis on the unfolding nature of events, the processive interaction between words, sounds, images, and emotions, even the unfinished aspect of conclusions, among other things, literature disturbs the empirical impersonality of facts and definitions. Not through a rejection of the latter, to be sure, but rather complicating them through a more wholesome and rounded approach. Literature might be said to provide, in lieu of sundry information, an intimate and intellectually more demanding account of the processes that go into their making. In other words, it is a description not so much of how things are in the present (or were in the past), but rather how they came to be.

Transposed from these general observations about the role of literature in the world, and relocated to the vast corpuses of literary texts and expressions in various languages and regions, most of which no single individual can claim mastery of, we might begin to describe the emergence of a critical schema of reading. This is the method whereby literatures of the world are transformed into comparative, and comparable, world literatures. Our attempt has been to capture and describe at some length this complex and multilayered socio-historical process in the twentieth century. Given the unwieldy scope of the subject at hand, we were restricted to providing specific examples in a particular context, India/South Asia, as symptomatic of the broad processes at work, illuminating the universal through the particular and – as Marx argued – the concrete from the abstract.

The book presented an early dialogue between the ideas of Rabindranath Tagore and Mao Zedong. This was based on the *visva-sahitya* lecture and the Yenan Forum talks – speeches that resonated with the vernacular energies unleashed in the East in the first half of the twentieth century. We ended with a contemporary novel, *The White Tiger*, and an equally phantasmal conversation occurring between another pair of Indian and Chinese figures: the characters of Balram Halwai and Wen Jiabao. Despite the symmetry between the two pairings, the implications of this latter (dialogue between Halwai and Jiabao) that is actually a monologue departs drastically from the first and anticipates a different future for the twenty-first century than was envisioned for the twentieth. Between these two episodes, no less real despite their fictive appearance, the previous century's vision of demotic equality has given way, one might say, to a graver nightmare of civilizational crisis.

Yet it would not do merely to describe the present century as different from the last one. Obviously, the current conjuncture embodies novel and specific challenges. At the same time, the great twentieth-century projects of human emancipation, national liberation, and anti-imperial socialism retain their continuing significance. This is perhaps easier for Western readers to appreciate now that in the past decade alone, the idiom of democratic socialism, in the United States and Great Britain, has become a part of the mainstream sociopolitical vocabulary. In the imperial metropoles as elsewhere, the popular demand for economic redistribution and social dignity is endlessly confronted by forces that once seemed distant and foreign: authoritarianism, the push for ironclad borders, cultural-religious fundamentalism, deep systemic poverty and conflict. If there is one silver lining to what Octavio Paz once called *tiempo nublado*, it is the welcome waning of banal indifference and antipathy to history. One risks immediate irrelevance in this scenario if one fails to acknowledge the mediated interrelations between the material social world and individual and collective consciousness.

The objective importance of the twentieth century and, especially, that of peripheral writers and intellectuals in this regard consists precisely in illuminating the worldly nature of creative work: of language and literature within the field of socio-historical relations. This constitutes the signal contribution of postcolonial literature, especially since the work of art was actively yet differently depoliticized in the West and the socialist second world in the postwar period. The reconfiguration of literary and cultural form beyond Euro-American contexts, such as the novel, drama, cinema, oral culture, nonfiction, in short the whole question of aesthetic innovation, might be reexamined in the light of such mimetic and realist impulse. Noteworthy too is the agonistic role of the intellectual, though one that is hardly unknown to counter-hegemonic groups and formations within the West. The activist history of art, and the artist, discussed in the book provides an opportunity to revisit the classic yet still relevant question of artistic and intellectual autonomy, and its resistance to capitalist commodification and regimentation.

Despite its benefits, however, any account of peripheral writing cannot (and indeed should not) be chalked up solely to correcting oversights about the non-Western world. As with any social practice, the production of knowledge in the metropolitan academy, and especially its techniques of recognition and methodology, necessitates unpacking and critique. The Anglophone and Francophone basis of the *theory* requires interrogating: to take the present case, for instance, one cannot have an intellectual history or literary criticism of South Asian literature without a sustained engagement with texts, languages, traditions, histories, affiliations, and movements – in Assamese, Bengali, Hindi, Malayalam, Marathi, Oriya, Punjabi, Urdu, Tamil, Telugu, and a host of other languages, as well as their variations and overlaps. Yet, as we noted, dominant assessments are often decontextualized and seldom venture beyond a handful of privileged texts and authors. The lack of historical context entailed in this approach is a problem. Additionally, the rapid and perhaps eclectic evolution of academic trends poses yet another obstacle. What might work for established fields, say, of British Victorian or American modernist literature, here hinders patient and collaborative assessment of the gains as well as shortcomings of extant work in postcolonial and comparative world literature.

Given this scenario, it is perhaps not unreasonable to insist that explorations of peripheral aesthetic and sociopolitical form be grounded in non-European languages. A historically attuned philology not only reveals the fault lines within the constituted time-space of nation-states but also uncovers alternative genealogies, exchanges, and emergences across state boundaries. In the preceding pages, we outlined the material basis for peripheral cognition and aesthetics: namely, its relation of dependence vis-à-vis the capitalist world-system and mode of production. On the one hand, this determination means the unhappy imposition of hegemonic structures from outside – as social relations, old or new ideas, and often both. On the other hand, peripherality engenders a "superior" vantage point for examining the total advances and backwardness of the world-system. Lived experience of the particular and its expression in the realms of conscious articulation and unconscious feeling – language, culture, orality, artwork, and so on – register the symptomatic, uneven, and exceptional incongruity of social form.

In this regard, the international acquires manifold and contradictory valences in the periphery. If the incursion of the foreign is an unavoidable fact, in the structural sense, this not only establishes the grounds for interrelation and comparison but also that of translation. In other words, the international continues to trouble the narrative of national exception – a sure sign of hegemony in culture – as much as it enables the reconfiguration of concepts and forms originating in other, sometimes vastly different, spaces and conjunctures. The latter enables the articulation of a decolonizing and solidaristic vision of national liberation, the only concrete option in an imperialized world, without ossifying the contents of the national. Accordingly, the possibilities of the international in this direction are activated – or elided – through conscious intent and effort, a point we have stressed in our discussion.

The practice of peripheral internationalism takes as its goal to render the demotic figure more and more legible. This, I would argue, is the task of contemporary criticism as well. The role of the critic, a partisan one clearly, is to resist selective remembering. The lost pathways, and alternate visions, of history offer different lineages of the present than those given by the dominant order. Yet, the critical excavation of the past need not be an antiquarian exercise driven by nostalgia or individual whim. Rather, it is determined by the urgencies and needs of the present. On the one hand, this means exploring the new and unprecedented relationships being forged between writers and the communities they address. On the other hand, approaching the vexed issue of tradition, it entails submitting to the criterion of mass politics what is useful and was not useful in the past. The various struggles of the marginalized, in different parts of the world, for emancipation and liberation articulate a collective vision of another world that is possible. It is to this singular imperative that our intellectual labor must, creatively and committedly, respond.

Works Cited

Aboul-Ela, Hosam M. *Domestications: American Empire, Literary Culture, and the Postcolonial Lens.* Chicago: Northwestern University Press, 2018.
Adiga, Aravind. *The White Tiger: A Novel.* New York: Free Press, 2008.
Adorno, Theodor. *Hegel: Three Studies.* Trans. Sherry W. Nicholsen. Cambridge: MIT Press, 1994.
　"Resignation." Trans. Wes Blomster. *Telos* 35 (1978): 165–168.
　"The Essay as Form." *Notes to Literature: Volume 1.* Ed. Rolf Tiedemann. Trans. Sherry W. Nicholsen. New York: Columbia University Press, 1991. 3–24.
Ahmad, Aijaz. *In Theory: Classes, Nations, Literatures.* London and New York: Verso, 1992.
　"Jameson's Rhetoric of Otherness and the 'National Allegory.'" *Social Text* 17 (Autumn 1987): 3–25.
　Lineages of the Present: Ideology and Politics in Contemporary South Asia. London and New York: Verso, 2000.
　On Communalism and Globalization: Offensives of the Far Right. New Delhi: Three Essays Collective, 2007.
　"Reading Arundhati Roy Politically." *Frontline,* August 8, 1997.
Ahmed, Siraj. *Archaeology of Babel: The Colonial Foundation of the Humanities.* Stanford: Stanford University Press, 2018.
Alonso, Isabel Huacuja. "M.N. Roy and the Mexican Revolution: How a Militant Indian Nationalist Became an International Communist." *South Asia: Journal of South Asian Studies* 40.3 (2017): 517–530.
Altbach, Philip. "Literary Colonialism: Books in the Third World." *Harvard Educational Review* 45.2 (1975): 226–236.
Ambedkar, B.R. *India and Communism.* Intro. Anand Teltumbde. New Delhi: Leftword Books, 2017.
　The Essential Writings of B.R. Ambedkar. Ed. Valerian Rodrigues. New Delhi: Oxford University Press, 2004.
Amin, Samir. *Eurocentrism: Modernity, Religion, and Democracy.* Trans. Russell Moore and James Membrez. New York: Monthly Review Press, 2009.
Anjaria, Ulka. *Realism in the Twentieth-Century Indian Novel: Colonial Difference and Literary Form.* New York: Cambridge University Press, 2012.
　"Realist Hieroglyphics: Aravind Adiga and the New Social Novel." *Modern Fiction Studies* 61.1 (2015): 114–137.

Apter, Emily. *Against World Literature: On the Politics of Untranslatability*. London and New York: Verso, 2013.
Armstrong, Elizabeth. *Gender and Neoliberalism: The All-India Democratic Women's Association and Globalization Politics*. New York: Routledge, 2014.
Auerbach, Erich. *Mimesis: The Representation of Reality in Western Literature*. Trans. William R. Trask. Intro. Edward W. Said. Princeton: Princeton University Press, 2003.
   "Philology and 'Weltliteratur.'" Trans. Maire Said and Edward Said. *The Centennial Review* 13.1 (Winter 1969): 1–17.
   Time, History, and Literature: Selected Essays of Erich Auerbach. Ed. James I. Porter. Trans. Jane O. Newman. Princeton: Princeton University Press, 2014.
Baer, Benjamin. *Indigenous Vanguards: Education, National Liberation, and the Limits of Modernism*. New York: Columbia University Press, 2019.
Badiou, Alain. *Metapolitics*. Trans. and Intro. Jason Barker. London and New York: Verso, 2005.
Bagchi, Amiya. "Rabindranath Tagore and the Human Condition." *Economic and Political Weekly* 49.12 (2014): 38–46.
Bagchi, Amiya and Amita Chatterjee. Eds. *Marxism: With and Beyond Marx*. New York: Routledge, 2014.
Bagchi, Barnita. "Ladylands and Sacrificial Holes: Utopias and Dystopias in Rokeya Sakhawat Hossain's Writings." *The Politics of the Im(Possible): Utopia and Dystopia Reconsidered*. Ed. Barnita Bagchi. New Delhi: Sage, 2012. 166–179.
Bagchi, Jasodhara. Ed. *The Changing Status of Women in West Bengal, 1970–2000: The Challenges Ahead*. Calcutta: Sage Publications, 2005.
Bajrange, Dakxin. "'Amma' and Budhan Theatre." *Himal Southasian*, August 22, 2016.
Bakhtin, Mikhail. *The Dialogic Imagination: Four Essays*. Trans. Caryl Emerson and Michael Holquist. Ed. M. Holquist. Austin: University of Texas Press, 1983.
Baldwin, Kate. *Beyond the Color Line and the Iron Curtain: Reading Encounters Between Black and Red, 1922–1963*. Durham: Duke University Press, 2002.
Bandopadhyay, Manik. "Atmahatyar Adhikar [The Right to Suicide]." *Sera Manik*. Ed. Shikha Ghosh. Calcutta: Bani Prokash, 1965. 471–479.
Bandopadhyay, Saroj. "Jiban ke Jante Jante Nijeke [Life and Self Knowledge]." *Samaresh Basur Sreshtha Golpo*. Calcutta: Proma, 1961. 9–16.
Banerjee, Sandeep. *Space, Utopia and Indian Decolonization: Literary Pre-Figurations of the Postcolony*. New York: Routledge, 2019.
Banerjee, Sumanta. *In the Wake of Naxalbari: A History of the Naxalite Movement in India*. Calcutta: Subarnarekha, 1980.
Bannerji, Himani. *Always Towards: Development and Nationalism in Rabindranath Tagore*. Kolkata: Institute of Development Studies Special Lectures, 2008.
   "Beyond the Binaries: Notes on Karl Marx's and Rabindranath Tagore's Ideas on Human Capacities and Alienation." *Marxism: With and Beyond Marx*.

Eds. Amiya Bagchi and Amita Chatterjee. New York: Routledge, 2014. 25–56.
The Mirror of Class: Essays in Bengali Theatre. Calcutta: Papyrus, 1998.
Bartolovich, Crystal. "Introduction: Marxism, Modernity, and Postcolonial Studies." *Marxism, Modernity, and Postcolonial Studies.* Eds. Crystal Bartolovich and Neil Lazarus. New York: Cambridge University Press, 2001. 1–17.
Basu, Samaresh. "Esmalgar [The Smuggler]." *Samaresh Basur Sreshtha Golpo* [Best Short Stories of Samaresh Basu]. Calcutta: Proma, 1961. 122–137.
Basu, Subho. "Framing China." Unpublished essay courtesy the author.
Basu, Subho and Auritro Majumder. ""Dilemmas of Parliamentary Communism: The Rise and Fall of the Left in West Bengal." *Critical Asian Studies* 45.2 (2013): 167–200.
Benjamin, Walter. *The Arcades Project.* Trans. Howard Eiland and Kevin McLaughlin. Cambridge, MA: Harvard University Press, 1999.
The Origin of German Tragic Drama. Trans. John Osborne. New York: Verso, 2003.
Bentes, Ivana. "'Cosmética da Fome' Marca Cinema do País [Cosmetics of Hunger Marks Cinema of the Country]." *Jornal do Brasil,* 8 (July 2001): n.p.
Benton, Gregor. Ed. *Prophets Unarmed: Chinese Trotskyists in Revolution, War, Jail, and the Return From Limbo.* Leiden: Brill, 2015.
Beverley, John. *Against Literature.* Minneapolis: University of Minnesota Press, 1993.
Bharucha, Rustom. *Rehearsals of Revolution: The Political Theatre of Bengal.* Honolulu: University of Hawaii Press, 1983.
Bhatia, Nandi. *Acts of Authority/Acts of Resistance: Theater and Politics in Colonial and Postcolonial India.* Ann Arbor: University of Michigan Press, 2004.
Bhatia, Varuni. *Unforgetting Chaitanya: Vaishnavism and Cultures of Devotion in Colonial Bengal.* New York: Oxford University Press, 2017.
Bhattacharya, Bijan. *Nabanna: Of Famines and Resilience: A Play.* Trans. Arjun Ghosh. Kolkata: Rupa Publications, 2018.
Bhattacharyya, Amit. *The Spring Thunder and Kolkata: An Epic Story of Courage and Sacrifice 1965–1972.* Calcutta: Setu, 2018.
Biswas, Hemango. *Abar Chin Dekhe Elam* [Another Trip to China]. Calcutta: Sribhumi Publishing, 1975.
Bose, Deb Kumar. "Unemployment in West Bengal." *Social Scientist* 6.6/7 (1978): 109–113.
Brandist, Craig *The Dimensions of Hegemony: Language, Culture, and Politics in Revolutionary Russia.* Leiden: Brill, 2015.
"The Eastern Side of the Circle: The Contribution of Mikhail Tubjanskij." *Studies in East European Thought* 67.3–4 (2015): 209–228.
Brecht, Bertolt. *Saint Joan of the Stockyards. Brecht Collected Plays,* Vol. 3. Ed. John Willett. London: Bloomsbury Methuen, 2015.
Brennan, Timothy. *Borrowed Light: Vico, Hegel and the Colonies.* Stanford: Stanford University Press, 2014.

"Joining the Party." *Postcolonial Studies* 16.1 (2013): 68–78.
Wars of Position: The Cultural Politics of Left and Right. New York: Columbia University Press, 2006.
Brouillette, Sarah. *Postcolonial Writers in the Global Literary Marketplace.* Basingstoke and New York: Palgrave Macmillan, 2007.
Brown, Nicholas. "Roberto Schwarz: Mimesis Beyond Realism." *The SAGE Handbook of Frankfurt School Critical Theory.* Eds. Beverley Best, Werner Bonefeld, and Chris O'Kane. London: Sage, 2018. 465–478.
Utopian Generations: The Political Horizon of Twentieth-Century Literature. Princeton: Princeton University Press, 2005.
Buck-Morss, Susan. *Hegel, Haiti, and Universal History.* Pittsburgh: University of Pittsburgh Press, 2009.
Cardoso, Fernando Henrique. "The Consumption of Dependency Theory in the United States." *Latin American Research Review* 12.3 (1977): 7–24.
Carpentier, Alejo. "On the Marvelous Real in America." Trans. Tanya Huntington and Lois Parkinson Zamora. *Magical Realism: Theory, History, Community.* Eds. Lois P. Zamora and Wendy B. Farris. Durham: Duke University Press, 1995. 75–88.
Casanova, Pascale. *The World Republic of Letters.* Trans. M.B. Debevoise. Cambridge, MA: Harvard University Press, 2004.
Census of India, 1971: Series 22, West Bengal, Volume II, *Issue 1.* New Delhi: Office of the Registrar General, 1975.
Césaire, Aimé. *Discourse on Colonialism.* Trans. Joan Pinkham. New York: Monthly Review Press, 2000.
Cevasco, Maria Elisa. "The São Paulo Fraction: The Lineaments of a Cultural Formation." *Mediations* 28.1 (2014): 75–103.
Chakrabarti, Arindam and Sibaji Bandyopadhyay. Eds. *Mahabharata Now: Narration, Aesthetics, Ethics.* New Delhi: Routledge, 2014.
Chakrabarty, Dipesh. "From Civilization to Globalization: The 'West' as a Shifting Signifier in Indian Modernity." *Inter-Asia Cultural Studies* 13.1 (2012): 138–152.
Chakraborty, Abin. "The Peasant Armed: Bengal, Vietnam and Transnational Solidarities in Utpal Dutt's *Invincible Vietnam.*" *Cultures of Decolonization: Transnational Productions and Practices, 1945–70.* Eds. Ruth Craggs and Claire Wintle. Manchester: Manchester University Press, 2016. 109–125.
Chakravarti, Sudeep. *Red Sun: Travels in Naxalite Country.* New Delhi: Penguin, 2008.
Chakravarty, Sumita. Ed. *The Enemy Within: The Films of Mrinal Sen.* London: Flick Books, 2000.
Chakravorty, Mrinalini. *In Stereotype: South Asia in the Global Literary Imaginary.* New York: Columbia University Press, 2014.
Chatterjee, Kalyan. "Lukács on Tagore: Ideology and Literary Criticism." *Indian Literature* 31.3 (1988): 153–160.
Chatterjee, Partha. *Nation and Its Fragments.* Princeton: Princeton University Press, 1993.

Chattopadhyay, Suchetana. *An Early Communist: Muzaffar Ahmad in Calcutta, 1913–1929*. New Delhi: Tulika Books, 2011.

Chattopadhyaya, Debiprasad. "Philosophy and Politics in Ancient India." *Defence of Materialism in Ancient India*. New Delhi: People's Publishing House, 2008. 110–126.

"Tagore and Indian Philosophical Heritage." *Science and Philosophy in Ancient India*. New Delhi: Aakar Books, 2013. 214–234.

Chaturvedi, Vinayak. "A Revolutionary's Biography: The Case of V.D. Savarkar." *Postcolonial Studies* 16.2 (2013): 124–139.

Mapping Subaltern Studies and the Postcolonial. London and New York: Verso, 2000.

Chaudhuri, Amit. *On Tagore: Reading the Poet Today*. New Delhi: Viking, 2012.

Chaudhuri, Supriya. "Singular Universals: Rabindranath Tagore on World Literature and Literature in the World." *Tagore: The World as His Nest*. Eds. Subhoranjan Das Gupta and Sangeeta Datta. Kolkata: Jadavpur University Press, 2016. 74–88.

"Translation and World Literature." *Literature Compass* 9.9 (2012): 593–598.

Cheah, Pheng. *What Is a World? On Postcolonial Literature as World Literature*. Durham: Duke University Press, 2016.

Chen, Xiaomei. "Remembering War and Revolution on the Maoist Stage." *Cold War Literature: Writing the Global Conflict*. Ed. Andrew Hammond. London: Routledge, 2006. 131–145.

Chibber, Vivek. *Postcolonial Theory and the Specter of Capital*. London and New York: Verso, 2012.

Choudhary, Shubranshu. *Let's Call Him Vasu: With the Maoists in Chhattisgarh*. New Delhi: Penguin, 2012.

Chowdhury, Kanishka. *The New India: Citizenship, Subjectivity and Economic Liberalization*. New York: Palgrave Macmillan, 2011.

Choudhury, Serajul Islam. *Nirbachito Sahityasamolochona* [Selected Literary Criticism]. Dhaka: Mouli Prakashani, 2002.

Chung, Tan, Amiya Dev et al. Eds. *Tagore and China*. London: Sage Publications, 2011.

Clark, Katerina. *Moscow, the Fourth Rome: Stalinism, Cosmopolitanism, and the Evolution of Soviet Culture, 1931–1941*. Cambridge, MA: Harvard University Press, 2011.

Cole, Andrew. *The Birth of Theory*. Chicago: University of Chicago Press, 2014.

Cypess, Sandra M. "The Dead Narrator in Modern Latin American Prose Fiction: a Study in Point of View." PhD Dissertation, University of Illinois Urbana–Champaign, 1968.

D'Mello, Bernard. "Arundhati Roy, Anuradha Ghandy, and 'Romantic Marxism.'" *Monthly Review Online*, January 25, 2012. https://mronline.org/2012/01/25/dmello250112-html/#gsc.tab=0

Dalit Panther Manifesto. *Untouchable! Voices of the Dalit Liberation Movement*. Ed. Barbara Joshi. London: Zed Press, 1986. 145.

Dalmia, Vasudha. *Poetics, Plays, and Performances: The Politics of Modern Indian Theatre*. New Delhi: Oxford University Press, 2006.
Damrosch, David. *What Is World Literature?* Princeton: Princeton University Press, 2003.
Das, Dhananjoy. *Marxbadi Sahitya Bitarka* [Marxist Literary Debates]. Calcutta: Karuna Prakashani, 2003.
Das, Jibanananda. *Banalata Sen and Other Poems*. Calcutta: Signet Press, 1952.
Das, Santanu. *India, Empire, and First World War Culture: Writings, Images, and Songs*. Cambridge: Cambridge University Press, 2018.
Das, Sisir Kumar. "The Controversial Guest: Tagore in China." *India and China in the Colonial World*. Eds. Madhavi Thampi et al. New Delhi: Social Science Press, 2005. 85–125.
Das, Srijana Mitra. "They Mocked Me Because I Did Not Know Who Lionel Richie Was." *The Times of India*, June 26, 2011. https://timesofindia.indiatimes.com/They-mocked-me-because-I-didnt-know-who-Lionel-Richie-was/articleshow/8995173.cms
Dasgupta, Shubhoranjan. *Elegy and Dream: Akhtaruzzaman Elias' Creative Commitment*. Kolkata: Shipra Publications, 2000.
Datta Gupta, Sobhanlal. "Gramsci's Presence in India." *International Gramsci Society Newsletter* 3 (March 1994): 18–21.
de Assis, Machado Joaquim Maria. *The Posthumous Memoirs of Brás Cubas*. Trans. Gregory Rabassa. New York: Oxford University Press, 1999.
Detention Conditions in West Bengal: Text of Report by Amnesty International. *Economic and Political Weekly* 9.38 (1974): 1612.
Devi, Jyotirmoyee. *The Impermanence of Lies: Stories by Jyotirmoyee Devi*. Intro. Mahasweta Devi. Trans. Ashoka Gupta. Kolkata: Bhatkal and Sen, 2001.
Devi, Mahasweta. *Agnigarbha* [The Womb of Fire]. Calcutta: Karuna Prakashani, 1977.
  "Draupadi." Translated with a foreword by Gayatri Chakravorty Spivak. *Critical Inquiry* 8.2 (1981): 381–402.
  Dust on the Road: Activist Writings. Intro. Maitreya Ghatak. Calcutta: Seagull, 1997.
  Jhansir Rani. *Mahasweta Debi Rachanasamagra* [Collected Works] Vol. 1. Ed. Ajay Gupta. Calcutta: Dey's Publishing, 2002.
  Lu Xun, Samaj o Sahitya [Lu Xun, Society and Literature]. Calcutta: Standard Publishers, 1981.
  The Queen of Jhansi. Trans. Sagaree and Mandira Sengupta. Kolkata: Seagull, 2010.
Dimock, Wai Chee. *Through Other Continents: American Literature Across Deep Time*. Princeton: Princeton University Press, 2006.
Dirlik, Arif. "Modernism and Antimodernism in Mao Zedong's Marxism." *Critical Perspectives on Mao Zedong Thought*. Eds. Arif Dirlik, Paul Healy, and Nick Knight. Atlantic Highlands: Humanities Press, 1997. 59–83.
  "The Postcolonial Aura: Third World Criticism in the Age of Global Capitalism." *Critical Inquiry* 20 (Winter 1994): 328–356.

Dunayevskaya, Raya. *Marxism and Freedom: From 1776 Until Today*. Atlantic Highlands: Humanities Press, 1987.
Dutt, Utpal. *Natoksamagra* [Collected Plays]. 12 vols. Eds. Sova Sen, Bishnupriya Dutt et al. Calcutta: Mitra Ghosh Publishers, 1994.
The Rights of Man. Trans. and Eds. Sudipto Chatterjee and Neilesh Bose. Calcutta: Seagull, 2009.
"Theater as a Weapon: An Interview." By A.J. Gunawardana. *The Drama Review* 15.2 (Spring 1971): 224–237.
Towards a Revolutionary Theatre. Kolkata: Seagull, 2009.
Dutta, Dipannita. *Ashapurna Devi and Feminist Consciousness in Bengal: A Bio-Critical Reading*. New Delhi: Oxford University Press, 2015.
Easterling, Stuart. *The Mexican Revolution: A Short History 1910–1920*. Chicago: Haymarket, 2013.
Edwards, Brent Hayes. *The Practice of Diaspora: Literature, Translation, and the Rise of Black Internationalism*. Cambridge, MA: Harvard University Press, 2003.
Ekotto, Frieda and Adeline Koh. Eds. *Rethinking Third Cinema: The Role of Anti-Colonial Media and Aesthetics in Postmodernity*. Munster: LIT Verlag, 2009.
Elias, Akhtaruzzaman. *Rachanasamagra* [Collected Works]. 4 vols. Dhaka: Mawla Brothers, 2012.
Esty, Jed. *Unseasonable Youth: Modernism, Colonialism, and the Fiction of Development*. New York: Oxford University Press, 2011.
Fanon, Frantz. *The Wretched of the Earth*. Trans. Richard Philcox. New York: Grove Press, 2004.
Fernandes, Leela. *India's New Middle Class: Democratic Politics in an Era of Economic Reform*. Minneapolis: University of Minnesota Press, 2006.
Fitzpatrick, Sheila. *The Cultural Front: Power and Culture in Revolutionary Russia*. Ithaca: Cornell University Press, 1992.
Frank, Andre Gunder. "Crisis of Ideology and Ideology of Crisis." *Dynamics of Global Crisis*. Eds. Samir Amin, Giovanni Arrighi, Andre Gunder Frank and Immanuel Wallerstein. New York: Monthly Review Press, 1982. 109–166.
ReORIENT: Global Economy in the Asian Age. Berkeley and Los Angeles: University of California Press, 1998.
Frazier, Robeson T. *The East Is Black: Cold War China in the Black Radical Imagination*. Durham: Duke University Press, 2014.
Friedman, Susan. *Planetary Modernisms: Provocations on Modernity Across Time*. New York: Columbia University Press, 2015.
Frydman, Jason. *Sounding the Break: African American and Caribbean Routes of World Literature*. Charlottesville: University of Virginia Press, 2014.
Gabriel, Teshome. *Third Cinema in the Third World: The Aesthetics of Liberation*. Ann Arbor: University of Michigan Research Press, 1982.
Gajarawala, Toral. *Untouchable Fictions: Literary Realism and the Crisis of Caste*. New York: Fordham University Press, 2013.
Ganguly, Keya. *Cinema, Emergence, and the Films of Satyajit Ray*. Berkeley: University of California Press, 2010.

Ganguly, Shyama Prasad. Ed. *The Kindred Voice: Reflections on Tagore in Spain and Latin America*. New Delhi: CSPILAS, Jawaharlal Nehru University, 2011.

Gangopadhyay, Agnibho. "Biography of a Pseudonym: Suprakash Ray, Bengal (1915–1990)." PhD Dissertation, Oxford University, 2018.

Gao, Mobo. *The Battle for China's Past: Mao and the Cultural Revolution*. London: Pluto Press, 2006.

Garo, Isabelle. "Deleuze, Marx and Revolution: What It Means to 'Remain Marxist.'" *Critical Companion to Contemporary Marxism*. Eds. Jacques Bidet and Stathis Kouvelakis. Leiden and Boston: Historical Materialism, 2008. 605–624.

Ghandy, Anuradha. *Scripting the Change: Selected Writings of Anuradha Ghandy*. Eds. Anand Teltumbde and Shoma Sen. New Delhi: Daanish Books, 2012.

Ghatak, Ritwik. *Rows and Rows of Fences: Ritwik Ghatak on Cinema*. Calcutta: Seagull, 2000.

Ghosh, Bishnupriya. "Melodrama and the Bourgeois Family: Notes on Mrinal Sen's Critical Cinema." *The Enemy Within: The Films of Mrinal Sen*. Ed. Sumita Chakravarty. London: Flick Books, 2000. 66–97.

Ghosh, Nirmal. *Mahasweta Devi: Aporajeyo Pratibadi Mukh* [The Unvanquished Face of Resistance]. Calcutta: Karuna Prakashani, 1998.

Ghosh, Pothik. *Akhtaruzzaman Elias: Beyond the Lived Time of Nationhood*. New Delhi: Aakar Books, 2008.

Gilly, Adolfo. *The Mexican Revolution*. Trans. Patrick Camiller. New York: New Press, 2005.

Giri, Saroj. "The Maoist 'Problem' and the Democratic Left in India." *Journal of Contemporary Asia* 39.3 (August 2009): 463–474.

Gnatyuk-Danil'chuk, A.P. *Tagore, India, and the Soviet Union*. Calcutta: Firma KLM, 1986.

Goh, Robbie. "Narrating 'Dark' India in *Londonstani* and *The White Tiger*: Sustaining Identity in the Diaspora." *The Journal of Commonwealth Literature* 46.2 (2011): 327–344.

Gopal, Priyamvada. "Concerning Maoism: Fanon, Revolutionary Violence, and Postcolonial India." *The South Atlantic Quarterly* 112.1 (2013): 115–128.

  The Indian English Novel: Nation, History, and Narration. Oxford: Oxford University Press, 2009.

  Literary Radicalism in India: Gender, Nation and the Transition to Independence. London: Routledge, 2005.

Gramsci, Antonio. *Prison Notebooks*, Vol. 1. Ed. Joseph A. Buttigieg. New York: Columbia University Press, 2011.

Green, Marcus. "On the Postcolonial Image of Gramsci." *Postcolonial Studies* 16.1 (2013): 90–101.

Gugelberger, Georg. Ed. *Marxism and African Literature*. Trenton: Africa World Press, 1986.

Guha, Ranajit *Dominance Without Hegemony: History and Power in Colonial India*. Cambridge, MA: Harvard University Press, 1997.

"On Some Aspects of Historiography in Colonial India." *Selected Subaltern Studies*. Eds. Ranajit Guha and Gayatri Spivak. New York: Oxford University Press, 1988. 37–44.

A Rule of Property for Bengal: An Essay on the Idea of Permanent Settlement. Durham: Duke University Press, 1996 [1963].

Guneratne, Anthony R., and Wimal Dissanayake, Eds. *Rethinking Third Cinema*. London: Routledge, 2003.

Gupta, Udayan. "New Visions in Indian Cinema: Interviews with Mrinal Sen, Girish Karnad, and Ketan Mehta." *Cineaste* 11.4 (1982): 18–24.

Gusdorf, Georges. "Conditions and Limits of Autobiography." *Autobiography: Essays Theoretical and Critical*. Ed. and Trans. James Olney. Princeton: Princeton University Press, 1980. 27–48.

Hanlon, Dennis. "Making Waves: Anand Patwardhan, Latin America, and the Invention of Indian Third Cinema." *Wide Screen* 5.1 (2014): 1–24.

Hansen, Kathryn. "Who Wants to Be a Cosmopolitan? Readings from the Composite Culture." *Indian Economic and Social History Review* 47.3 (2010): 291–308.

Hartley, Daniel. *The Politics of Style: Towards a Marxist Poetics*. Leiden: Brill, 2016.

Haywood, Harry. *Black Bolshevik: Autobiography of an Afro-American Communist*. Chicago: Liberator Press, 1978.

Hegel, Georg W.F. *Lecture on the Philosophy of World History*. Trans. H.B. Nisbet. New York: Cambridge University Press, 1975.

Phenomenology of Spirit. Trans. A.V. Miller. London: Oxford University Press, 1979.

Heidegger, Martin. *Introduction to Metaphysics*. Trans. Gregory Fried and Richard Polt. New Haven: Yale University Press, 2014.

Higgins, Charlotte. "Out of the Darkness: Adiga's White Tiger Rides to Booker Victory against the Odds." *The Guardian* October 14, 2008. www.theguardian.com/books/2008/oct/14/booker-prize-adiga-white-tiger

Hobsbawm, Eric. *Nations and Nationalism Since 1780: Programme, Myth, Reality*. New York: Cambridge University Press, 1990.

Holcomb, Gary. *Claude McKay, Code Name Sasha: Queer Black Marxism and the Harlem Renaissance*. Gainesville: University of Florida Press, 2009.

Hood, John. *Chasing the Truth: The Films of Mrinal Sen*. Calcutta: Seagull, 1993.

Hossain, Rokeya S. *Sultana's Dream and Padmarag: Two Feminist Utopias*. Trans. Barnita Bagchi. New Delhi and London: Routledge, 2007.

Huggan, Paul. *The Postcolonial Exotic: Marketing the Margins*. London and New York: Routledge, 2001.

Hui, Wang. *China's Twentieth Century: Revolution, Retreat, and the Road to Equality*. Ed. Saul Thomas. London and New York: Verso, 2016.

Hutnyk, John. "Music for Euro-Maoists: On the Correct Handling of Contradictions among Pop Stars." *Theory, Culture, and Society* 17.3 (2006): 136–158.

Jalal, Ayesha. *The Pity of Partition: Manto's Life, Times, and Work Across the India-Pakistan Divide*. Princeton: Princeton University Press, 2013.

James, C.L.R. *Notes on Dialectics: Hegel, Marx, Lenin*. London: Allison and Busby, 1980.
Jameson, Fredric. *Fables of Aggression: Wyndham Lewis, the Modernist as Fascist*. Berkeley: University of California Press, 1979.
— *Marxism and Form: Twentieth-Century Dialectical Theories of Literature*. Princeton: Princeton University Press, 1972.
— "On Magical Realism in Film." *Critical Inquiry* 12.2 (Winter 1986): 301–325.
— *Postmodernism: Or, the Cultural Logic of Late Capitalism*. Durham: Duke University Press, 1992.
— "Third-World Literature in the Era of Multinational Capitalism." *Social Text* 15 (Autumn 1986): 65–88.
— *Valences of the Dialectic*. London: Verso, 2010.
Jani, Pranav. "Beyond 'Anticommunism': The Progressive Politics of *The God of Small Things*." *Globalizing Dissent: Essays on Arundhati Roy*. Eds. Ranjan Ghosh and Antonia Navarro Tejero. New York: Routledge, 2009. 63–86.
Jelnikar, Ana. *Universal Hopes in India and Europe: The Worlds of Rabindranath Tagore and Srecko Kosovel*. New Delhi: Oxford University Press, 2016.
Joseph, Betty. "Neoliberalism and Allegory." *Cultural Critique* 82 (Fall 2012): 68–94.
Kaiwar, Vasant. *The Postcolonial Orient: The Politics of Difference and the Project of Provincializing Europe*. Leiden: Brill, 2014.
Kang, Liu. *Aesthetics and Marxism: Chinese Aesthetic Marxists and Their Western Contemporaries*. Durham: Duke University Press, 2000.
— "The Legacy of Mao and Althusser: Problematics of Dialectics, Alternative Modernity, and Cultural Revolution." *Critical Perspectives on Mao Zedong Thought*. Eds. Arif Dirlik, Paul Healy, and Nick Knight. Atlantic Highlands: Humanities Press, 1997. 234–265.
Karl, Rebecca. *The Magic of Concepts: History and the Economic in Twentieth-Century China*. Durham: Duke University Press, 2017.
Kaup, Monica. *Neobaroque in the Americas: Alternative Modernities in Literature, Visual Art and Film*. Charlottesville: University of Virginia Press, 2012.
Khor, Lena. "Can the Subaltern Right Wrongs? Human Rights and Development in Aravind Adiga's *The White Tiger*." *South Central Review* 29.1-2 (2012): 41–67.
Kipling, Rudyard. *The City of Dreadful Night and Other Stories*. New York: Barnes and Noble Digital Library, 2011.
Knight, Nick. *Rethinking Mao: Explorations in Mao Zedong's Thought*. Lanham: Lexington Books, 2007.
Kosambi, Damodar Dharmanand. *Myth and Reality: Studies in the Formation of Indian Culture*. Bombay: Popular Prakashan, 2005.
— "Social and Economic Aspects of the Bhagavad Gita." *Journal of the Economic and Social History of the Orient* 4.2 (1961): 198–224.
Köves, Margit and Shaswati Mazumdar. Eds. *Contributions on Lukács: Papers of the 1985 Delhi Seminar*. New Delhi: ABC Publishing, 1989.

Kruger, Loren. *Post-Imperial Brecht: Politics and Performance, East and South.* Cambridge: Cambridge University Press, 2004.

Kumar, Aishwary. *Radical Equality: Ambedkar, Gandhi, and the Risk of Democracy.* Stanford: Stanford University Press, 2015.

Kunnath, George. *Rebels from the Mud Houses: Dalits and the Making of the Maoist Revolution in Bihar.* New Delhi: Social Science Press, 2012.

Larsen, Neil. *Determinations: Essays on Theory, Narrative and Nation in the Americas.* New York and London: Verso, 2001.

Modernism and Hegemony: A Materialist Critique of Aesthetic Agencies. Minneapolis: University of Minnesota Press, 1990.

Lazarus, Neil. *The Postcolonial Unconscious.* New York: Cambridge University Press, 2011.

Lazarus, Sylvain. *Anthropology of the Name.* Trans. Gila Walker. London and New York: Seagull, 2015.

Lecercle, Jean-Jacques. *A Marxist Philosophy of Language.* Trans. Gregory Elliott. Leiden: Brill, 2006.

"Deleuze, Guattari and Marxism." *Historical Materialism* 13.3 (2005): 35–55.

Lee, Christopher. Ed. *Making a World After Empire: The Bandung Moment and Its Political Afterlives.* Athens: Ohio University Press, 2010.

Lenin, Vladimir. *The Development of Capitalism in Russia: The Process of the Formation of a Home Market for Large-Scale Industry.* Moscow: Foreign Languages Publishing House, 1956.

Lifshitz, Mikhail. *The Philosophy of Art of Karl Marx.* Trans. Ralph B. Winn. London: Pluto Press, 1973.

Loomba, Ania. *Revolutionary Desires: Women, Communism, and Feminism in India.* London and New York: Routledge, 2018.

López, Silvia. "Dialectical Criticism in the Provinces of the 'World Republic of Letters': The Primacy of the Object in the Work of Roberto Schwarz." *A Contracorriente* 9.1 (Fall 2011): 69–88.

Losurdo, Domenico. *Hegel and the Freedom of Moderns.* Trans. Jon and Marella Morris. Durham: Duke University Press, 2004.

Liberalism: A Counter-History. Trans. Gregory Elliott. London and New York: Verso, 2011.

War and Revolution: Rethinking the Twentieth Century. Trans. Gregory Elliott. London and New York: Verso, 2015.

Louro, Michele L. *Comrades Against Imperialism: Nehru, India, and Interwar Imperialism.* New York: Cambridge University Press, 2018.

Lukács, Georg. *Goethe and His Age.* Trans. Robert Anchor. London: Merlin Press, 1979.

"Narrate or Describe?" *Writer and Critic: And Other Essays.* Ed. and Trans. Arthur Kahn. Lincoln: Authors Guild, 2005. 110–148.

"Realism in the Balance." *Aesthetics and Politics.* Trans. Rodney Livingstone. New York: Verso, 1977. 28–59.

"Reportage or Portrayal?" *Essays on Realism.* Ed. Rodney Livingstone. Cambridge, MA: MIT Press, 1981. 45–75.

 Studies in European Realism. New York: Grosset and Dunlap, 1964.
 "Tagore's Gandhi Novel." Die rote Fahn, 1922, marxists.org/archive/lukacs/works/1922/tagore.htm. Accessed August 6, 2017.
 The Destruction of Reason. Trans. Peter Palmer. Atlantic Highlands: Humanities Press, 1980.
 The Theory of the Novel: A Historico-Philosophical Essay on the Forms of Great Epic Literature. Trans. Anna Bostock. London: Merlin Press, 1971.
Majumdar, Nivedita. "Silencing the Subaltern." *Catalyst* 1.1 (2017), n.p.
Majumder, Auritro. "Caste, Race, and Intellectual History: Notes on a Singular Modernity." *Crossing Borders: Essays on Literature, Culture and Society in Honor of Amritjit Singh*. Eds. Tapan Basu and Tasneem Shahnaaz. Lanham: Fairleigh Dickinson University Press, 2017. 135–146.
 "Gayatri Spivak, Planetarity, and the Labor of Imagining Internationalism." *Mediations* 30.2 (2017): 15–28.
 "The Poetics and Politics of Blackness: Literature as a Site of Transnational Contestation in Chanakya Sen's *The Morning After* and Utpal Dutt's *The Rights of Man*." *Journal of Postcolonial Writing* 50.4 (2014): 423–436.
 "Toward a Materialist Critique of the Postnational: Haile Gerima's Lukácsian Realism in *Harvest 3000 Years*." *Research in African Literatures* 49.1 (2018): 209–225.
Makalani, Minkah. *In the Cause of Freedom: Radical Black Internationalism from Harlem to London, 1917–1939*. Chapel Hill: University of North Carolina Press, 2011.
Manjapra, Kris "The Impossible Intimacies of M.N. Roy." *Postcolonial Studies* 16.2 (2013): 169–184.
 M.N. Roy: Marxism and Colonial Cosmopolitanism. New Delhi: Routledge, 2010.
Manto, Saadat Hassan. *Letters to Uncle Sam*. Trans. Khalid Hasan. Islamabad: Alhamra, 2001.
Marasco, Robyn. *The Highway of Despair: Critical Theory After Hegel*. New York: Columbia University Press, 2015.
Mariátegui, Jose Carlos. *Seven Interpretive Essays on Peruvian Reality*. Trans. Marjori Urquidi. Austin: University of Texas Press, 1988.
Markandeya, D. *Bastarlo Janatana Jaitrayatra* [People's Victorious Journey in Bastar]. Hyderabad: Viplava Rachayitala Sangham, 2013.
Martin, Michael T. Ed. *New Latin American Cinema*. Vol. 1: *Theories, Practices, and Transcontinental Articulations*. Detroit: Wayne State University Press, 1997.
Marx, Karl. *Capital: A Critique of Political Economy*. Vol. 1. Moscow: Progress Publishers, 1977.
 The Eighteenth Brumaire of Louis Bonaparte. Ed. C.P. Dutt. New York: International Publishers, 1975.
Marx, Karl and Friedrich Engels. *The German Ideology: Part 1 With Selections from Parts 2 and 3*. Ed. C.J. Arthur. New York: International Publishers, 1970.
Matilal, Bimal Krishna. "Krishna: In Defence of a Devious Deity." *Essays on the Mahabharata*. Ed. Arvind Sharma. Leiden: Brill, 1991. 401–418.

Maxwell, William. *New Negro, Old Left: African-American Writing and Communism Between the Wars.* New York: Columbia University Press, 1999.
McKay, Claude. *A Long Way from Home.* Ed. and Intro. Gene Andrew Jarrett. New Brunswick: Rutgers University Press, 2007.
Mendes, Ana Christina. "Exciting Tales of Exotic Dark India: Aravind Adiga's *The White Tiger.*" *The Journal of Commonwealth Literature* 45.2 (2010): 275–293.
Menon, Nirmala. *Remapping the Indian Postcolonial Canon: Remap, Reimagine and Retranslate.* London: Palgrave Macmillan, 2016.
Migraine-George, Thérèse. *From Francophonie to World Literature in French: Ethics, Poetics, and Politics.* Lincoln: University of Nebraska Press, 2013.
Misch, Georg. *A History of Autobiography in Antiquity* 2 vols. London: Kegan Paul, 1950.
Misri, Deepti. "'Are You a Man?': Performing Naked Protest in India." *Signs* 36.3 (2011): 603–625.
Mitra, Ananda. "Imaging of the 1970s: Calcutta and West Bengal." *The Enemy Within: The Films of Mrinal Sen.* Ed. Sumita Chakravarty. London: Flick Books, 2000. 37–65.
Mitra, Ashok. *Calcutta Diary.* London: Frank Cass, 1976.
Mookerjea-Leonard, Debali. *Literature, Gender, and the Trauma of Partition: The Paradox of Independence.* New York: Routledge, 2017.
Moretti, Franco. "Conjectures on World Literature." *New Left Review* 1 (Jan.-Feb. 2000): 54–68.
Moretti, Franco. "More Conjectures." *New Left Review* 20 (March-April 2003), n.p.
Mufti, Aamir. *Forget English! Orientalisms and World Literatures.* Cambridge, MA: Harvard University Press, 2018.
Mukherjee, Ankhi. *What Is a Classic? Postcolonial Rewriting and Invention of the Canon.* Stanford: Stanford University Press, 2014.
Mukhopadhyay, Ashoke Kumar. "Through the Eyes of the Police: Naxalites in Calcutta in the 1970s." *Economic and Political Weekly* 41.29 (2006): 3227–3233.
Mukhopadhyay, Deepankar. *The Maverick Maestro: Mrinal Sen.* Calcutta: Indus, 1995.
Mullen, Bill. "By the Book: Quotations From Chairman Mao and the Making of Afro-Asian Radicalism, 1966–1975." *Mao's Little Red Book: A Global History.* Ed. Alexander Cook. New York: Cambridge University Press, 2014. 245–265.
Nag, Dulali. "Little Magazines in Calcutta and a Postsociology of India." *Contributions to Indian Sociology* 31.1 (1997): 109–133.
Namboodiripad, E.M.S. *History, Society, and Land Relations: Selected Essays.* New Delhi: Leftword Books, 2010.
Naoroji, Dadabhai. *Poverty and Un-British Rule in India.* New Delhi: Publications Division, Ministry of Information and Broadcasting, Govt. of India, 1962.
Nathan, Robert Stuart. *The White Tiger: A Novel.* New York: Simon and Schuster, 1987.

Navlakha, Gautam. *Days and Nights in the Heartland of Rebellion*. New Delhi: Penguin, 2012.
Nickels, Joel. "Claude McKay and Dissident Internationalism." *Cultural Critique* 87 (2014): 1–37.
　World Literature and the Geographies of Resistance. New York: Cambridge University Press, 2018.
Nielsen, Kenneth B., and Patrick Oskarsson. Eds. *Industrializing Rural India: Land, Policy and Resistance*. London: Routledge, 2016.
Orsini, Francesca. "India in the Mirror of World Fiction." *New Left Review* 13 (Jan.-Feb. 2002): 75–88.
Ortiz, Fernando. *Cuban Counterpoint: Tobacco and Sugar*. Trans. Harriet De Onis. Durham: Duke University Press, 1995.
Palumbo, Liu, Bruce Robbins, and Nirvana Tanoukhi. Eds. *Immanuel Wallerstein and the Problem of the World: System, Scale, Culture*. Durham: Duke University Press, 2011.
Parry, Benita. "Aspects of Peripheral Modernisms." *ARIEL: A Review of International English Literature* 40.1 (2009): 27–55.
Paswan, Sanjay and Pramanshi Jaideva. Eds. *The Encyclopedia of Dalit Literature* Vol. 11: *Literature*. New Delhi: Kalpaz Publications, 2002.
Patil, Sharad. *Dasa-Sudra Slavery: Studies in the Origins of Indian Slavery and Feudalism and Their Philosophies*. New Delhi: Allied, 1982.
Patnaik, Utsa and Prabhat Patnaik. *A Theory of Imperialism*. New York: Columbia University Press, 2017.
Phule, Jyotirao. *Selected Writings of Jyotirao Phule*. Ed. G. Deshpande. New Delhi: Leftword Books, 2002.
Pines, Jim and Paul Willeman. Eds. *Questions of Third Cinema*. London: British Film Institute, 1989.
Pizer, John David. *The Idea of World Literature: History and Pedagogical Practice*. Baton Rouge: Louisiana State University Press, 2006.
Popescu, Monica. *South African Literature Beyond the Cold War*. New York: Palgrave Macmillan, 2010.
Prashad, Vijay. Ed. *Communist Histories*: Vol. 1. New Delhi: Leftword Books, 2016.
　The Darker Nations: A People's History of the Third World. New York: New Press, 2007.
　Ed. *The East Was Read: Socialist Culture in the Third World*. New Delhi: Leftword Books, 2018.
Prendergast, Christopher. Ed. *Debating World Literature*. London and New York: Verso, 2004.
Protopopova, Darya. "Virginia Woolf's Versions of Russia." *Postgraduate English* 13 (2006): 2–29.
Rak, Julie. "Are Memoirs Autobiography? A Consideration of Genre and Public Identity." *Genre* 36 (Fall/Winter 2004): 305–326.
Rama, Ángel. *The Lettered City*. Trans. John Charles Chasteen. Durham: Duke University Press, 1996.

Ramaswamy, Sumathi. *Passions of the Tongue: Language Devotion in Tamil India, 1891–1970*. Berkeley: University of California Press, 1997.
Ramnath, Maia. *Decolonizing Anarchism: An Antiauthoritarian History of India's Liberation Struggle*. Oakland: AK Press, 2011.
  Haj to Utopia: How the Ghadar Movement Charted Global Radicalism and Attempted to Overthrow the British Empire. Berkeley: University of California Press, 2011.
Ranadive, B.T. *Caste, Class, and Property Relation*. Calcutta: National Book Agency, 1982.
Rao, Anupama. *The Caste Question: Dalits and the Politics of Modern India*. Los Angeles: University of California Press, 2009.
Rao, Nagesh. "The Politics of Genre and the Rhetoric of Radical Cosmopolitanism; Or, Who's Afraid of Arundhati Roy?" *Prose Studies* 30.2 (2008): 159–176.
Raza, Ali, Franziska Roy and Benjamin Zachariah. Eds. *The Internationalist Moment: South Asia, Worlds, and World Views 1917–1939*. New York: Sage, 2019.
Riddell, John. Ed. *Workers of the World and Oppressed Peoples, Unite! Proceedings and Documents of the Second Congress of the Communist International 1920*. 2 vols. New York: Pathfinder Press, 1991.
Robbins, Bruce. "Introduction Part I: Actually Existing Cosmopolitanism." *Cosmopolitics: Thinking and Feeling Beyond the Nation*. Eds. Bruce Robbins and Pheng Cheah. Minneapolis: University of Minnesota Press, 1998. 1–19.
Robinson, Andrew. *Satyajit Ray: The Inner Eye*. Berkeley: University of California Press, 1989.
Rocha, Glauber. "The Aesthetics of Hunger." *Cinema in Focus: Writings*. Ed. Pranjali Bandhu. Thiruvananthapuram: Odyssey Press, 1992. 94–97.
Rodney, Walter. *How Europe Underdeveloped Africa*. London and New York: Verso, 2018.
  The Russian Revolution: A View From the Third World. Eds. Robin D.G. Kelley and Jesse Benjamin. London and New York: Verso, 2018.
Roy, Anuradha. *Cultural Communism in Bengal 1936–1952*. New Delhi: Primus Books, 2014.
Roy, Arundhati. "Instant Mix Imperial Democracy, Buy One Get One Free." *An Ordinary Person's Guide to Empire*. New Delhi: Penguin, 2006. 135–170.
  The God of Small Things. London: Random House, 1997.
  Walking with the Comrades. London: Penguin Random House, 2011.
  "The Great Indian Rape Trick I and II." *Sunday Magazine*, August 1994.
Roy, Biswanath. *West Bengal Today: A Fresh Look*. New Delhi: Mittal Publications, 1993.
Roy, M.N. *Fascism: Its Philosophy, Professions and Practice*. Calcutta: Renaissance Publishers, 1976.
  Heresies of the 20th Century: Philosophical Essays. Moradabad: Pradeep Karyalay, 1940.
  India in Transition. New Delhi: India Renaissance Institute, 1971.

Materialism: An Outline of the History of Scientific Thought. Calcutta: Renaissance Publishers, 1940.
Memoirs. Bombay and New York: Allied Publishers, 1964.
Reason Romanticism and Revolution, Vol. 1. Calcutta: Renaissance Publishers, 1952.
Revolution and Counter-Revolution in China. Calcutta: Renaissance Publishers, 1946.
Selected Works of M.N. Roy, Vols. 1 and 2. Ed. Sibnarayan Ray. New Delhi and New York: Oxford University Press, 1987.
Roy, Mallarika Sinha. *Gender and Radical Politics in India: Magic Moments of Naxalbari (1967–1975).* London: Routledge, 2011.
Roy, Modhumita. "Englishing India: Reinstituting Class and Social Privilege." *Social Text* 39 (Summer 1994): 83–109.
Roy, Sabitri. *Harvest Song: A Novel on the Tebhaga Movement.* Trans. Chandrima Bhattacharya and Aditi Mukherjee. Calcutta: Stree, 2006.
Roy, Samaren. *Twice-Born Heretic: M.N. Roy and the Comintern.* Calcutta: Firma KLM, 1986.
Rudra, Ashok. *Non-Eurocentric Marxism and Indian Society.* Calcutta: People's Book Society, 1988.
Saha, Poulomi. *An Empire of Touch: Women's Political Labor and the Fabrication of East Bengal.* New York: Columbia University Press, 2019.
Said, Edward. *Humanism and Democratic Criticism.* New York: Columbia University Press, 2004.
The World, the Text, and the Critic. Cambridge, MA: Harvard University Press, 1983.
Salgado, Minoli. "Tribal Stories, Scribal Worlds: Mahasweta Devi and the Unreliable Translator." *Journal of Commonwealth Literature* 35.1 (2003): 131–145.
Sanyal, Probodh Kumar. *Angar.* Calcutta: Mitra Ghosh, 1944.
Sanyal, Sulekha. *Nabankur: The Seedling's Tale.* Trans. Gouranga P. Chattopadhyay. Calcutta: Stree, 2001.
Sarkar, Bhaskar. *Mourning the Nation: Indian Cinema in the Wake of Partition.* Durham: Duke University Press, 2009.
Sarkar, Sumit. *The Swadeshi Movement in Bengal, 1903–1908.* New Delhi: People's Publishing House, 1973.
Writing Social History. New Delhi: Oxford University Press, 2009.
Satnam. *Jangalnama: Inside the Maoist Guerrilla Zone.* Trans. Vishav Bharti. New Delhi: Penguin, 2010.
Schotland, Sara D. "Breaking Out of the Rooster Coop: Violent Crime in Aravind Adiga's *The White Tiger* and Richard Wright's *Native Son.*" *Comparative Literary Studies* 48.1 (2011): 1–19.
Schwarz, Roberto" Brecht's Relevance: Highs and Lows." Trans. Emilio Sauri. *New Left Review* 57 (2009): 85–104.
"City of God." *New Left Review* 12 (Nov.-Dec. 2001): 102–112.

A Master on the Periphery of Capitalism: Machado de Assis. Trans. John Gledson. Durham: Duke University Press, 2001.
Misplaced Ideas: Essays on Brazilian Culture. Ed. John Gledson. New York: Verso, 1992.
Seely, Clinton B. *A Poet Apart: A Literary Biography of the Bengali Poet Jibanananda Das.* Newark: University of Delaware Press, 1991.
Sehanobish, Chinmohan. *Rabindranather Antorjatik Chinta* [Tagore's Internationalist Thought]. Calcutta: Navana, 1983.
Sembène, Ousmane. *La Noire de* [Black Girl]. Dakar: Doomireew Films, 1965.
Sen, Mrinal. *Ami Ebong Chalacchitra* [Cinema and Me]. Calcutta: Bengal Publishers, 1972.
Calcutta 71. Calcutta: Angel Digital, 2003.
Cinema, Adhunikata [Cinema, Modernity]. Ed. Shiladitya Sen. Calcutta: Pratikkhan, 1992.
Montage: Life, Politics, Cinema. Calcutta: Seagull, 2002.
Over the Years: An Interview with Samik Bandyopadhyay. Calcutta: Seagull, 2003.
Views on Cinema. Calcutta: Ishan, 1977.
Sengupta, Debjani. *The Partition of Bengal: Fragile Borders and New Identities.* New Delhi: Cambridge University Press, 2016.
Seth, Sanjay. "Interpreting Revolutionary Excess: The Naxalite Movement in India, 1967–1971." *New Asian Marxisms.* Ed. Tani Barlow. Durham: Duke University Press, 2002. 333–358.
Marxist Theory and Nationalist Politics: The Case of Colonial India. New Delhi: Sage, 1995.
Shapiro, Stephen and Neil Lazarus. "Translatability, Combined Unevenness and World Literature in Antonio Gramsci." *Mediations* 32.1 (2018): 1–36.
Shah, Alpa. *Nightmarch: Among India's Revolutionary Guerrillas.* Chicago: University of Chicago Press, 2019.
Shah, Alpa and Dhruv Jain. "Naxalbari at Its Golden Jubilee: Fifty Recent Books on the Maoist Movement in India." *Modern Asian Studies* 51.4 (2017): 1165–1219.
Shingavi, Snehal. "Capitalism, Caste and Con-Games in Aravind Adiga's *The White Tiger.*" *Postcolonial Text* 9.3 (2014): 1–16.
The Mahatma Misunderstood: The Politics and Forms of Literary Nationalism in India. London: Anthem Press, 2014.
Siskind, Mariano. *Cosmopolitan Desires: Global Modernity and World Literature in Latin America.* Chicago: Northwestern University Press, 2014.
Slate, Nico. *Colored Cosmopolitanism: The Shared Struggle for Freedom in the United States and India.* Cambridge, MA: Harvard University Press, 2012.
Smith, John. *Imperialism in the Twenty-First Century: Globalization, Super-Exploitation, and Capitalism's Final Crisis.* New York: Monthly Review Press, 2016.

Smith, Neil. *Uneven Development: Nature, Capital and the Production of Space.* Athens: University of Georgia Press, 2008.
Sofa, Ahmed. *Nirbachito Probondho* [Selected Essays]. Dhaka: Mawla Brothers, 2002.
Solanas, Fernando and Octavio Getino. "Towards a Third Cinema: Notes and Experiences for the Development of a Cinema of Liberation in the Third World." *New Latin American Cinema.* Vol. 1: *Theories, Practices, and Transcontinental Articulations.* Ed. Michael T. Martin. Detroit: Wayne State University Press, 1997. 33–58.
Spenser, Daniela. *Stumbling Its Way through Mexico: The Early Years of the Communist International.* Trans. Peter Gellert. Tuscaloosa: University of Alabama Press, 2011.
Spivak, Gayatri C. *Death of a Discipline.* New York: Columbia University Press, 2003.
Other Asias. Oxford: Blackwell, 2008.
Srivastava, Neelam and Baidik Bhattacharya. Eds. *The Postcolonial Gramsci.* London: Routledge, 2012.
Subrahmanyam, Sanjay. "Diary." *London Review of Books* November 6, 2008.
Szeman, Imre. *Zones of Instability: Literature, Postcolonialism and the Nation.* Baltimore: Johns Hopkins University Press, 2003.
Tagore, Rabindranath. *Letters from Russia.* Trans. Sashadhar Sinha. Calcutta: Visvabharati, 1984.
Talks in China. Calcutta: Rupa & Co., 2002.
"Visva-sahitya." *Rabindra Rachanabali* [Collected Works], Vol. 8, *Visvabharati*, 1941, Bichitra: Online Tagore Variorum bichitra.jdvu.ac.in/index.php. Accessed Aug. 6, 2018.
"World Literature." Trans. Swapan Chakravorty. *Selected Writings on Literature and Language.* Ed. Sukanta Chaudhuri. New Delhi: Oxford University Press, 2001. 138–150.
Thiong'o, Ngũgĩ W. *Decolonizing the Mind: The Politics of Language in African Literature.* London: James Currey, 1986.
Moving the Center: The Struggle for Cultural Freedoms. Nairobi: EAEP, 1993.
Thiong'o, Ngũgĩ W. et al. "On the Abolition of the English Department." *The Postcolonial Studies Reader.* Eds. Bill Ashcroft, et al. New York: Routledge, 1995. 438–442.
Thomas, Peter *The Gramscian Moment: Philosophy, Hegemony, and Marxism.* Leiden: Brill, 2009.
"Refiguring the Subaltern." *Political Theory* 46.6 (2018): 861–884.
Trotsky, Leon. *The History of the Russian Revolution.* Trans. Max Eastman. London: Gollancz, 1965.
Urban Guerrillas in Calcutta. *Economic and Political Weekly* 6.28 (1971): 1378–1382.
Vadde, Aarthi. *Chimeras of Form: Modernist Internationalism Beyond Europe, 1914–2016.* New York: Columbia University Press, 2016.
Varughese, Emma Dawson. *Beyond the Postcolonial: World Englishes Literature.* New York: Palgrave Macmillan, 2012.

Vico, Giambattista. *The New Science of Giambattista Vico*. Trans. Thomas G. Bergin and Max H. Fisch. Ithaca: Cornell University Press, 1984.

Viswanath, Rupa. *The Pariah Problem: Caste, Religion and the Social in Modern India*. New York: Columbia University Press, 2014.

Wagner, Erica. "Aravind Adiga Wins Man Booker Prize with The White Tiger." *The Times*, October 15, 2008. www.thetimes.co.uk/article/aravind-adiga-wins-man-booker-prize-with-the-white-tiger-lw7rjpr390m

Warren, Rosie. Ed. *The Debate on Postcolonial Theory and the Specter of Capital*. London and New York: Verso, 2016.

Warwick Research Collective (WReC). *Combined and Uneven Development: Towards a New Theory of World-Literature*. Liverpool: Liverpool University Press, 2015.

Wayne, Mike. *Political Film: The Dialectics of Third Cinema*. London: Pluto Press, 2001.

Wenzel, Jennifer. "Epic Struggles over India's Forests in Mahasweta Devi's Short Fiction." *Alif: Journal of Comparative Poetics* 18 (1998): 127–158.

"Reading the Politics of Survival in Mahasweta Devi's 'Dhowli.'" *Postcolonial Ecologies: Literatures of the Environment*. Eds. Elizabeth DeLoughrey and George B. Handley. New York: Oxford University Press, 2011. 136–158.

Williams, Raymond *The Country and the City*. London: Vintage, 1975.

Marxism and Literature. London: Oxford University Press, 1977.

Wolin, Richard. *The Wind from the East: French Intellectuals, the Cultural Revolution, and the Legacy of the 1960s*. Princeton: Princeton University Press, 2018.

Woolf, Virginia. "Modern Fiction." *Theory of the Novel: A Historical Approach*. Ed. Michael McKeon. Baltimore and London: Johns Hopkins University Press, 2000. 739–744.

Wordsworth, William. "Preface to Lyrical Ballads." *Wordsworth and Coleridge: Lyrical Ballads and Other Poems*. Ware, Hertfordshire: Wordsworth Editions, 2003.

Wright, Richard. *Native Son*. New York: Harper and Bros., 1940.

Wu, Yiching. *The Cultural Revolution at the Margins: Chinese Socialism in Crisis*. Cambridge, MA: Harvard University Press, 2014.

Xavier, Ismail. *Allegories of Underdevelopment: Aesthetics and Politics in Modern Brazilian Cinema*. Minneapolis: University of Minnesota Press, 1997.

Yadav, Yogendra. "What Is Living and What Is Dead in Ram Manohar Lohia?" *Economic and Political Weekly* 45.40 (October 2–8, 2010): 92–107.

Yokokawa, Noboharu, Jayati Ghosh, and Robert Rowthorn. Eds. *Industrialization of India and China: Their Impact on the World Economy*. New York: Routledge, 2013.

Zamora, Lois P. *The Inordinate Eye: New World Baroque and Latin American Fiction*. Chicago: University of Chicago Press, 2006.

Zavaleta Mercado, René. *Towards a History of the National Popular in Bolivia*. Trans. Anne Freeland. London: Seagull Books, 2016.

Zedong, Mao. "Analysis of the Classes in China." Peking: Foreign Languages Press, 1968.

On New Democracy. Honolulu: University Press of the Pacific. 2003.

Talks at the Yenan Forum on Art and Literature. Beijing: Foreign Languages Press, 1960.

Zene, Cosimo. Ed. *The Political Philosophies of Antonio Gramsci and B. R. Ambedkar: Itineraries of Dalits and Subalterns*. Oxford and New York: Routledge, 2013.

Zhang, Longxi. *From Comparison to World Literature*. Albany: State University of New York Press, 2016.

Žižek, Slavoj. *Less Than Nothing: Hegel and the Shadow of Dialectical Materialism*. London: Verso, 2012.

Zubel, Marla. "Literary Reportage and the Poetics of Cold War Internationalism." PhD Dissertation, University of Minnesota, 2017.

Index

Adiga, Aravind, xii, 20
  The White Tiger, 164–175
Adorno, Theodor, 21, 23, 25, 26, 38, 157, 158
aesthetics. *See* literary form; peripheral aesthetics
Africa, x, 12, 20, 49, 53, 91, 120, 125, 126, 137, 138, 182
  Algeria, 127
  Congo, ix, 125, 127
  Egypt, 1, 70, 181, 182
  Ethiopia, 37
  Kenya, 1, 12, 126, 129, 161, 192
  Mozambique and Angola, 102
  Nigeria, 12
  Uganda, 126
African-American, 12, 53, 70, 74, 75, 128, 169, 170, 191, *See* Black radicalism
Afro-Asia, 1, 49, 51, 73, 74, 75, 171
Ahmad, Aijaz, 31, 162, 188, 191
  critique of Jameson, 29, 32, 179–184
  on hegemony, 189
allegory, 85, 87, 88, 96, 102
  national allegory. *See* Jameson, Fredric
Ambedkar, Bhimrao Ramji, 49, 50, 70, 73, 186
America. *See* Latin America; United States
Anglo-American, x, 3, 28, 44, 46, 50, 51, 78, 118, 121, 182, 188
Anglophone, ix, x, xii, 3, 20, 40, 43, 45, 119, 121, 136, 143, 159, 160, 165, 166, 179, 183, 184, 187, 190, 199
  Indian Anglophone, 159, 165, 169, 178, 192, 193
anticolonialism. *See* national liberation; nationalism; periphery
Aryanism, 60, 61, 68, 78, 80, 132, 186
Asia, x, 2, 3, 4, 7, 14, 16, 19, 20, 24, 27, 39, 41, 47, 49, 53, 54, 56, 62, 74, 77, 91, 118, 120, 125, 137, 138, 162, 166, 171, 172, 182, 185, 187, 192, 194, *See* China; India; Vietnam
  Arab, 44, 90, 164, 183
  Indonesia, 55, 125, 127, 181
  Japan, 2, 3, 23, 53, 54, 58, 171
  Korea, 3, 28, 138, 172, 194

Turkey, 3
Auerbach, Erich, 1, 120, 160
authoritarianism, 33, 64, 186, 198
autobiography, 50, 51, 52, 60, 74, 77
autonomy, 5, 9, 21, 25, 34, 38, 57, 64, 181, 199

backwardness, 8, 9, 24, 25, 27, 64, 79, 86, 89, 93, 174, 177, 200
Bakhtin, Mikhail, 41, 45, 120, 160
Bandopadhyay, Manik, x, xi, 103, 104, 106, 107, 114
Bandung, 16, 31, 49, 63, 75, 76, 85, 126, 181, 185
Bangalore, 164, 166, 167, 175, 190, 193
Bangladesh, 16, 17, 42, 67, 117, 136, 161
Basu, Samaresh, x, xi, 103, 104, 108, 109
Bengal
  1905 partition of, 3
  famine in, 98, 102, 106, 109
  Renaissance in, 17, 39
Benjamin, Walter, 31, 102, 103, 114, 115
Berlin, 53, 54, 62, 65, 66, 73, 74, 79
Bhagavad-Gita, 139, 162
Bhashani, (Maulana) Abdul HK, 17
Bhattacharya, Bijan, x, 95, 126, 127, 161
Bihar, 167, 175, 185, 186, 192
Biswas, Hemango, 17, 18, 43
Black radicalism, xi, 19, 42, 49, 51, 54, 59, 74, 75, 78, 82, 126, 138, 157
  Black Panther Party, xii, 128, 162
  Black Power, 127
  Blackness, 137, 138, 156
Bloch, Ernst, 32, 41, 178
bourgeois, 3, 8, 10, 13, 15, 16, 17, 18, 33, 45, 63, 64, 65, 66, 67, 69, 70, 71, 76, 77, 79, 87, 96, 100, 104, 105, 106, 113, 114, 120, 123, 130, 133, 134, 148, 152, 153, 174, 181, 182, 195
Brahminism, 15, 42, 57, 61, 69, 78, 81, 125, 129, 173, 186
Brazil, 23–25, 28, 36, 37, 40, 85, 89–91, 93, 97, 130, 148, 194

221

Brecht, Bertolt, 18, 20, 127, 129, 132, 134, 135, 139, 140, 144, 161
Brennan, Timothy, 1, 2, 39, 46, 80, 159
Briggs, Cyril, 54
Buddhism, 40, 80, 81, 99, 110, 115, 185
bureaucracy, 18, 95, 96, 134, 135, 140, 172

Calcutta, 4, 53, 66
  culture and politics in, 83–115
capital. *See* labor; valorization; world-system
  precapitalist, 29, 69, 71
caricature, 134, 139, 141, 156, 172, 186
Carpentier, Alejo, 31, 37, 46
Casanova, Pascale, 21, 22, 23, 24, 183, 194
caste, xi, xii, 42, 53, 61, 68, 69, 70, 74, 113, 122, 125, 128, 131, 133, 148, 160, 163, 164, 167, 168, 169, 170, 172, 173, 175, 176, 177, 178, 185, 191, 193
  Dalit, 70, 167, 170, 172, 173, 175, 185, 191, 192, 193
  Dalit Panthers, 138, 162
Césaire, Aimé, 37, 46, 50, 76
Chatterjee, Partha, x, 68, 76
Chattopadhyay, Bankim Chandra, 53
Chattopadhyaya, Debiprasad, 13, 124
Chhattisgarh, 144, 149, 153
Chicago, 134, 169, 170
China, 3, 16, 54, 65, 113
  Cultural Revolution, 33, 85, 93, 112, 127, 181
  impact in South Asia, 16–18
  in the twenty-first century, 170, 186
  May Fourth Movement, 3, 8, 18
  Revolution of 1949, 3, 11, 14, 33
Choudhury, Serajul Islam, 16, 42
circulation, 22, 23, 61, 79, 118, 143, 147, 179, 180, 194
civil society, 81, 146, 147, 148, 154, 159, 176
class. *See* labor
classical, 10, 50, 71, 93, 101, 121, 134, 135, 139, 156, 176, 190
cognition, 123, 199
Cold War, xii, 12, 50, 51, 75, 127, 129, 137, 140, 157, 181, 182, 183, 195
comedy, 97, 132, 141
Comintern, 41, 47, 48, 49, 51, 54, 56, 58, 63, 64, 66, 67, 71, 74, 75, 78, 79, 81
Communism, 11, 19, 48, 49, 51, 73, 100, 181
consciousness, 6, 7, 8, 9, 10, 30, 35, 37, 46, 57, 64, 68, 78, 84, 93, 96, 111, 119, 123, 125, 127, 128, 136, 137, 138, 139, 141, 142, 154, 156, 157, 172, 190, 198
constellation, ix, xi, 10, 19, 20, 21, 50, 51, 73, 102, 103, 114, 115, 143, 153, 157, 189
core, xii, 2, 21, 22, 25, 26, 27, 30, 34, 109, 170, 174, 187, 190, 191

cosmopolitanism, x, 21, 33, 82, 86, 108, 152, 157, 158, 160, 162
counter-insurgency, 119, 130, 139, 140, 144, 150, 152, 162
critical theory, x, 40, 44, 52

Dante Alighieri, 1, 31, 45
Das, Jibanananda, xi, 99, 100, 103, 117
de Assis, Machado, 45, 97
De Sica, Vittorio, 36, 92
dependency, 25, 27, 29, 50, 70, 87, 106, 107, 158, 180, 190, 195
determination, ix, 6, 29, 69, 136, 138, 148, 180, 181, 184, 187, 188, 190, 200
development
  combined and uneven, 22, 27, 67, 72, 76, 81, 87, 158, 178, 180, 187
  underdevelopment, 26, 68, 71, 72, 85, 89
Devi, Ashapurna, 122
Devi, Jyotirmoyee, 122
Devi, Mahasweta, xi, 20
  "Draupadi", 130–142
  early writings of, 123–125
  theatrical adaptations of, 142
dialectic, 3, 5, 10, 26, 27, 30, 39, 61, 65, 85, 86, 88, 90, 100, 103, 107, 109, 133, 138, 140, 155, 157, 158, 161, 180, 181, 183, 187, 192
difference, xi, 32, 49, 50, 65, 77, 80, 89, 90, 112, 118, 119, 125, 133, 161, 163, 174, 184, 187, 188, 191
Dovzhenko, Alexander, 36, 37
Dravidian, 60, 61, 78
Du Bois, WEB, 6, 12, 40, 42, 50
Dunayevskaya, Raya, 57, 78
Dutt, Utpal, x, 75, 138
  in cinema, 95
  in theater, 126–130
  on intellectuals and politics, 18–19
Dutta, Saroj, 14, 111, 112

East, 3, 19, 26, 36, 43, 47, 59, 61, 65, 74, 78, 79, 101, 161, 164, 167, 172, 181, 184, 186, 187, 198
Eisenstein, Sergei, 36, 109
Elias, Akhtaruzzaman, 136
emancipation, x, 3, 18, 21, 22, 24, 28, 30, 32, 33, 48, 49, 56, 57, 65, 66, 67, 69, 72, 73, 76, 90, 120, 136, 160, 163, 179, 198, 200
Enlightenment, x, 2, 24, 50, 195
epic, 37, 52, 53, 97, 105, 109, 112, 132, 133, 134, 139, 156
epistolary, xii, 169, 170, 171, 185, 186
Espinosa, Julio, xi, 90, 91
Eurocentrism, 14, 27, 29, 32, 45, 61, 63, 78, 125
Europe
  England, 24, 36, 54, 71, 135

Index

France, 24, 54, 102, 135
Germany, 18, 19, 24, 53, 54, 56, 62, 135
Italy, 8, 71, 92
exotica, 37, 89, 108, 119, 121
exploitation, 15, 69, 70, 71, 96, 100, 106, 123, 136, 148

family, 80, 97, 104, 105, 106, 107, 108, 109, 113, 123, 128, 167, 168, 177, 178, 186
Fanon, Frantz, 33, 72, 76, 90, 107
fascism, 15, 47, 48, 68, 73, 80, 81, 140, 141, 186, 187, 191, 195
feudalism, 10, 13, 15, 31, 67, 113, 127, 128, 134, 135, 136, 168, 169, 185, 195
figuration, 2, 97, 99, 100, 102, 106, 108, 111, 112, 115, 124, 128, 133, 134, 147, 149, 152, 155, 165, 171, 178, 179, 186, 187, 191, 192, 193, 200
folk, 1, 9, 43, 95, 110, 114, 120, 130, 135, 172
fragmentation, 52, 55, 61, 65, 77, 85, 87, 98, 102, 103, 114, 131, 136, 158
Frank, Andre Gunder, 26, 27, 45

Gandhi, Mohandas Karamchand, 14, 43, 48, 49, 72, 73, 80, 82, 125, 139, 151, 155, 157
gender, 24, 35, 69, 72, 76, 80, 90, 108, 119, 123, 130, 142, 155, 162, 189
Ghadar Party, 53, 54, 74, 77
Ghatak, Ritwik, 88, 93, 95, 105
globalization, 7, 29, 45, 90, 142, 143, 146, 147, 155, 158, 163, 164, 174, 176, 183, 187, 190, 191, 195
Goethe, JWV, 1, 24, 130, 134, 179
Gramsci, Antonio, 8, 33, 41, 45, 46, 50, 53, 72, 81, 124, 159, 189, 195
guerrilla, 91, 97, 113, 114, 124, 128, 132, 133, 140, 150, 167
Guevara, Ernesto "Che", 52, 91, 112
Guha, Ranajit, x, 68, 79, 81

Haywood, Harry, 74, 75, 82
Hegel, GWF, 1, 2, 4, 7, 8, 24, 26, 35, 40, 62
Hegelianism, 2, 3, 5, 40, 41, 43, 56, 78, 103
hegemony, xii, 3, 11, 15, 19, 48, 49, 72, 81, 105, 110, 111, 114, 115, 119, 125, 130, 132, 133, 140, 141, 148, 152, 183, 188, 189, 199, 200
Heisnam, Sabitri, 142, 143
Hindi, x, 95, 96, 121, 143, 144, 183, 188, 195, 196, 199
Hindu, 15, 40, 42, 54, 57, 58, 73, 74, 77, 80, 82, 110, 115, 122, 127, 129, 132, 133, 136, 160, 169, 195
history, intellectual, x, xii, 3, 13, 19, 50, 80, 81, 82, 119, 192, 199
universal history, 45, 78, 103, 125
world-history, 3, 62, 136
Ho Chi Minh, 54, 74, 75, 126

Hochhuth, Rolf, 140
Hossain, Rokeya Sakhawat, 122, 125
humanism, xii, 2, 7, 13, 14, 15, 20, 24, 41, 48, 50, 57, 90, 125, 129, 160
posthuman, x, 7

identity, 18, 26, 31, 34, 37, 58, 77, 87, 88, 90, 108, 123, 135, 141, 142, 144, 150, 155, 158, 164, 173, 180, 184, 187, 193
ideology, 8, 20, 41, 57, 76, 81, 108, 114, 127, 137, 160, 165, 176, 178, 183, 186, 194
imagination, ix, x, 2, 4, 5, 6, 7, 8, 20, 39, 45, 61, 64, 77, 105, 133, 138, 147, 149, 176
imperialism, 3, 15, 27, 29, 30, 32, 37, 40, 45, 48, 49, 61, 62, 66, 74, 88, 127, 147, 172, 180, 192
India
  economic liberalization in, 165, 188–190
  independence and partition, 11, 12, 48, 49, 98, 109, 122, 125, 126, 170
  Indian National Congress, 48, 73
indigeneity, ix, x, xii, 3, 16, 20, 38, 40, 61, 88, 96, 101, 109, 110, 115, 121, 127, 129, 135, 148, 153, 169, 172, 186, 191
insurgency, 123, 155. See counter-insurgency
internationalism. See periphery
Iqbal, (Allama) Muhammad, 40, 172, 191
irony, 83, 147, 174, 188
Islam, 17, 40, 77, 110, 115
Islam, (Kazi) Nazrul, 41

James, CLR, 57, 78
Jameson, Fredric
  on third world literature, 28–35, 179–180, 182, 191
Joyce, James, 41, 132

Kipling, Rudyard, 100, 103
Kosambi, 124, 139

labor, 2, 5, 7, 15, 17, 21, 26, 31, 69, 88, 108, 133, 155, 158, 159, 190, 200
  agricultural, 118, 165, 167
  capitalist wage, 29, 177, 196
  division of, 26, 27, 69, 70
  formal freedom of, 69
  labor movement, 53, 55
  real subsumption of, 183
  slave, 25
Larsen, Neil, 31, 38
Latin America, x, 19, 26, 31, 37, 91, 113, 125, See Brazil
  Argentina, 90, 125
  Bolivia, 125, 148, 159
  Cuba, ix, 18, 28, 33, 75, 112, 125, 127
  Mexico, xi, 49, 52, 56, 59–60, 61, 62, 65

Latin America (cont.)
  Peru, 8, 40, 71
Lazarus, Neil, 32, 119
Lenin, Vladimir, xi, 6, 45, 47, 61, 62, 63, 64, 67, 73, 75, 117, 172
liberalism, 46, 178
  neoliberalism, 165, 179
Lifshitz, Mikhail, 16, 43
literary form, xi, xii, 10, 20, 23, 25, 51, 65, 77, 120, 135, 158, 180
literary marketplace, 174, 179, 180, 190
Lohia, Ram Manohar, 185, 186
Lu Xun, 33, 41, 135, 136, 170
Lukács, Georg, 1, 14, 15, 16, 23, 24, 34, 42, 43, 45, 46, 77, 102, 114, 117, 120, 128, 144, 170
lumpen, xi, 18, 20, 75, 76, 84–85, 110, 113–115
Luxemburg, Rosa, 50, 62, 80, 172

Mahabharata, 132, 133, 134, 136, 139, 162
Manto, Saadat Hassan, 170, 171, 191, 193
Mao Zedong, 1, 33, 72, 112, 185, 198, *See* China
  Yenan Forum talks, 7–11
Mariátegui, José Carlos, 41, 50, 67, 70, 72, 79
Marx, Karl, 4, 7, 27, 35, 47, 57, 69, 71, 84, 114, 186, 198
  and Friedrich Engels, 1, 7, 24, 70
Mazumdar, Charu, 16, 111, 164
McKay, Claude, 50, 51, 58, 73, 74, 75, 163, 193
mediation, 24, 32, 89, 121, 155, 158, 159, 169, 177, 179, 180, 185, 187
melodrama, 105, 112, 114, 117
metropolitan, 20, 22, 23, 25, 29, 36, 38, 62, 81, 87, 89, 96, 143, 147, 152, 154, 179, 180, 182, 186, 187, 199, *See* core
mimesis, 23, 37, 158, 199
mixed style, 131, 138, 139, 156
modernism, x, 11, 24, 36, 37, 102, 123, 180, *See* postmodernism
  in the periphery, x, 23, 28, 32, 38, 99, 117
  modernismo, 38
modernity, xii, 2, 5, 7, 37, 50, 70, 87, 93, 94, 96, 161, *See* capital
modernization, 86, 87, 88, 93, 95, 143
Moretti, Franco, 21, 22, 23, 24, 166, 183
Morrell, David, 140
myth, 2, 8, 35, 37, 100, 114, 123, 130, 132, 133, 135

Nasser, Gamal Abdel, 181, 182
Nathan, Robert Stuart, 172, 191
national liberation, 3, 14, 19, 65, 66, 85, 117, 127, 198, 200
nationalism, ix, xi, 6, 13, 15, 17, 30, 50, 56, 57, 58, 65, 66, 73, 74, 88, 181, 182
naturalism, 131, 149, 152

Naxalism, 18, 83, 84, 95, 97, 111, 112, 114, 118, 143, 149, 164, 165, 167, 168, 175
Naxalbari, 19, 118, 126, 129, 138
negation, 5, 7, 21, 26, 37, 106, 188
Nehru, Jawaharlal, 14, 48, 181, 182
New Delhi, 106, 164, 167, 169, 170, 177
New York, 53, 55, 59, 66, 87
Nietzsche, Friedrich, 2, 35, 37, 46, 80
noir, 105, 106, 107, 114
non-fiction, xii, 19, 119, 123, 131, 135, 142, 143, 145, 148, 149, 151, 199
novel
  novella, 52, 104, 118, 122, 133
  political novel, 125, 126
  protest novel, xii, 168, 169, 171
  third world novel, 180

orality, 1, 7, 8, 9, 110, 114, 120, 124, 135, 146, 147, 184, 199, 200
Ortiz, Fernando, 129

Pakistan, 16, 17, 67, 74, 146, 150, 170
Pan-Africanism, 49, 157
pan-Asianism, 12, 40
Parichay magazine, 14, 45, 120, 160
parody, 95, 96, 139, 140, 170, 175, 180, 184, 185, 187, 188
partisan, 25, 200
patriarchy, 69, 73, 96, 106, 107, 108, 122, 128, 141, 148, 177, 189
peasantry
  landless, 20, 66, 118, 121, 162
  revolutionary, 85, 168
  sharecropper, 111, 123, 133, 168
periphery, 26–27
  peripheral aesthetics, 27–29, 37–39
  peripheral internationalism, ix, 19, 20, 21, 38, 49, 119, 165, 168, 175, 182, 191, 200
philology, 9, 39, 42, 199
photography, 85, 102, 154, 155
Phule, Jyotirao, 50, 69, 70, 186
poetic, 3, 57, 99, 100, 120, 125, 130, 148
postcolonial theory, 23, 39, 46, 51, 79, 119, 122, 159, 179
postmodernism, 26, 33, 36, 65, 181, 182
postwar, 16, 36, 39, 41, 50, 51, 75, 92, 199
poverty, 67, 84, 86, 87, 89, 98, 100, 104, 108, 119, 170, 198
print, 94, 120, 144, 147, 184, 194
production, 9, 22, 24, 66, 69, 70, 71, 126, 140, 142, 184, 194, 199
  mode of, 10, 27, 29, 30, 41, 69, 70, 200
  relations of, 27, 133, 179, 194
progressive literature, xii, 13, 120, 170
  in cinema, 92, 94

Index

Progressive Writers Association, 1
proletariat, 7, 8, 9, 10, 62, 64, 66, 70–72, 75, 76, 93, 130, 134, *See* lumpen
public sphere, 33, 120, 154

race. *See* Black radicalism; caste
Raihan, Zahir, 93, 117
Rama, Ángel, 86, 129
rationality, 2, 5, 6, 7, 27, 95
   humanist reason, 7, 47, 57
   irrational, 15, 37, 46
Ray, Satyajit, 88, 92–94, 95, 101
Ray, Suprakash, 124, 160
realism, x, 16, 35, 43, 91, 102, 105, 108, 117, 119, 121, 123, 158, 168
   socialist, 9, 12, 41, 104, 114, 122
   surrealism, 36, 37
reportage, 20, 142–145, 149, 151
Rocha, Glauber, 36–37, 85, 89–91, 92, 93, 108
Rodney, Walter, 57, 78
Roy, Arundhati, xi, 20, 165, 174
   Walking With the Comrades, 142–144, 148–156
Roy, Manabendra Nath, xi, 19, 86, 190
   debate with Lenin, 63–64
   India in Transition, 65–73
   Memoirs, 47–65
Roy, Sabitri, 122

Said, Edward, 14, 22, 39, 44
San Francisco, 53, 55, 66
Sanjinés, Jorge, 90, 92
Sanyal, Probodh Kumar, 103, 104
Sanyal, Sulekha, 122, 123
satire, 101, 133, 135, 156, 173, 191
Satnam, 144, 145, 148, 149, 154
Schwarz, Roberto, 28, 87, 114, 134
   and world literature, 23–26
   principle of composition, 186, 194
Sembène, Ousmane, 90, 156
semi-colonial, 41, 63, 67, 135, 168
semi-periphery, 8, 22, 30, 166
Sen Katayama, 54, 75
Sen, Bhabani, 14, 43, 45
Sen, Chanakya, 126
Sen, Mrinal, x, xi, 20, 37
   Calcutta 71, 83–84, 97–115
   early films of, 94–97
short story, 107, 120, 135
Sikder, Siraj, 16
Smedley, Agnes, 75, 143
socialism, 28, 34, 62, 66, 119, 135, 192, 198
   in colonial Bengal, 53
   in Latin America, 52, 61
   in the third world, 181–184
   in *The White Tiger*, 184–187

Islamic, 17
socialist intellectuals, 4, 10, 18, 33, 74, 105
socialist realism. *See* realism
socialist universalism, 4, 13
Sofa, Ahmed, 16, 42
Solanas, Fernando and Octavio Getino, xi, 85, 91, 104
South Asia. *See* Bangladesh; India; Pakistan
Soviet Union. *See* Comintern; Communism; Lenin, Vladimir; Stalin, Josef
   Bolshevik revolution, 3, 48, 51, 61
   Moscow, 50, 54, 66, 72, 73, 74
Spivak, Gayatri, x, xii, 45, 118, 119, 132, 141, 155, 159, 161, 192
Stalin, Josef, 47, 64
   Stalinism and anti-Stalinism, 13, 41, 51, 57, 73
subalternity, ix, xii, 50, 76, 115, 169, 173, 175, 188
   and Subaltern Studies, 68
   social movements and internationalist writing, 118–159

Tagore, Rabindranath, xi, 24, 73, 76, 105, 139, 198
   on world literature (*visva sahitya*), 2–7
   reception of, 11–16, 17–18
testimonio, 52–53, 65, 150
theater, x, 19, 95, 119, 121, 131, 142
   Chinese model plays, 127
   Indian People's Theater Association (IPTA), 17, 75, 96, 127
   jatra, 127, 128, 129, 133
   tamasha, 169, 172, 173
Third Cinema, 36, 85, 88–94, 105, 111, 112
third world. *See* periphery
tragedy, 97, 106, 111, 134
transculturation, 31, 129, 130, 139
translation, 3, 12, 14, 39, 42, 43, 51, 60, 61, 64, 66, 112, 120, 121, 123, 131, 132, 136, 156, 160, 161, 183, 186, 187, 200
Trent, Evelyn, 54, 59, 60, 65, 79
tribal, xi, 38, 118, 133, 140, 159
   Gond, 143, 144, 146, 148, 149, 150, 152, 154, 155
   Santhal, 118, 127, 130, 132, 133, 137, 157
Trotsky, Leon, 22, 44, 48, 50, 67, 70, 71, 79
Trotskyism, 12, 48, 57, 81

United States, xi, 19, 49, 54, 58, 74, 101, 127, 129, 135, 137, 140, 148, 169, 170, 180, 181, 198
universalism, xi, 40, 50, 129, *See* humanism
Urdu, 170, 172, 183, 193, 196, 199

Vaishnavism, 40, 110
   Chaitanya, 110, 117, 125
valorization, x, 36, 88, 166, 169, 187
vernacular, ix, x, 1, 43, 79, 94, 99, 119–122, 123, 125, 126, 143, 158, 194, 195, 198

Vico, Giambattista, 1, 4, 16, 35, 48, 57, 62, 120
  The New Science, 7, 10, 41, 43, 47
Vietnam, ix, 18, 28, 74, 75, 93, 102, 125, 138, 140, 157
  in West Bengal theater, 126–129

Wa Thiong'o, Ngũgĩ, 1, 12, 129
Wallerstein, Immanuel, 22, 27, 44
West Bengal, 14, 16, 18, 19, 43, 83, 85, 92, 100, 101, 113, 115, 118, 119, 126, 130, 136
West, Western. *See* Anglo-American; Eurocentrism
Williams, Raymond, 11, 15, 23, 25, 184
women writers, 78, 120, 125
  in Bengali, 122–123
Woolf, Virginia, 35–36
Wordsworth, William, 34–35
world literature, ix, x, xii, 10, 50, 180, 183, 190, 191, 197, 199, *See* Tagore, Rabindranath on world literature
  critique of, 21–26
world war
  first, 40, 76
  second, 135, 137
world-system, 21–23, 26–27, 28, 50, 165, 190, 200
Wright, Richard, 169–171, 188

Zetkin, Clara, 73, 75

For EU product safety concerns, contact us at Calle de José Abascal, 56–1°, 28003 Madrid, Spain or eugpsr@cambridge.org.

www.ingramcontent.com/pod-product-compliance
Lightning Source LLC
LaVergne TN
LVHW041628060526
838200LV00040B/1488